ADVANCES IN APPLIED MICRO-ECONOMICS

Volume 5 • 1990

ADVANCES IN APPLIED MICRO-ECONOMICS

A Research Annual

Guest Editor: ALBERT N. LINK
Department of Economics
University of North Carolina at Greensboro

Series Editor: V. KERRY SMITH
Department of Economics and Business
North Carolina State University

VOLUME 5 • 1990

JAI PRESS INC.

Greenwich, Connecticut *London, England*

55 Old Post Road, No. 2
Greenwich, Connecticut 06830

JAI PRESS LTD.
118 Pentonville Road
London N1 9JN
England

ISBN: 0–89232–797–9

Manufactured in the United States of America

CONTENTS

PART II. THE VALUATION OF RECREATION RESOURCES

LIST OF CONTRIBUTORS

Sanford V. Berg	Department of Economics University of Florida Gainsville
Nancy E. Bockstael	Department of Agricultural and Resource Economics University of Maryland College Park
Wesley M. Cohen	Department of Social and Decision Sciences Carnegie Mellon University Pittsburgh
Kathryn L. Combs	Department of Economics and Statistics California State University Los Angeles
Barry T. Hirsch	Department of Economics University of North Carolina at Greensboro
Donn M. Johnson	Department of Agricultural and Resource Economics Colorado State University Fort Collins
Catherine L. Kling	Department of Agricultural Economics University of California at Davis
Daniel A. Levinthal	The Wharton School University of Pennsylvania Philadelphia

Albert N. Link — Department of Economics
University of North Carolina at Greensboro

Kenneth E. McConnell — Department of Agricultural and Resource Economics
University of Maryland
College Park

John R. McKean — Department of Agricultural and Resource Economics
Colorado State University
Fort Collins

Edward R. Morey — Department of Economics
University of Colorado
Boulder

John T. Scott — Department of Economics
Dartmouth College
Hanover

W. Douglass Shaw — Department of Economics
Vassar College
Poughkeepsie

V. Kerry Smith — Division of Economics and Business
North Carolina State University
Raleigh

Ivar E. Strand — Department of Agricultural and Resource Economies
University of Colorado
Boulder

Richard G. Walsh — Department of Agricultural and Resource Economics
Colorado State University
Fort Collins

Marca Weinberg — Department of Agricultural Economics
University of California at Davis

INTRODUCTION TO VOLUME V

This fifth volume of *Advances in Applied Microeconomics* repeats the practice I initiated with Volume III of inviting a guest editor to work with me in composing the papers to be included. Two topics have been selected: current developments in modeling factors that affect technological change and the issues associated with modeling the demand for and valuation of recreation resources. Albert Link of the University of North Carolina at Greensboro, a leading researcher in the analysis of the factors influencing firms' research and development decisions, as well as a wide range of other issues in modeling the innovation process, agreed to edit the first part of the volume, and I assumed responsibility for the second.

While this volume was planned some time ago and the papers in each part developed independently, they do address two sets of very relevant issues on the "front burner" of current national policy debates. Of course, they appear under somewhat different headings. For example, we cannot consider seriously the issues involved in restoring

American competitiveness in the world marketplace without understanding the factors influencing the pace and direction of innovation and technological change. Likewise, the national and international news media reflect a renewal of interest and concern about many dimensions of environmental quality.

Interest in measuring consumers' valuations for environmental amenities is widespread. Moreover, estimates from these exercises have played an increasingly important role in developing information used in formulating environmental policy. This may not seem to be a new development for the United States, where this type of information has been considered, albeit informally, in evaluating aspects of environmental policy for some time.[1] But the current experience is different in at least two respects.

With Executive Order 12291 issued by President Reagan in 1981, benefit cost analysis was required for major regulations where the law did not preclude its use and encouraged the information to be provided for predefined regulations, even in cases where statute suggested it could not be considered in the initial standard-setting process. After over eight years, benefit cost information has become a routine part of the regulation development process. Prior to this period, the use of benefit cost analysis was haphazard. The Executive Order's mandate gave "economists a place at the table."[2] This does not mean they now control the process or will ever do so. Rather it implies their input is recognized as *one* of the ingredients in the evaluation of policy.

Secondly, the direct introduction of its use at the federal level for evaluating regulations has spread to the state level, and, more recently, to international policy. This last impact is certainly not due entirely to the U.S. mandate. Nonetheless, the U.S. practice has encouraged interest in benefit cost analysis and to estimation of the benefits provided by nonmarketed resources in the market economies of Europe, as well as in several newly developing countries of the Pacific Basin.

The connection of all these developments to a set of papers on modeling the demand for recreational resources may still seem tenuous until one further aspect of the literature is noted. Over the past half decade, recreational demand analysis has become the center of exceptionally active research integrating modern econometric methods for dealing with individual decisions reflected in mixed discrete and continuous demand responses. Factors contributing to the surge of interest in recreation demand analysis include increased availability of micro data on households' recreational choices, increased policy interest in values of changes in resource quality, and overall trends in policy analysis. Thus, the issues described in modeling how individuals use and value the improvements in outdoor recreation resources have broader relevance.

The next step in the research process is to explore connections between these two areas. To what extent are nonmarket amenities influenced by innovation? Are there mechanisms that reflect the values of these amenities in directing technical change? The obvious answer to this second question is through policy instruments that rely on incentives (e.g., effluent charges or marketable permits), but there may be others. This remains an area for further research. I hope that by putting these two topics in the same volume, some indirect encouragement may be given to the process of exploring them.

NOTES

1. The issue of benefit cost analysis in prospect evaluation has a long history. Indeed, Kneese and Schulze (1985) describe mention of this approach by Thomas Jefferson's Treasury Secretary, Albert Gallatin. Two Presidents prior to Reagan called for increased use of benefit-cost analysis in evaluating proposed regulatory programs. He was the first to mandate its use.

2. I owe this insight to Dale Whittington's description of the implications of benefit cost analysis during a forum on the Ethical Issues in Benefit Cost Analysis at the 1988 annual meetings of the Southern Economic Association in San Antonio, Texas.

REFERENCE

Kneese, Allen V. and William D. Schulze. 1985. "Ethics and Environmental Economics," in *Handbook of Natural Resource and Energy Economics,* edited by A. V. Kneese and J. L. Sweeney (Amsterdam: North Holland).

V. Kerry Smith
Series Editor

PART I

FACTORS AFFECTING TECHNOLOGICAL CHANGES

INTRODUCTION:

THE PROCESS OF TECHNOLOGICAL DEVELOPMENT

Albert N. Link

Economic activity is often represented in terms of an input-to-output relationship. For an ith firm, economic activity is frequently expressed by a production function of the general form:

$$q_i = A_i(K_i, L_i, T_i) \tag{1}$$

where q_i represents output, A_i is a shift factor characterizing the firm's efficiency in transforming inputs into output, K_i represents capital inputs, L_i represents labor inputs, and T_i represents technology inputs.

The value of q_i is determined in the marketplace. Through market development (the interaction between the product's characteristics and market factors), value is added.

Thc tcchnological component in the production function requires

Advances in Applied Micro-Economics, Volume 5, pages 3–6.

ISBN: 0-89232-797-9

scrutiny. T_i is itself an output from a separate production process expressed as

$$T_i = G_i(PT_i, BT_i, IT) \quad (2)$$

where G_i is a shift factor characterizing the firm's efficiency in transforming technology-related inputs into a technology output, PT_i represents proprietary (self-financed through R&D) technical knowledge, BT_i represents borrowed (or purchased) technical knowledge, and IT refers to all related infratechnologies.

These two production processes are related in a way described by the model of technological development illustrated in Figure 1.

Underlying much new technology is our science base. This base comes from basic research, funded primarily by the public sector. Basic research is the search for fundamental scientific principles without consideration of practical applications. Discovery of these principles does not lead, nor is it intended to lead, to new product or process applications.

Generic technology and the associated research process represent the organization of knowledge into the conceptual form of an eventual application and the laboratory testing of the concept. Its foundation is usually the science base, but (unlike scientific knowledge) it has a functional focus. Cooperative research among firms is one organiza-

Figure 1. A model of the process of technological development.

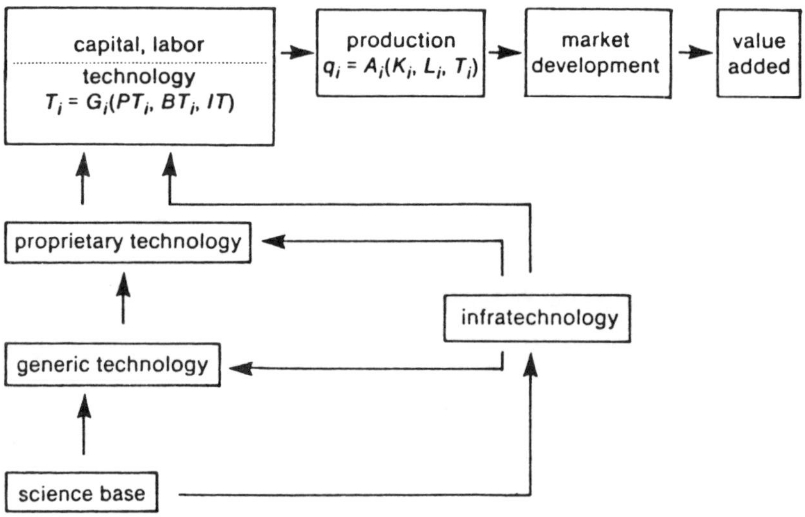

tional form intended to increase the base of generic technology. The paper by Combs adds much to our understanding of cooperative research activity.

Proprietary technologies are in the private domain; they are fully appropriable by the firm so long as they are secret. Such product and process technologies result from self-financed R&D or, more precisely, from development activities concerned with creating the marketable, technologically based product or process. The paper by Cohen and Levinthal discusses the important activities served by R&D.

Infratechnologies, as the name implies, support R&D, production, and marketing in industries. As such, they have a neutral competitive influence at the firm level, affecting all firms in an industry to the same degree (hence no subscript on IT). Infratechnologies include evaluated scientific data use in the conduct of R&D, measurement and test methods used in research, production control, and acceptance testing for market transactions and various technical procedures such as those used in the calibration of equipment. Infratechnologies are not generally embodied in an industry's product technology in the same way as the generic technology (the knowledge that is organized into the conceptual form of an eventual application). Instead, infratechnologies facilitate development of generic technology by, for example, providing highly precise measurements and creating organized and evaluated scientific and engineering data necessary for understanding, characterizing, and interpreting relevant research findings. Typically, they tie, at root, to the fundamental units of measurement. They also provide both the measurement and testing concepts as well as the techniques that enable higher quality and greater reliability at lower cost of production. Finally, infratechnologies provide buyers and sellers mutually acceptable, low-cost methods of ensuring that specified performance levels are met when technologically sophisticated products enter the marketplace. The paper by Berg chronicles the important role played by infratechnologies in the telecommunications industry.

Economists have devoted very little attention to technological development as described in Figure 1. Efforts have been made within the confines of Eq. (1) to isolate the role of R&D expenditures (a flow into the stock of T) in increasing productivity. These efforts, while important, are limited in three respects. First, they implicitly ignore the role of the other elements of technology in the overall process of economic activity. Second, they explicitly ignore the overall environment (a term not intended to be synonymous with just market structure) of the firm—such as unionism as discussed in the paper by Hirsch—and its impact on the process of innovation and technology. And third, they overemphasize the importance of internal R&D and ignore both the strategic nature of the composition of R&D and the influence of exogenous factors that may leverage the efficiency of internal R&D. The paper by Scott illustrates well the strategic role of purposeful diversification in R&D.

As noted in the discussion above, the five papers in this section of the Volume make a positive contribution to filling these voids in the research agenda associated with the study of the economics of technological change.

REFERENCES

Link, Albert N. and Gregory Tassey, *Strategies for Technology-Based Competition: Meeting the New Global Challenge*. Lexington, MA: Lexington Books, 1987.

PURPOSEFUL DIVERSIFICATION OF R&D AND TECHNOLOGICAL ADVANCEMENT

John T. Scott

I. INTRODUCTION

Schumpeter was surely right that in the long run the type of competition that matters most is the competition from new products, new processes, or new organizational forms. However, there has been scant empirical support for his proposition that firm size and monopolistic power promote technological advance.[1] In this paper, I explore the possibility that previous empirical tests have been incapable of revealing proof of the Schumpeterian hypothesis because the phenomenon of purposeful diversification has been ignored. By purposeful diversification of research and development (R&D), I mean a firm's systematic attempt to improve the net value of innovative investment by diversify-

Advances in Applied Micro-Economics, Volume 5, pages 7–28.

ISBN: 0-89232-797-9

ing its R&D across a group of industry categories for which research efforts are complementary. The complementary research efforts may share facilities and personnel and knowledge may spill from the R&D in one activity to that in another.[2]

Section II reviews the recent evidence that suggests that firm size, among the largest 1000 U.S. manufacturers, and monopolistic power, as measured by seller concentration in manufacturing industries, do not clearly matter one way or another for technological progress. The rest of the paper will reframe the tests using the concept of purposeful diversification of research and development (R&D) expenditures. Section III explains that concept, and then Section IV explains the methodology for discerning purposeful diversification and illustrates it by developing new evidence at the level of broad manufacturing industries.

Section V demonstrates that differences in the extent and type of purposeful diversification of R&D provide firm characteristics associated with differences in firms' R&D behavior even within the same industry category. Size per se may not matter, but differences among firms in purposeful diversification do matter.

Section VI pursues the idea that the pertinent competition in R&D is taking place within the groups of related industries combined by firms that have purposely diversified in similar ways. The firms in each such group are likely to be competing in R&D with strategies aimed at introducing similar innovations. So arguably concentration of R&D resources among the firms in a given group of related activities and its effect on behavior should be the focus of any exploration, via the relationship between seller concentration and R&D intensity, of the "Schumpeterian" hypothesis about monopolistic power. Previous work has examined seller concentration in sales within the industry categories determined by the old, existing products. True, Schumpeter would argue that monopolistic power in old product markets gives firms the extra revenue needed to support R&D and provide "insurance," while expected monopolistic profits in new product markets provides the incentive. But, our review in Section II of the behavioral reasons for a link between seller concentration and R&D intensity suggests that the concentration of R&D resources would be a key determinant of R&D behavior. Key are expectations about the ability to coordinate price competition in the postinnovation market and the ability to coordinate nonprice competition in the preinnovation market. Both should depend on the number and size distribution of sellers competing in R&D in the preinnovation market. Thus, Section VI explores the impact of concentration of R&D resources in the groups, holding constant all relevant firm-wide and industry category-wide variables (including their nonlinear effects) assuming only that the true model is linear in the parameters (but not linear in the variables).

After assessing the findings in this paper, Section VII concludes by pointing up how the concept of purposeful diversification provides new directions for research about industrial R&D.

II. RECENT EVIDENCE ABOUT THE SCHUMPETERIAN HYPOTHESIS

Studies of firm size and innovation have most often explored the relationship between size and R&D intensity, usually measured as the ratio of R&D expenditures to sales. In an exploration of the differences in R&D intensity across the over 3000 lines of business (LBs)[3] of the over 400 firms reporting to the Federal Trade Commission's (FTC's) Line of Business (LB) Program in the 261 four-digit FTC manufacturing industry categories, I found that after controlling for all four-digit FTC industry effects, LB (i.e., business unit) size had no effect on R&D intensity.[4] Cohen et al. (1987) use direct measures of appropriability and opportunity differences across industries to provide controls and corroborate my finding regarding business unit size as well as the finding of previous literature that firm size does not, among the largest U.S. manufacturing firms, affect R&D intensity once one controls for industry differences.[5]

But there is another prominent firm characteristic, arguably more meaningful a priori than size, namely, the diversification of the firm's R&D effort. Nelson (1959) advanced and exposited the hypothesis that a firm's size in the form of the extent of its diversification—production in several industry categories—would increase its ability to carry out and to benefit from R&D activity, especially basic research. With research designs allowing examination of basic research, Link (1981, 1982, 1983) and Link and Long (1981) provide interesting support for the hypothesis. Scherer (1984, p. 236) examines *applied* R&D and in a variety of experiments finds only a small but statistically significant effect of diversification on patenting, ceteris paribus.[6]

Scott and Pascoe (1987) provide support for the idea that *purposive* (purposeful herein) diversification of *applied* R&D across FTC four-digit industry categories is an important determinant of behavioral differences in that R&D. Section V will add to that evidence by observing the purposeful diversification of R&D (and its effects on behavior) at the level of the broad two-digit manufacturing industries. I then explore the idea that this firm characteristic—the extent and type of purposeful diversification—is the key to understanding why the industry level tests of the relationship between concentration and R&D intensity have been so inconclusive. The firms in a given industry are typically pursuing very different R&D strategies. They are not all competing in one industry group, but rather fall into different groups according to their different strategies. Each firm competes in R&D with those firms with similar strategies and expecting similar products in the future. Thus, the type of purposeful diversification pursued by a firm should be used to determine the extent of competition that it faces in its R&D.

Studies of the hypothesis that monopolistic power promotes innovation have most often focused on the relationship between R&D intensity and seller concentration. In my 1981 NBER conference paper (Scott, 1984), I was able to show that the effect of seller concentration was only a small percentage of the systematic variance in R&D intensity across the over 3000 business units. Further, control for firm effects and two-digit industry effects eliminated the significance of seller concentration. Without the controls, seller concentration was significant and exhibited the familiar inverted-U relationship with R&D intensity.[7]

The inverted-U relationship is one where R&D intensity first rises with concentration but then after some point decreases as concentration increases. Assuming seller concentration does measure the ability to coordinate behavior, the behavioral reason for such a relationship is a difference in the ability to coordinate price competition in the postinnovation market as contrasted with the ability to coordinate nonprice competition in the preinnovation market. At very high levels of concentration, coordination of both price and nonprice competitive devices is possible. At intermediate levels of concentration, R&D performers may anticipate more cooperation on price in the postinnovation market than they are able to coordinate for R&D in the preinnovation market. With low levels of seller concentration, the competition among substitutes (patented or not) in the postinnovation market may severely reduce appropriation of returns and hence R&D in the preinnovation market.

The distinction between cooperation before and after an innovation is often forced in the theoretical models by assuming Cournot behavior in R&D while maintaining that the R&D competitors are competing for a fixed total amount of rent to accrue to the winner of the R&D race or to be shared among several winners. Hence, although there is monopoly in the postinnovation market or implicitly a joint profit maximizing coordination of price by multiple sellers in that market, coordination does not occur in the preinnovation market. Instead, there is a Cournot outbreak of "wasteful" nonprice competition in the form of rivalrous innovative investments. Of course, if the monopoly solution would have resulted in too little R&D investment because of the monopolist's inability to appropriate all of the social returns, the rivalry in R&D, although reducing private profits, may increase R&D toward the socially optimal level. Thus, the inverted-U results when, in a middle range of seller concentration, overbidding (from a private rather than a social perspective) for innovative rewards dominates any appropriability problems in the postinnovation market.

Support for the inverted-U has been found in numerous data sets and in numerous papers. But based on my findings (Scott, 1984), I concluded that we have no evidence supporting the "Schumpeterian" notion that seller concentration is an important determinant of R&D intensity, since in all studies finding such a relationship the result was arguably an artifact of insufficient control for differences in the value, cost, and opportunity for R&D across firms and industries apart from the differences caused because seller concentration differed. In my work, the effect of concentration disappeared despite its considerable variance within the sets of observations isolated to allow control of opportunity and appropriability differences other than those generated by concentration itself. At the FTC four-digit industry level, Levin et al. (1985) replicate my elimination of the inverted-U effect by directly controlling for the variance in appropriability and opportunity conditions across industries.[8]

I think one obvious problem with the previous tests has been the failure to take account of purposeful diversification. Section III explains why such diversification occurs; then subsequently, we can explore the impact of the concentration of R&D resources across the multiindustry groups of firms resulting from purposeful diversification.

III. WHY FIRMS DIVERSIFY PURPOSELY[9]

Figure 1 depicts the value V (before deduction of any R&D costs) of innovative investment x for a firm competing in an area of industrial R&D. V and x are present values (i.e., discounted streams of expected

Figure 1.

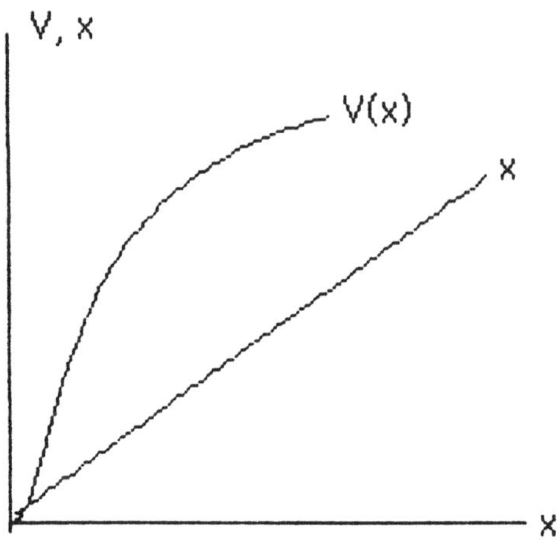

outcomes), and V is a function of x. After an initial range of increasing returns, decreasing returns result as further gains in the speed and quality of the development become more difficult. The firm's optimal investment in R&D is x such that $dV/dx = 1$, i.e., at the optimum the marginal value of another dollar invested is one dollar.

Competition in R&D will reduce the expected net benefit from innovative investment, but may increase the total R&D expenditures in the given area of industrial research up to the equilibrium in which net present value of innovative investment is zero and the internal rate of return equals the required rate of return on the investment. With higher values for the parameter h denoting a greater degree of competition, Figure 2 depicts a case where the representative firm spends more on R&D as competitive pressures increase. The sequence of short-run equilibria [for which the slopes of the curves V(x) and x are equal] reveals that the optimal x increases with competitive pressure. Long-run equilibrium occurs when $V = x$, and each firm believes that its strategy cannot be improved upon given the strategies of its rivals. Although the case depicted in Figure 2 is not the only possibility, it is an important one that is consistent with many models reviewed in Baldwin and Scott (1987).[10]

Purposeful diversification can be explained as an attempt by the firm to increase the net present value of innovative investment and escape the normal rate of return implicit in the equilibrium, shown in Figure 2, where $V = x$.

Figure 2.

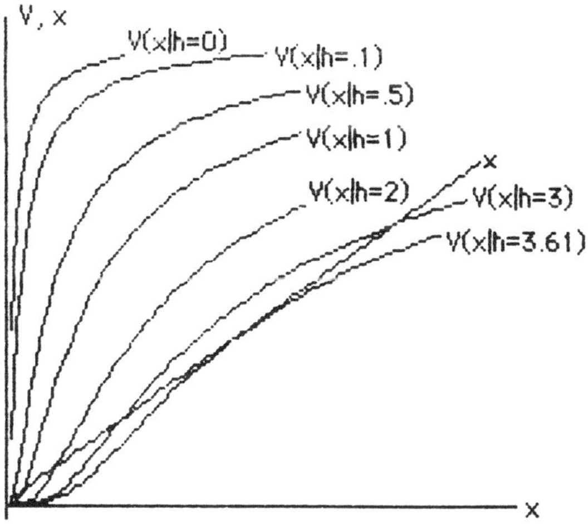

Diversification could reduce the probability of preemption by rivals, because the firm would be more likely to quickly see the applicability of research findings and beat its rivals to market with innovations. Diversification would then lower h, the rivalry parameter in Figure 2, if the firm considered its rivals less likely to beat it to the punch. In the research area covered by its diversified strategy, the firm might perceive fewer rivals, and in that case h, denoting a hazard rate measuring the conditional density of rivals' introduction, would fall. As shown in Baldwin and Scott (1987, pp. 32–41), this will raise V, and, at least temporarily, the net present value of innovative investment. With a more general argument, Nelson (1959) emphasized that diversification may increase appropriability, because the firm that continually explores many areas is more likely to recognize applications or get the proper gestalt for innovations combining insights from several fields of research. If so, the appropriability gain shifts up V. Arrow (1962) explained that moral hazard precludes complete insurance against failure of innovative investment, and, hence, diversification may lower the risk as the firm provides its own insurance. If financial markets value such diversification, the discount rate falls and V increases.

Diversification may also lower R&D costs, in effect raising V. For a given V, the firm needs less x as the costs of specialized R&D resources—say laboratory equipment or scientists—are spread over several areas of R&D investments. When economies of scope (Baumol et al. 1982) require common inputs not readily traded across markets, a diversified enterprise can lower the cost of economic activity (Teece, 1980). Teece identifies two general classes of such common inputs—know-how and specialized, indivisible physical assets. R&D investment requires those inputs in a context where the transactional difficulties for arms-length trading of technological proprietary information preclude efficient market transactions. "This is because the protection of the ownership of technological knowhow often requires suppressing information in exchange possibilities" (Teece, 1980, p. 227).

The favorable effects on net present value because of the effects of diversification on V's position for the firm do not necessarily imply that the firm's innovative investment, x, will increase. The data reviewed in Section V show that purposeful diversification of a particular type affects R&D intensity, sometimes lowering it and in other cases raising it above the average for all other firms in a given industry category. However, the data suggest that in a preponderant number of cases purposeful diversification typically increases the R&D expenditures of the firm in an industry category as compared with those firms in the category that have not purposely diversified in any way.

IV. DISTINGUISHING PURPOSEFUL DIVERSIFICATION OF R&D EFFORT

If a firm diversifies its R&D effort purposely for the reasons discussed in Section III, and if similar opportunities are available to other firms, we should find significant grouping of firms. Firms purposely combining a particular set of multicategory R&D activities will meet in the "group" of those activities more than would occur by chance from random diversification.

To find "the groups," I examined every possible pair of firms in the subset (376 large U.S. manufacturing firms) of the FTC LB sample (U.S. FTC, 1981) which was used and described in Scott and Pascoe (1984, 1986). Groups of multiple categories within which spillovers of knowledge are a priori likely are, using the methodology introduced in Scott (1982), defined to be those sets of categories where "significant" (0.01 level) meetings are found.

Scott and Pascoe (1987) find and report significant groups of FTC four-digit industries. Here I work with the broad two-digit SIC (and FTC) manufacturing industry categories, both to provide new evidence while illustrating the methodology for discerning purposeful diversification and because subsequently I focus on the effect of competition within these broad groups. In his seminal article hypothesizing the importance of diversification, Nelson (1959, pp. 302–303) emphasized the breadth of the large technological leaders in manufacturing:

> A broad technological base insures that, whatever direction the path of research may take, the results are likely to be of value to the sponsoring firm. It is for this reason that firms which support research toward the basic-science end of the spectrum are firms that have their fingers in many pies. The big chemical companies producing a range of products as wide as the field of chemistry itself, the Bell Telephone Company, General Electric, and Eastman Kodak immediately come to mind. It is not just the size of the companies. . . . Rather it is their broad underlying technological base, the wide range of products they produce or will be willing to produce if their research efforts open possibilities.

Here I work with the *applied* R&D of large U.S. manufacturing firms, yet Nelson's (1959) reasoning and the ideas of others reviewed in Section III suggest that technological leaders in manufacturing will compete for positions in the markets of the future within groups of the broad industry categories.

I let n denote the number (20 here) of two-digit SIC manufacturing categories in which the firms have R&D expenditures. For each pair of firms, s is the number of two-digit categories in which one firm has R&D, while t ($t \leq s$) is the number of two-digit categories in which the other firm does R&D. I let g denote the number of categories in which the two firms meet, while $C_{x,y}$ denotes the combination of x things taken y at a time. Then for each pair of firms for which both firms have R&D activity, I can compute a probability

$$AP = 1 - \sum_{f=0}^{g-1} p(f) = 1 - \sum_{f=0}^{g-1} [(C_{t,f}C_{n-t,s-f})/C_{n,s}],$$

the probability that the firms would meet as much or more than they do if diversification were random. Note that $C_{t,f}$ is the number of different combinations of f activities in which the two firms could meet. Conditional on the two firms meeting in a particular f activities, $C_{n-t,s-f}$ is the number of possibilities for $s - f$ categories that do not coincide with the t activities of the other firm. $C_{n,s}$ is the total number of ways the firm with s activities can be configured. So p(f) gives the proportion of $C_{n,s}$ taken by all the cases where the two firms meet in f categories. When AP is less than or equal to 0.01, the null hypothesis of random diversification is rejected and the alternative, purposeful diversification, is accepted. Scott (1982) provides numerical illustrations.

The procedure finds (after elimination of duplicates) 165 groups of related categories, and an illustrative set of examples is given in Table 1. Table 1 shows, for example, that 32 of the sample's firms performed R&D in both the two-digit SIC categories 20 (food) and 28 (chemicals). Note that a given firm can be a competitor in more than one group [with some of its lines of business (LBs) in one group and others of its LBs in other groups—but note that the same LB can be a member of more than one group], one (with some or all of its LBs in that group), or none.

V. PURPOSEFUL DIVERSIFICATION AND R&D INTENSITY

To study the effect of purposeful diversification on LB R&D intensity, I used the three years, 1974 through 1976, for which data were available. Total (applied) R&D expenditure in each line of business (a firm's operations in a given industry category, sometimes called a "business unit") for a firm was used. I chose total R&D because the decision to combine R&D in various industry categories is expected to take account of the fact that both government-financed R&D and R&D performed under contract more generally provide knowledge spillovers to the firm.[11] To lessen the importance of outliers that could result

Table 1. Some of the 165 Groups: Examples from Those Combining Research in Chemicals with Research in Other Areas

Industry categories in the group	*Number of firms in the sample and in the group*
20, food and kindred products; 28, chemicals and allied products	32
22, textile mill products; 23, apparel and other fabric products; 28, chemicals and allied products; 30, rubber and miscellaneous plastics products	4
28, chemicals and allied products; 29, petroleum refining and related industries; 30, rubber and miscellaneous plastics products	11
28, chemicals and allied products; 33, primary metal industries; 34, fabricated metal products, except machinery and transportation equipment	23
28, chemicals and allied products; 35, machinery except electrical; 36, electrical and electronic machinery, equipment, and supplies; 38, measuring, analyzing, and controlling instruments; photographic, medical and optical goods; watches and clocks	10

because of startups or catastrophies destroying sales, I used RS, the sales-weighted average of R&D expenditures to sales during the 3 years for each line of business, for the 355 firms in the sample that maintained R&D expenditures throughout the 3 years in one or more two-digit manufacturing industry categories. Thus, there were 21 firms in the sample of 376 that had no nonsporadic two-digit R&D activities.

Purposeful diversification of a particular type has a significant effect on the behavior of the firms with that particular type of diversification strategy. The firms in a purposeful diversification group behave differently from the other firms in any particular industry category in common, even when among the other firms are those that also, in their own way, have purposely diversified. To make that point, rather than comparing within each industry category the firms of each type of purposeful diversification with firms that have not purposely diversified at all, Table 2 examines the difference, industry category by industry category, of the mean of R&D intensity, RS, for firms within each type of purposeful diversification group and a matched set of firms outside the group. Recall that RS is, for each two-digit line of business (an LB—i.e., the operations of a firm in a two-digit industry category), the sum of the three years of total applied R&D—company-financed R&D plus R&D billed to the federal government plus R&D billed to other outsiders—divided by the sum of the 3 years of LB sales. Table 2 shows that the firms purposely diversified in a particular way do not necessarily have greater R&D intensity in a particular industry category than the average R&D intensity in that category of the firms not so

Table 2. Difference in R&D Intensity[a]

Significance level, *p* (two tails)	*The sign of the difference* +	*The sign of the difference* −
$p \leq 0.10$	8.9	5
$0.10 < p \leq 0.30$	16.1	13
Insignificant	28.5	28.5

[a] Using each of the 165 groups, and each two-digit industry category within each group, the percentage of cases at each level of significance for the difference in mean R&D intensity, RS, between firms within the group and an equal number of firms randomly selected (each firm had an equal chance of being chosen) from those having R&D expenditures within the two-digit category but not within the group. For the 740 cases for which the matched sample could be formed.

diversified. The R&D intensity of the particular purposely diversified firms is clearly significantly different, but the difference may be positive or negative.

To assess the statistical significance of the results in Table 2, imagine a random distribution of m items across n boxes of equal size. Let x_i be the random variable that is one if the ith item appears in a particular box and zero otherwise. Then a measure of the number of items appearing in a particular box is the random variable $X = \sum_{i=1}^{m} x_i$. Its expected value is

$$E(X) = \sum_{i=1}^{m} [1 \cdot 1/n + 0 \cdot (1 - 1/n)] = m/n.$$

Its variance is

$$\begin{aligned} var(X) &= \sum_{i=1}^{m} var(x_i) \\ &= m\ var(x_i) \\ &= m\{[1 - 1/n]^2(1/n) + [0 - 1/n]^2(1 - 1/n)\}. \end{aligned}$$

Considering the top two categories on the left as a single "box," or the top two categories on the right as a single "box," $n = 1/0.15 = 6\frac{2}{3}$. This is true because a two-tailed test at the 30% level implies that there should be 15% of the cases in each tail. There are then 100%/15% = $6\frac{2}{3}$ such equally likely categories or "boxes" into which cases can fall under the null hypothesis. Then, since 740 cases are examined in Table 2, $E(X) = m/n = 740/(6\frac{2}{3}) = 111$, and $\sqrt{var(X)} = 9.71$. Now, in the top two "boxes" on the left, there are 25% of the 740 items, or 7.62 standard deviations above the expected number if the behavior or purposely diversified firms is no different from that of others. In the top two "boxes" on the right, there are 18% of the items, or 2.29 standard deviations above the expected number.

As Scott and Pascoe (1987) show by also comparing purposely diversified firms with matched sets of firms not purposely diversified, firms purposely diversified in different ways are more alike in their R&D intensity than are purposely diversified firms and firms that have not so diversified. And although purposely diversified firms may have higher or lower R&D intensities in particular industry categories than the firms that have not purposely diversified, there is a significant tendency for the R&D intensity of the purposely diversified firms to be higher.

VI. R&D CONCENTRATION WITHIN MULTIINDUSTRY GROUPS AND R&D INTENSITY

Despite the elimination in Scott (1984) of the effect of seller concentration on R&D intensity and the corroboration of that result in Levin et al. (1985) where direct controls for appropriability and opportunity were used, a simple descriptive relation consonant with a simplified view that competition promotes technological progress is still possible. Arguably seller concentration should be measured by the concentration of R&D resources, and concentration within industry categories should arguably be replaced by concentration within complementary R&D activities. In this section, I explore both possibilities. If I find that, using R&D concentration within complementary sets of R&D activities, the relationship between concentration and R&D intensity survives the controls for other differences across firms and industries, then the simple descriptive relation is resurrected. However, if the relation again disappears, we are clearly left with the need to explore more intricate models.

First, the experiments of Scott (1984) and Levin et al. (1985) at most caution that previously estimated inverted-U relations between seller concentration and R&D intensity may not reflect the theory of competition in R&D. Further, the observations on seller concentration may be incorrect if effective competition in R&D occurs within industry boundaries that differ from those conventionally defined. With R&D, the customary distinction between "the food industry" and "the chemical industry" may—unfortunate as it may seem—be blurred. Finally, seller concentration in R&D activity may well be the relevant factor. Traditional sales concentration measures have previously been used, yet the anticipation of the degree of competition in the postinnovation market as well as conjectural variations in the preinnovation market may well depend on the concentration of R&D activity.

With CR denoting four-firm concentration ratios and H denoting Herfindahl indices, and with I denoting conventional industry categorization and G denoting our group categorization, and D_i and T_j denoting firm and industry dummy variables, respectively, Tables 3 and 4 undertake the new experiments suggested by these thoughts. These tests are rough, because we must capture the variance in the number and size

Table 3. Industry R&D Concentration and Line of Business (LB) R&D Intensity, with the Concentration Associated with an LB Observation Being the Concentration for the Conventional Industry to Which the LB Belongs

(1) $RS = -0.018 + 0.17\ ICR - 0.17(ICR)^2$
$(t = -0.90)\quad (t = 2.3)^{b}\quad (t = -2.4)^{b}$
F value = 3.1,[c] $R^2 = 0.0049$, degrees of freedom = 1256

(2) $RS = 0.018 + 0.12\ IH - 0.53\ (IH)^2$
$(t = 2.8)^{b}\quad (t = 1.3)^{d}\quad (t = -2.0)^{c}$
F value = 3.5,[c] $R^2 = 0.0055$, degrees of freedom = 1256

(3) $RS = 0.027 - 0.0073\ ICR$
$(t = 3.6)^{b}\quad (t = -0.52)$
F value = 0.27, $R^2 = 0.00021$, degrees of freedom = 1257

(4) $RS = 0.029 - 0.050\ IH$
$(t = 7.9)^{a}\quad (t = -1.7)^{c,i}$
F value = 3.0,[d,i] $R^2 = 0.0024$, degrees of freedom = 1257

(5) $$RS = z + \sum_{i=2}^{355} \beta_i D_i - 0.010\ ICR - 0.017\ (ICR)^2$$
$(F = 1.5)^{a,e}\quad (t = -0.11)\quad (t = -0.20)$
F value = 1.5,[a] $R^2 = 0.37$, degrees of freedom = 902

(6) $$RS = z + \sum_{i=2}^{355} \beta_i D_i - 0.14\ IH + 0.22\ (IH)^2$$
$(F = 1.5)^{a,f}\ (t = -1.4)^{d}\quad (t = 0.74)$
F value = 1.5,[a] $R^2 = 0.38$, degrees of freedom = 902

(7) $$RS = z + \sum_{i=2}^{355} \beta_i D_i - 0.028\ ICR$$
$(F = 1.5)^{a,g}\ (t = -1.8)^{c}$
F value = 1.5,[a] $R^2 = 0.37$, degrees of freedom = 903

(8) $$RS = z + \sum_{i=2}^{355} \beta_i D_i - 0.068\ IH$$
$(F = 1.5)^{a,h}\ (t = -2.2)^{c}$
F value = 1.5,[a] $R^2 = 0.38$, degrees of freedom = 903

[a] Significance level (one-tail) = 0.0001.
[b] Significance level (one-tail) = 0.01.
[c] Significance level (one-tail) = 0.05.
[d] Significance level (one-tail) = 0.10.
[e] To reduce the size of the X′X matrix, the firm effects were absorbed. Nonetheless, the F test is for the effects when fitted last. That is, F for the company effects is the ratio of the reduction in residual sum of squares, as we go from Eq. (1) to Eq. (5), divided by 354, to the residual sum of squares for Eq. (5) divided by 902.
[f] This is the F test for the effects when fitted last. The F value was derived using Eqs. (2) and (6) in the manner described in note *e* for Eqs. (1) and (5).
[g] Fitted last, using Eqs. (3) and (7).
[h] Fitted last, using Eqs. (4) and (8).
[i] Note that the discrepancy between the significance of the slope coefficient and the significance of the equation as a whole results because we are using a one-tailed test to determine the significance of the t value. With a two-tailed test, the probability of $|t|$ being larger is of course the same as the probability of F being larger, which in this case is 0.085.

Table 4. Group R&D Concentration and Line of Business (LB) R&D Intensity[a]

---

(1) $RS = -0.0067 + 0.12\ GCR - 0.11\ (GCR)^2$

$(t = -0.29) \quad (t = 1.7)^{d} \quad (t = -2.1)^{d}$

F value $= 5.5^{c}$ $R^2 = 0.0087$, degrees of freedom $= 1256$

(2) $RS = 0.025 - 0.0038\ GH - 0.018\ (GH)^2$

$(t = 5.5)^{b} \quad (t = -0.13) \quad (t = -0.46)$

F value $= 1.4$, $R^2 = 0.0022$, degrees of freedom $= 1256$

(3) $RS = 0.040 - 0.024\ GCR$

$(t = 6.0)^{b} \quad (t = -2.6)^{c}$

F value $= 6.6^{c}$ $R^2 = 0.0052$, degrees of freedom $= 1257$

(4) $RS = 0.027 \quad 0.017\ GII$

$(t = 9.2)^{b}\ (t = -1.6)^{e,h}$

F value $= 2.6^{h}$ $R^2 = 0.0021$, degrees of freedom $= 1257$

(5) $RS = z + \sum_{i=2}^{355} \beta_i D_i + \sum_{j=2}^{20} \gamma_j T_j - 0.050\ GCR + 0.014\ (GCR)^2$

$(F = 1.4)^{c,f} \quad (F = 3.5)^{b} \quad (t = -0.40) \quad (t = 0.16)$

F value $= 1.7^{b}$ $R^2 = .42$, degrees of freedom $= 883$

(6) $RS = z + \sum_{i=2}^{355} \beta_i D_i + \sum_{j=2}^{20} \gamma_j T_j - 0.063\ GH + 0.050\ (GH)^2$

$(F = 1.4)^{c,g}\ (F = 3.7)^{b} \quad (t = -1.0) \quad (t = 0.74)$

F value $= 1.7^{b}$ $R^2 = 0.42$, degrees of freedom $= 883$

(7) $RS = z + \sum_{i=2}^{355} \beta_i D_i + \sum_{j=2}^{20} \gamma_j T_j - 0.031\ GCR$

$(F = 1.4)^{c,g}\ (F = 3.5)^{b} \quad (t = -1.4)^{e}$

F value $= 1.7,^{a}$ $R^2 = 0.42$, degrees of freedom $= 884$

(8) $RS = z + \sum_{i=2}^{355} \beta_i D_i + \sum_{j=2}^{20} \gamma_j T_j - 0.020\ GH$

$(F = 1.4)^{c,g} \quad (F = 3.7)^{b} \quad (t = -0.85)$

F value $= 1.7^{b}$ $R^2 = 0.42$, degrees of freedom $= 884$

---

[a] The concentration associated with an LB observation is that for the group (or the average for the groups) to which that LB belongs, or for the conventional industry to which the LB belongs if the LB is not part of a group.

[b] Significance level (one-tail) = 0.0001.

[c] Significance level (one-tail) = 0.01.

[d] Significance level (one-tail) = 0.05.

[e] Significance level (one-tail) = 0.10.

[f] Although the firm effects were absorbed to reduce the size of the X′X matrix, this F value is for the 354 firm effects when fitted last. It is the ratio of the reduction in the sum of squared residuals, as we move from the specification with industry effects, GCR, and $(GCR)^2$ to that including additionally the firm effects, divided by 354, to the sum of squared residuals in Eq. (5) divided by 883. Thus, when fitted last, F for the company effects is 1.4 with 354 and 883 degrees of freedom. This is obviously highly significant, but unlike the 1.5 case in Table 3, I have not worked out the integral, which is tedious (using Simpson's rule) when the number of degrees of freedom in the numerator and the denominator are so large. Although the result is actually more significant, I have conservatively labeled it as "c."

[g] This F value is for the firm effects when fitted last, in the same manner as explained in note f. Again, "c" is very conservative; the result is actually more significant.

[h] Note that the discrepancy between the significance of the slope coefficient and the significance of the equation as a whole results because we are using a one-tailed test to determine the significance of the t value. With a two-tailed test, the probability of $|t|$ being larger is of course the same as the probability of F being larger, which in this case is 0.11.

distribution of R&D performers with their distribution in our sample. For example, suppose that industry categories A and B each has 10 firms and each firm has the same R&D expenditures. ICR is 0.40 for industry A and 0.40 for industry B, while IH is 0.1 for A and 0.1 for B. But if in fact industry categories A and B constitute a group of complementary activities, and for a simple example we counterfactually assume A's firms are all different from B's, then the R&D intensity for an LB in either industry A or B would be matched in Table 4's statistics with GCR = 0.20 or GH = 0.05.

Equation (1) in Table 3 shows that, using conventional industry categories and no controls for other effects, there is the conventional inverted-U relation between R&D intensity and concentration. R&D intensity peaks for a four-firm R&D concentration ratio of 0.50 (i.e., when 50% of an industry's R&D is controlled by the four firms with the largest R&D expenditures). Equation (1) of Table 4 shows that when the R&D concentration of our multimarket groups is used, the peak of R&D intensity occurs when four-firm R&D concentration is 0.55 (or 55%).

However, the tests show that although firm effects (βs), or firm and industry effects (γs) where both can be estimated,[12] eliminate the inverted-U in the data, a statistically significant negative effect of sellers' (R&D activity) concentration on LB R&D intensity remains. As comparison of the two tables shows, however, the result is not markedly different when concentration within the group rather than concentration within the industry category is used to condition the R&D behavior of a line of business. A simplified view that competition stimulates R&D is weakly supported. However, the concentration variables explain only a minuscule proportion of the variance in R&D at the two-digit line of business level. Thus, my attempt to resurrect a simple empirical relationship between concentration and R&D intensity has failed.[13]

VII. SUMMARY

The results are promising for our exploration of the effects of "size" along the dimension of purposeful diversification across several industry categories. As the theory reviewed in Section III predicts, purposely diversified firms clearly behave differently from those that are not purposely diversified. There is also a tendency for purposely diversified firms to have higher R&D intensity, ceteris paribus.

The results were not promising for concentration in any simple form, although it may well be that in interactions with other industry variables it has a lot to do with the variance in behavior explained by industry effects. In any case, the implication from the work here in conjunction with that in Scott (1984) is that seller concentration does not, ceteris paribus, appear to be an important determinant of LB R&D intensity, whether measured in terms of current sales or R&D expenditures, and whether measured for conventional industry categories or for the multicategory groups of related categories combined by purposely diversifying firms.

More generally, the idea of purposeful diversification has a lot to add, even if it cannot save the simple view of concentration and Schumpeterian competition. I think progress in the empirical research about market structure and technological change will require measures of behavior other than R&D intensity and measures of performance other than patenting.[14]

Since productivity growth is in part determined by R&D, it provides one possible alternative variable that can be used to frame and test hypotheses about Schumpeterian competition. For example, Scherer (1983) has explored the association between concentration, R&D intensity, and productivity growth.[15] Purposeful diversification could usefully be considered in such tests, because, as the theory of Section III would predict, analysis of productivity data affords evidence of spillovers of knowledge among the industry categories in each set combined by purposeful diversification (Scott and Pascoe, 1987).

Scott's model (1987) of "component gestalt"—the integrated product structure or components' performance-attribute pattern necessary for a complex innovation—provides a framework for further analysis of "Schumpeterian" hypotheses and purposeful diversification. Many industrial R&D projects require the integration of several components. Purposeful diversification undoubtedly results in part because the development of multiple component projects requires integration of research in several industry categories.

Scott and Pascoe (1987) find that firms in the same four-digit industry category have different patterns of purposeful diversification and in many cases do not purposely diversify at all. That same phenomenon occurs at the two-digit industry level observed in this paper. Scott's work on "component gestalt" (1987) describes the sample space for industrial R&D and suggests the reason that firms differ so dramatically in their extent and type of purposeful diversification is that they find it profitable to research different niches in that sample space. Some will focus on isolated components while others will attempt their integration in a grand R&D project.

Perhaps surprisingly, R&D rivalry may improve the prospects for an integrated product structure rather than a set of isolated components (Scott, 1987). The new direction suggested for research is to ask if more competition does lead to a filling up of more niches in the sample space and a desirable increase in expected product integration in areas of R&D where appropriability problems would otherwise reduce the extent of "component gestalt" below the socially optimal level. Empirical work could usefully study the effects of firm size and R&D rivalry on the extent of product component integration. More generally, although the simplest concentration–R&D intensity tests offer little support for theories about R&D rivalry, even when defined over the multiindustry groups determined by purposeful diversification, I expect that sophisticated tests of Schumpeterian hypotheses will ultimately reveal that R&D competition must be viewed within such groups.

ACKNOWLEDGMENTS

I thank William L. Baldwin, Albert N. Link, V. Kerry Smith, and an anonymous referee for helpful comments. My evidence uses the Line of Business (LB) data from the Federal Trade Commission (FTC). George Pascoe provided the expert data processing needed to obtain the results. The FTC's Disclosure Avoidance Officer has certified that these results do not identify individual company LB data. The conclusions presented herein are those of the author and have not been adopted by the FTC or any entity within the Commission.

NOTES

1. See Baldwin and Scott (1987, pp. 1–4) for quotes from Schumpeter (1939, 1942) with discussion documenting his vision about the competition that counts and the need for large firms with market power in order to have good performance on the score of technological change. Baldwin and Scott (1987, pp. 63–113) also provide a review of the empirical literature exploring the Schumpeterian hypothesis about firm size and market power.

2. The idea of purposeful diversification is developed in Scott (1982), Scott and Pascoe (1987), and Scott (1988).

3. A line of business (LB, sometimes called a business unit) is a firm's operations in a particular industry category. In Scott (1984) and Scott and Pascoe (1987) each LB is the operations of a firm in an FTC four-digit industry category. For the present paper, where I want to focus on the competition within broad industry categories, each LB is the operations of a firm in a SIC (and equivalently FTC) two-digit industry category.

4. The elasticity of R&D with respect to business unit size was essentially one (Scott, 1984, p. 243).

5. The previous literature is reviewed in Baldwin and Scott (1987, pp. 63–113). There is of course the possibility that the insignificant effect of firm size results because the estimated coefficients are biased by the left-out firm-wide variables. Such variables are important, since differences across firms explain a large and significant amount of the variance in business-unit R&D intensity even after control for industry effects (Scott, 1984, 1987). Yet the only firm variable controlled, firm size, appears to be unimportant. Inclusion of the missing firm variables could change our current understanding of the data.

6. See Baldwin and Scott (1987) for a review of these and other studies examining the relationships between diversification and technological advance.

7. Baldwin and Scott (1987) review the theories predicting such a relationship as well as the empirical studies that have found it.

8. Scott's work eliminated the relation completely. Levin et al. replicate this result in the sense that the significance of the relation between concentration and R&D intensity is dramatically reduced. Again, the lack of control for firm level variables may be a problem. The Levin et al. (1985) estimation is at the FTC four-digit industry level. Therefore, the coefficients on the appropriability and opportunity variables (as well as on seller concentration) may be reflecting left-out variables describing the firms or business units. This problem has perhaps been best understood in the literature about market structure and profits. The links between industry characteristics and profits that appear in industry level data look very different once one looks at disaggregated firm or especially business unit data and controls for firm and business unit effects. See Scott and Pascoe (1986).

9. This section is based on the discussion in Scott (1988).

10. See Baldwin and Scott (1987, pp. 4–63) and Scott (1988) where Figure 2 is seen to be a simulation of one of the models of Kamien and Schwartz (1982) and where other models of rivalry in R&D are discussed in the context of the general relationships in Figures 1 and 2.

11. Using FTC LB data, Scott (1984), at the LB level, and Levin et al. (1985), at the industry level, have documented a complementary relationship between government-financed and company-financed R&D expenditures. Levy and Terleckyj (1983) find that government contract R&D induced private R&D expenditure and that the stock of government contract R&D has a discernible effect on private sector productivity. Lichtenberg (1987) has noted that the effect of government-financed R&D on company-financed R&D may be in part because along with greater government-financed R&D comes greater sales to the government, and there may be an identifiable component of the company-financed R&D that is associated with such sales. Serious misspecification problems plague his estimation, though, because (except for a time trend in the aggregate time series and time dummies in the pooled cross-section and time series) he has no control variables other than government-financed R&D and two sales variables (sales to the government and sales to others). Yet he does not use LB data and cannot control for firm effects across the many industry categories over which the firms in his sample spread their R&D. Further, he does not control for industry effects, although a rough attempt at such control would be possible even with his data. Because firm and industry effects are important (Scott, 1984, 1987), many firm variables and industry variables should be controlled given the firm-level observations Lichtenberg uses. Finally, note that the firm and industry dummies in Scott (1984) control for the systematic differences across firms and industries in the proportion of

sales to the government. The relevant differences will have been controlled if, after taking out the firm and industry differences, little difference remained at the LB level. If not, though, it is possible that the effect of government-financed R&D on corporate-financed R&D does not reflect spillovers but instead a compartmentalized link between sales to the government and government funding of R&D effort.

12. The industry effects cannot be estimated for the specifications in Table 3, because the necessary dummy variables would be completely collinear with the concentration measures.

13. Note that in the results of Table 4, where firm *and* industry effects can be controlled because the concentration measures (having been observed for the multiindustry groups) are not perfectly collinear with the industry effects, we have in effect controlled for all relevant firm-level variables, any relevant powers of those variables, and their interactions, as well as all relevant industry-level variables, their powers, and their interactions, assuming only that the true model is linear in the parameters, although not linear in the variables. From the linear algebra and the Gauss–Markov theorem, the expected value of the intercept is the weighted sum of the entire set of coefficients for the true variables characterizing firms and industries, with the weight of each coefficient being the value its associated variable takes for the base firm or base industry. The expected value of the coefficient of the dummy variable for each remaining industry (or firm) is the difference from the intercept of the weighted sum of the entire set of coefficients for the true variables characterizing industries (or firms), with the weight of each coefficient being the value its associated variable takes for that industry (or firm). Scott and Pascoe (1986, pp. 284–285) provide the simple linear algebra for this interpretation.

14. New ways of observing behavior and framing Schumpeterian hypotheses are needed not only because of the lack of conclusive evidence from existing tests, but additionally because rather special and exacting circumstances, difficult to obtain in practice, are necessary for interpretation of the tests focusing on the relationship between size and R&D intensity (Kohn and Scott, 1982).

15. See also Link and Lunn (1984).

REFERENCES

Arrow, K. J., "Economic Welfare and the Allocation of Resources for Invention." In Universities-National Bureau Committee for Economic Research, *The Rate and Direction of Inventive Activity*. Princeton: Princeton University Press, 1962.

Baldwin, W. L. and J. T. Scott, "Market Structure and Technological Change." *Fundamentals of Pure and Applied Economics* 17. London: Harwood Academic Publishers, 1987.

Baumol, W. J., J. C. Panzar and R. D. Willig, *Contestable Markets and the Theory of Industry Structure*. New York: Harcourt, Brace Jovanovich, 1982.

Cohen, W. M., R. C. Levin and D. C. Mowery, "Firm Size and R&D Intensity: A Re-Examination." *Journal of Industrial Economics* 35(June 1987):543–565.

Kamien, M. I. and N. L. Schwartz, *Market Structure and Innovation*. Cambridge: Cambridge University Press, 1982.

Kohn, M. and J. T. Scott, "Scale Economies in Research and Development: the

Schumpeterian Hypothesis." *Journal of Industrial Economics* 30(March 1982):239–249.

Levin, R. C., W. M. Cohen and D. C. Mowery, "R&D Appropriability, Opportunity, and Market Structure: New Evidence on Some Schumpeterian Hypotheses." *American Economic Review* 75(May 1985):20–24.

Levy, D. M. and N. E. Terleckyj, "Effects of Government R&D on Private R&D Investment and Productivity: A Macroeconomic Analysis." *The Bell Journal of Economics* 14(Autumn 1983):551–561.

Lichtenberg, Frank R., "The Effect of Government Funding on Private Industrial Research and Development: A Re-Assessment." *The Journal of Industrial Economics* 36(September 1987):97–104.

Link, A. N., *Allocating R&D Resources: A Study of the Determinants of R&D by Character of Use*. Washington: U.S. National Science Foundation, 1981.

Link, A. N., "An Analysis of the Composition of R&D Spending." *Southern Economic Journal* 49(October 1982): 342–348.

Link, A. N., "Alternative Sources of Technology: An Analysis of Induced Innovations." *Managerial and Decision Economics* 4(1983):40–43.

Link, A. N. and J. E. Long, "The Simple Economics of Basic Scientific Research: A Test of Nelson's Diversification Hypothesis." *Journal of Industrial Economics* 30(1981):105–109.

Link, A. N. and J. Lunn, "Concentration and the Returns to R&D." *Review of Industrial Organization* 1(1984):232–239.

Nelson, R. R., "The Simple Economics of Basic Scientific Research." *Journal of Political Economy* 67(June 1959):297–306.

Scherer, F. M., "Concentration, R&D, and Productivity Change." *Southern Economic Journal* 50(July 1983):221–225.

Scherer, F. M., "Corporate Size, Diversification, and Innovative Activity." In F. M. Scherer (ed.), *Innovation and Growth: Schumpeterian Perspectives*. Cambridge: MIT Press, 1984.

Schumpeter, J. A., *Business Cycles,* 2 vol. New York: McGraw-Hill, 1939.

Schumpeter, J. A., *Capitalism, Socialism, and Democracy*. New York: Harper, 1942.

Scott, J. T., "Multimarket Contact and Economic Performance." *Review of Economics and Statistics* 64(August 1982):368–375.

Scott, J. T., "Firm versus Industry Variability in R&D Intensity." In Zvi Griliches (ed.), *R&D, Patents, and Productivity,* Chapter 10. Chicago: University of Chicago Press for the National Bureau of Economic Research, 1984.

Scott, J. T., "Diversification versus Cooperation in R&D Investment." *Managerial and Decision Economics* 9 (September 1988): 173–186.

Scott, J. T., "Component Gestalt and Industrial R&D: Firm Effects and the Sample Space for Industrial R&D." Dartmouth College Working Paper 87-7, presented at the 57th annual conference of the Southern Economic Association in Washington, D. C., November 22–24, 1987.

Scott, J. T. and G. Pascoe, "Capital Costs and Profitability." *International Journal of Industrial Organization* 2(September 1984):217–233.

Scott, J. T. and G. Pascoe, "Beyond Firm and Industry Effects on Profitability in Imperfect Markets." *Review of Economics and Statistics* 68(May 1986):284–292.

Scott, J. T. and G. Pascoe, "Purposive Diversification of R&D in Manufacturing." *The Journal of Industrial Economics* 36(December 1987):193–205.

Teece, D. J., "Economies of Scope and the Scope of the Enterprise." *Journal of Economic Behavior and Organization* 1(September 1980):223–247.

U.S. Federal Trade Commission, Bureau of Economics, "The Survey Plan," pp. 340–341, *Statistical Report: Annual Line of Business Report: 1974*. Washington, D. C., September 1981.

THE IMPLICATIONS OF SPILLOVERS FOR R&D INVESTMENT AND WELFARE:

A NEW PERSPECTIVE

Wesley M. Cohen and Daniel A. Levinthal

I. INTRODUCTION

Since Nelson (1959) and Arrow (1962), economists have argued that research spillovers diminish firms' incentives to invest in R&D, and, thus, dampen firms' innovativeness by undermining the appropriability of returns to inventive activity. This proposition assumes that technological knowledge that is in the public domain is a public good. Like a radio signal or smoke pollution, its effects are costlessly realized by all firms located within the neighborhood of the emission. This view, however, ignores an important feature of the assimilation of research spillovers. The firm's ability to recognize and assimilate useful knowl-

Advances in Applied Micro-Economics, Volume 5, pages 29–45.

ISBN: 0-89232-797-9

edge from the environment depends to a great extent on the firm's prior and ongoing R&D. This observation implies that although spillovers discourage R&D by undermining appropriability, they also encourage R&D since only through its own R&D may a firm exploit the knowledge generated by its competitors.[1] Recognizing this role of R&D changes our view of the effect of appropriability conditions on R&D spending. In this paper, we develop a model that explores the implications for R&D investment and social welfare of these offsetting incentives associated with spillovers.

To place this discussion in the broader context of the determination of firms' inventive activity, it is useful to understand that three broad classes of industry-level determinants are typically considered to drive R&D spending: demand, appropriability, and technological opportunity conditions. In this paper, we are suggesting that the effect of the research spillovers that often underlie appropriability conditions is less straightforward than commonly believed, and depend critically upon the ease of learning within an industry.

In order to assimilate research spillovers, the firm conducts its own research. While some of this activity involves the immediate task of information processing, we suggest that it is principally the firm's prior R&D experience that shapes its ability to assimilate external knowledge. Specifically, a firm's research experience prepares it to identify, assimilate, and use new knowledge from the environment. This observation is confirmed by a number of scholars of technological change who have shown that firms must invest in own R&D to be able to utilize information that is available externally.[2] Thus, we argue that although R&D obviously generates innovations, it also develops the firm's ability to learn from the environment. R&D satisfies a dual role within the firm. In other words, if we refer to the ability to learn from the environment as a firm's "absorptive capacity," then innovations and absorptive capacity are joint products of the same process.

Once the role of R&D in building absorptive capacity is recognized, it follows that the appropriability of the output of other firms' R&D is endogenous with respect to a firm's own R&D spending. As a consequence, spillovers yield two offsetting effects on firms' incentives to conduct R&D. The first is the well-known negative incentive effect associated with the appropriation of the firm's R&D output by others. Second, other firms' spillovers provide a firm with greater incentive to conduct its own R&D because only through its own R&D may the firm tap into the knowledge and associated benefits generated by other firms.

Recognition of the dual role of R&D clarifies a paradox noted by Spence (1984). If spillovers dampen R&D investment, then why do we observe in some industries, such as semiconductors and engineering and scientific instruments, a high level of spillovers coexisting with high levels of R&D investment?[3] The perspective presented here provides one possible explanation. Although spillovers dilute rents to innovation, they also provide an incentive for a firm to invest in R&D in order to be able to assimilate its competitors' R&D spillovers. In some industries, this positive incentive effect may be sufficient to more than offset the negative incentive associated with the imperfect appropriation of rents due to R&D.

To explore the implications of the endogeneity of absorptive capacity for both R&D investment and social welfare, we construct a simple model of the generation of a firm's technological knowledge. To do so, we extend the model of industry spillovers developed by Spence (1984), which represents the role of R&D in terms of cost-reducing technical change. Section II of the paper develops the model structure, which is analyzed in Section III. Although suggestive of the forces affecting the firm's incentives to conduct R&D, the results of the general analysis are, however, often ambiguous. Thus, in Section IV we develop a numerical example to both explore the conditions under which particular results are obtained and evaluate the robustness of these results. We then explore the welfare implications of our model.

II. MODEL STRUCTURE

The marginal cost of production is assumed to be constant and is represented by c_i, where i denotes firm i. R&D affects the firm's performance through c_i, which is assumed to be a function of the level of technological and scientific knowledge available to the firm. We represent additions to firm i's stock of knowledge by z_i. The firm's cost is related to changes in the stock of knowledge by the function F(•); $c_i = F(z_i)$, where F is a declining function of z_i. The key element of the model structure is the determination of the knowledge increment, z_i. We postulate the following relationship:

$$z_i = M_i + \gamma_i \, \theta \sum_{j \neq i} M_j \tag{2.1}$$

The firm's new knowledge, z_i, reflects not only the firm's own investment in research and development, indicated by M_i, but other firms' investment in research and development, represented by M_j for $j \neq i$. The degree to which the research efforts of one firm may spill over to a pool of knowledge potentially available to all other firms is characterized by θ. A θ value of one means that the R&D effort of one firm increases the pool of knowledge available to other firms by the total amount of the firm's R&D. A value of zero means that the benefits of research are exclusively appropriated by the firm conducting the research. Exogenous factors such as patent policy or the nature of an industry's technology presumably shape θ.

Our analysis enriches prior treatments of spillovers with the notion that a firm's capacity to absorb externally generated knowledge depends on the firm's own research efforts. We represent a firm's absorptive capacity in Eq. (2.1) by $\gamma_i(M_i, \beta)$, where $0 \leq \gamma_i \leq 1$. When $\gamma_i = 1$, the firm absorbs all knowledge that is in the public domain; alternatively, when $\gamma_i = 0$, the firm absorbs none. Firm R&D increases absorptive capacity, $\gamma_M \equiv \partial\gamma/\partial M > 0$, though at a decreasing rate, $\gamma_{MM} \equiv \partial^2\gamma/\partial M\partial M < 0$.

The importance of R&D to developing and maintaining a firm's absorptive capacity will, however, vary. We consider γ to be a function of not only M_i, but of the variable β, which represents the degree to which a firm must conduct R&D to be able to assimilate new knowledge. We suggest that β may be determined by the cumulative character of technological advance in an industry, the pace of that advance, or the complexity of the underlying knowledge base. For example, in fields in which technology is mature and fairly stable, β would take on a low value, while in fields of rapidly changing technology, such as genetic engineering, β would take on a high value. We assume that as β increases the greater will be the marginal impact of own R&D on absorptive capacity, such that $\gamma_{M\beta} \equiv \partial^2\gamma/\partial M\partial\beta > 0$.[4] We also assume that for a given level of M, absorptive capacity decreases with β, ceteris paribus (i.e., $\gamma_\beta < 0$).[5] Thus, we are assuming that increasing β increases the marginal effect of R&D on absorptive capacity, but diminishes the level of absorptive capacity. This second effect indicates that when external knowledge becomes more difficult to assimilate, the firm will assimilate less of it for a given R&D effort.

In highlighting the importance of an endogenous absorptive capacity, γ, we are not suggesting that spillovers themselves do not play an important role. Rather, we assume the appropriation of other firms' research is realized through the interaction of θ and γ, reflecting the notion that the firm cannot assimilate what is not spilled out. In addition, the firm cannot passively assimilate externally available knowledge and must invest in its own R&D to absorb any of the R&D output of its competitors.

The non-R&D elements of the model structure are outlined as follows. There are n firms in the industry with symmetric R&D policies producing a homogeneous good. The output of firm i is represented by x_i. The market price when x units of the good are sold, where $x \equiv \sum_{i=1}^{n} x_i$, is represented by P(x). Each firm chooses its level of R&D to maximize profits, taking the R&D levels of the other firms as given. Thus, we are modeling a symmetric Nash equilibrium in R&D levels. However, the firms anticipate the effect of changes in their R&D investments on their competitor's knowledge levels and the effect of this on competitors' output decisions. The optimal production level for a firm depends not only on its own costs, which depend upon z_i, but on the costs of its competitors as well. As a result, the firm's output is a function not only of its own level of knowledge, z_i, but the knowledge level of all firms in the industry, represented by the vector $z \equiv (z_1, z_2, z_3, \ldots, z_n)$. Therefore, we can represent the firm's production level by $x_i(z)$ and the market output by $x(z)$. The profits of the firm, gross of research expenditures, can be written as follows:

$$\Pi^i(z) = x_i(z)P[x(z)] - c_i(z_i)x_i(z). \tag{2.2}$$

Differentiating Π^i with respect to M_i yields

$$R(M, \theta, \beta) \equiv \Pi^i_{z_i}\left[1 + \gamma_{M_i}\theta \sum_{j \neq i} M_j\right] + \theta \sum_{j \neq i} \gamma_j \Pi^i_{z_j} \tag{2.3}$$

where $\Pi^i_{z_i}$ is the derivative of gross profits with respect to the firm's own knowledge and $\Pi^i_{z_j}$ is the derivative with respect to other firms' knowledge. The function $R(M, \theta, \beta)$ is the marginal return to firm i of conducting its own R&D. If we derive this expression for each firm and set it equal to one, the per unit cost of R&D, this generates a set of equations characterizing the firms' optimal R&D policy given their competitors' R&D levels. When solved for simultaneously, these equations yield the equilibrium values of firm R&D.

III. ANALYSIS

In this section, we consider the effect of changes in the structural parameters of the model on the firm's equilibrium R&D expenditures. Given Eq. (2.3), the following equation characterizes the firm's optimal level of R&D:

$$\Pi^i_{Z_i}\left[1 + \gamma^{M_i}\theta \sum_{j\neq i} M_j\right] + \theta \sum_{j\neq i} \gamma_j \Pi^i_{Z_j} = 1. \qquad (3.1)$$

If we define the optimal level of firm R&D to be M* and substitute this into the above equation, then (3.1) holds as an identity. Given this relationship, we may examine the effect on equilibrium R&D expenditures of the spillover rate, θ. In the context of our n-firm symmetric equilibrium, we can show that the sign of $\partial M^*/\partial\theta$ equals the sign of R_θ, where R is defined in Eq. (2.3) above.[6] Therefore, to simplify the presentation of our comparative static results, we only present R_θ to establish the sign of $\partial M^*/\partial\theta$.[7]

To explore how equilibrium R&D expenditures, M*, change with the spillover rate, we differentiate Eq. (3.1) with respect to θ,

$$\begin{aligned}\operatorname{sign}\left\{\frac{\partial M^*}{\partial\theta}\right\} = \operatorname{sign}(R_\theta) = \operatorname{sign}\Big\{&\Pi^i_{Z_i}\gamma_M(n-1)M + (n-1)\gamma\Pi^i_{Z_j}\\ &+ \gamma(n-1)M\Big[\Big\langle\Pi^i_{Z_iZ_i} + (n-1)\Pi^i_{Z_iZ_j}\Big\rangle\Big[1 + \gamma_M\theta(n-1)M\Big]\\ &+ \theta(n-1)\gamma\Big[\Pi^i_{Z_iZ_j} + \Pi^i_{Z_jZ_j} + (n-2)\Pi^i_{Z_jZ_k}\Big]\Big]\Big\}, \qquad (3.2)\end{aligned}$$

where $i\neq j\neq k$. A natural question to ask is whether spillovers have the traditional negative effect on equilibrium R&D expenditure if absorptive capacity is not endogenous, meaning $\gamma \equiv 1$. This negative effect is obtained if, first, we assume that $\Pi^i_{Z_i} > 0$ and $\Pi^i_{Z_j} < 0$. Increases in own knowledge increases profits, while increases in other firms' knowledge decreases profits. These properties are the same as those assumed by Spence (1984), and can be derived in the context of the example developed in Section IV. Second, we must also assume either that the second-order effects of knowledge, z, on own profits, are negative or relatively small, or that the sufficient condition holds for the reaction function to be downward sloping when $\gamma \equiv 1$.[8]

However, if absorptive capacity is endogenous, meaning $\gamma_M > 0$, then the sign of $\partial M^*/\partial\theta$ is ambiguous regardless of the signs of the second order terms of Π^i. Indeed, a sufficient condition for the sign of $\partial M^*/\partial\theta$ to be ambiguous is that $\Pi^i_{z_i} > 0$, $\Pi^i_{z_j} < 0$, and $\gamma_M > 0$. Under these conditions, ambiguity is a consequence of two offsetting first-order effects. These two effects can be clearly seen if we assume that the second-order terms of firm profits with respect to knowledge equal zero. In this case,

$$\text{sign}\left\{\frac{\partial M^*}{\partial\theta}\right\} = \text{sign}\left\{\Pi^j_{z_i}\gamma_M(n-1)M + (n-1)\gamma\Pi^i_{z_j}\right\} \qquad (3.3)$$

The term, $(n-1)\gamma\Pi^i_{z_j}$, reflects the negative incentive associated with the diminished appropriability of rents generated by R&D. This term embodies Arrow's observation that a higher spillover rate makes R&D more of a public good, thus lessening the incentive of any single firm to conduct R&D.

However, with an endogenous absorptive capacity, a higher spillover rate also provides an offsetting positive incentive effect on R&D because a higher rate of absorption is more valuable to the firm. This is reflected in the positive first-order effect, $\Pi^i_{z_i}\gamma_{M_i}(n - 1)M$, which indicates that a higher spillover rate, by increasing the pool of knowledge, provides an incentive to increase the rate of absorption via further research expenditures. The positive impact of changing θ is greater the greater is γ_M, and smaller the greater is other firms' absorptive capacity. The fact that γ interacts with θ is critical. Higher θ makes increasing the absorptive capacity more attractive, ceteris paribus. Thus, our introduction of absorptive capacity changes the traditional result in two ways. Most importantly, the desire to assimilate the knowledge generated by other firms provides a positive incentive to invest in R&D as θ increases. Second, the disincentive associated with other firms' assimilation of the firm's R&D output is dampened because other firms' absorptive capacities are less than unity. Therefore, contrary to the proposition that increasing spillovers necessarily reduces the incentive to invest in R&D, the net effect here is ambiguous.[9]

As suggested above, we find that the positive impact of θ is typically greater the larger is β, the impact of own R&D on absorptive capacity. To formally examine this requires considering the cross partial derivative, $\partial^2M^*/\partial\theta\partial\beta$. If we focus only on terms that are first-order effects of z on profit and also assume that $\gamma_{MM} = 0$, then we can show that $R_{\beta\theta}$ is positive.[10] There are three distinct effects. First, a higher β value enhances the positive incentive to invest in R&D associated with building absorptive capacity. Second, by reducing competitors' absorptive capacity, a higher level of β mitigates the negative effect of spillovers, ceteris paribus. Finally, a higher level of β increases the optimal level of R&D.[11] In terms of the first order effects, β increases the optimal M_j, which causes both the pool of knowledge available to firm i to increase, but also increases firm j's absorptive capacity to firm i's detriment. However, as long as the marginal return to own knowledge exceeds in magnitude the marginal effect on profits of a change in a competitor's knowledge level (i.e., $|\Pi^i_{z_i}| > |\Pi^i_{z_j}|$), this last effect is positive.

At this point we can clarify our intuition with respect to the various influences on R&D incentives in our model. We have two broad countervailing incentives at work. First, anything that adds to the marginal benefit of R&D via the role of R&D in augmenting absorptive capacity constitutes a positive "absorption incentive effect." The second factor shaping incentives is the extent to which own R&D effort contributes to the public pool of knowledge, diminishing own profits relative to what they would be otherwise. In our framework, this occurs as either the degree of spillovers or the level of other firms' absorptive capacity increases. We will call this the "appropriability incentive effect."

The analysis of this section is only suggestive of the effect of spillovers on the firm's incentives to conduct R&D. In all the effects we considered, the signs of those effects are ambiguous. We are able to sign the derivatives only by ignoring selected second-order effects. For this reason, we develop a numerical example to consider the robustness of our results and to explore how the magnitudes of the results change with the underlying parameter values. We also use the numerical example to explore the welfare implications of our model.

IV. AN EXAMPLE

In the example, we focus on the relationship between spillovers and R&D effort. We analyze Nash equilibria in which the firms' R&D policies are assumed to be symmetric. The industry is assumed to face a demand curve of constant elasticity, $x = AP^{-b}$, where b is the price elasticity of demand.[12] The base values used for these variables are b = 2 and A = 50. The unit costs of each firm are assumed to have the following functional form: $c_i = q_0 + c_0e^{-fz_i}$, where q_0 represents fixed costs, c_0 represents initial variable costs, and f indicates the potential for cost reduction given some level of new knowledge, z_i. The base values for these variables are $q_0 = 1$, $c_0 = 1$, and $f = 0.5$.

These parameter settings generate results that are reflective of outcomes under a wide range of parameter values. Where these results are not representative, we indicate the sensitivity of the results to the parameter values.

Following Eq. (2.1), the firm's stock of new knowledge is

$$z_i = M_i + \theta\gamma_i \sum_{j \neq i} M_j. \tag{4.1}$$

Consistent with the characterization of γ in Section III, we assume that

$$\gamma_i = \begin{cases} 1 - \dfrac{\beta}{M_i} & \text{if } M_i > \beta, \\ 0 & \text{otherwise.} \end{cases} \tag{4.2}$$

This functional form for γ has the desired properties that increases in M increase the absorptive capacity, though at a decreasing rate. If $\beta = 0$, firm R&D has no impact on absorptive capacity. Own firm R&D has a greater impact on absorptive capacity the greater is β.

Given firm i chooses its output to maximize profits, its market share equals $b(1 - c_i/P)$.[13] Since the sum of all the market shares is one, it follows that $P = \hat{c}/w$, where $w = 1 - 1/bn$, $\hat{c} = \Sigma c_i/n$, and n equals the number of firms. Thus, Π^i may be expressed as a function of the cost of production, the price elasticity, and the number of firms:

$$\Pi^i = b(1 - wc_i/\hat{c})^2 Aw^{b-1}\hat{c}^{1-b}. \tag{4.3}$$

After differentiating (4.3) with respect to M_i, we then assume that firms' R&D strategies are symmetric, such that $M_i = M_j$ for all j, which in turn implies that $c_i = c_j$. As a result, we can represent the firm's marginal incentive to invest in R&D as follows:

$$R(M, \theta, \beta) = \frac{1}{n^2} Aw^{b-1}c_i^{-b} fc_0 e^{-fz} \left\{ \left[2w(n - 1) - (1 - b)(1 - w) \right] \left[1 + \beta\,(n - 1)\theta/M \right] + (n - 1)\theta \left\langle \left[1 - \beta/M \right] \left[- 2w - (1 - w)(1 - b) \right] \right\rangle \right\}. \tag{4.4}$$

This is analogous to Eq. (2.3). Setting this equal to 1, the per unit cost of R&D, yields an implicit expression for the optimal R&D level. We explore numerically how equilibrium R&D moves with the level of spillovers. The numerical example also allows us to consider the welfare implications of our model. Since we are unable to solve analytically for the integral, which equals producers' surplus, we use a Riemann sum to approximate it.[14]

Table 1 indicates how equilibrium R&D expenditures move with β and θ when $f = 0.5$, $n = 5$, $b = 2$, and $A = 50$. For a given value of β, we observe the traditional result; equilibrium R&D expenditures, M^*, tend to decline as spillovers, θ, increase. This relationship does not hold, though, for all parameter settings. M^* often increases with θ, as shown in Table 2. Here, the value of A is set at 45, the price elasticity of demand is increased to 3, and the number of firms increased to 6. In this case, given any positive value of β, M^* is typically an increasing function of θ. Thus, Table 2 demonstrates that under some parameter settings a positive relationship may exist between equilibrium R&D expenditures and spillovers when absorptive capacity is endogenous. When $\beta = 0$, M^* declines to zero as θ increases; however, for larger values of β there is a positive relationship between M^* and θ. Indeed, we observe that introducing an endogenous absorptive capacity allows equilibrium R&D to increase with respect to θ under a wide range of parameter settings.

Our analysis in Section III indicates that as spillovers increase, R&D may not decline once we recognize that a firm must conduct its own R&D in order to assimilate the knowledge "spilled out" by other firms. The numerical analysis presented here demonstrates that a reversal of the traditional proposition indeed occurs with a simple perturbation of the basic model—the addition of an endogenous absorptive capacity. How can we account for the positive impact of spillovers on the incentive to conduct R&D? As spillovers increase, the pool of

Table 1. Firm R&D Levels: β vs θ[a]

	θ				
β	*0.00*	*0.25*	*0.50*	*0.75*	*1.00*
0.00	3.00	0.00	0.00	0.00	0.00
0.25	3.00	0.86	0.61	0.59	0.63
0.50	3.00	1.38	1.13	1.12	1.12
0.75	3.00	1.63	1.53	1.36	1.50
1.00	3.00	2.13	1.88	1.69	1.73

[a] $f = 0.5$, $n = 5$, $b = 2$, $A = 50$.

Table 2. Firm R&D Levels: β vs θ[a]

β	θ				
	0.00	*0.25*	*0.50*	*0.75*	*1.00*
0.00	0.03	0.00	0.00	0.00	0.00
0.25	0.03	0.25	0.44	0.44	0.53
0.50	0.03	0.86	0.81	0.88	0.88
0.75	0.03	1.38	1.26	1.28	1.29
1.00	0.03	1.63	1.50	1.63	1.50

[a] $f = 0.5$, $n = 6$, $b = 3$, $A = 45$.

potential knowledge that can be absorbed for a given level of firm investment in R&D increases. Thus, as θ increases, the firm has a greater incentive to increase γ, its capacity to absorb external knowledge. There is a positive absorption incentive effect. However, at low values of β, we do observe that incentives may decline with θ. Thus, for low values of β the appropriability incentive dominates the absorption incentive, while for larger values of β the reverse occurs.

An interesting question is how the qualitative relationship between M^* and θ is affected by the structural parameters other than β. Of our structural parameters, clear patterns emerge with respect to n and b after conducting numerous numerical experiments. We find that as the price elasticity of demand, b, increases in absolute value, $\partial M^*/\partial\theta$ tends to be positive. With respect to market structure, we find that as the number of firms in the industry, n, increases, the relationship also tends to be positive. We can interpret this result to suggest that as firms face a more competitive environment, in the sense that they are less interdependent due to either an increase in demand elasticity or lower concentration, we find that spillovers are more likely to encourage R&D investment. The intuition is that as an industry becomes more competitive, the private loss associated with the public good character of R&D spillovers diminishes relative to the private benefit of being able to exploit competitors' spillovers.

A. Welfare Implications

Thus far we have considered the implications of an endogenous absorptive capacity for industry R&D spending. We now consider the social welfare implications of changing θ. Given our demand equation, the consumer surplus is

$$H(M, n, b, \beta) = \left[bA/(b-1)\right]w^{b-1}c^{1-b}. \tag{4.5}$$

Assuming symmetry, the earnings for a firm gross of its R&D expenditures is

$$E(M, n, b, \beta) = \frac{1}{bn^2}Aw^{b-1}c^{1-b}. \tag{4.6}$$

Thus, the total social surplus, S is

$$S(M, n, b, \theta, \beta) = Aw^{b-1}c^{1-b}\left[\frac{b}{(b-1)} + \frac{1}{bn}\right] - nM. \tag{4.7}$$

Substituting the equilibrium value of M into (4.7) yields the social surplus in market equilibrium.

In order to consider the social welfare impacts of spillovers, we examine their effects on the total social surplus in market equilibrium relative to the first-best social surplus. To do so, we examine the ratio of the value of (4.7) under market equilibrium relative to the first-best surplus. We calculate a first-best surplus from Eq. (4.7) by assuming that there is a social welfare maximizing monopolist.[15] Since there is only one firm, questions of appropriability do not arise. In addition, since the monopolist maximizes social welfare, price is set equal to marginal cost. More formally, we have $n = 1$ and $c = P$. Under these conditions, Eq. (4.7) becomes

$$\hat{S} \equiv (Abc^{1-b})/(b - 1) - z, \tag{4.8}$$

where $\hat{S}$ represents the first-best social surplus and z is the firm's stock of knowledge as defined in Eq. (2.2). The first-best value of z is that which maximizes $\hat{S}$.

Table 3 presents the ratio of the social surplus in market equilibrium to the first-best surplus as the degree of spillover, θ, and the dependence of absorptive capacity on own R&D, β, vary.[16] Using the same parameter settings as in Table 1, we observe in Table 3 that the social surplus ratio increases with respect to θ for values of β equalling 0.25 or greater. In addition, surplus increases with β while holding θ constant. These qualitative results are replicated under a broad range of parameter settings. These results show that in the context of our model social surplus need not move in the same direction as the associated

Table 3. Ratios of Surplus (%): β vs θ[a]

β	θ 0.00	0.25	0.50	0.75	1.00
0.00	69	52	52	52	52
0.25	69	66	66	69	74
0.50	69	72	74	79	84
0.75	69	72	78	80	86
1.00	69	76	80	81	86

[a]f = 0.5, n = 5, b = 2, A = 50.

equilibrium R&D expenditures. Recall that with the same parameter settings in Table 1, we found equilibrium R&D expenditures tend to decline with θ. To probe the relationship between R&D and the components of social surplus, we consider in Table 4 how the value of total producers' surplus moves with respect to θ, again using the same parameter values as set for Tables 1 and 3. We observe the same qualitative result for the movement in producers' surplus as for total social surplus. With a β value of 0.25 or greater, producers' surplus moves up, although the associated R&D equilibrium expenditures is moving down with θ. A comparison of Tables 1 and 4 indicates that even when the marginal incentives to conduct R&D decline as spillovers increase, producers' surplus, reflecting the returns to the inframarginal units of R&D, may increase. In contrast, when absorptive capacity is exogenous, producers' surplus and marginal incentives move together. The former occurs because at lower R&D expenditure levels, competitors are less able to exploit the research output of the firm since, with declining R&D expenditures, their absorptive capacities are declining. In addition, for a given level of industry R&D, the returns to building absorptive capacity increase. Thus, with an endogenous absorptive capacity, there is an effect on the social benefits associated with the

Table 4. Producers' Surplus: β vs θ[a]

β	θ 0.00	0.25	0.50	0.75	1.00
0.00	4.16	0.00	0.00	0.00	0.00
0.25	4.16	2.78	4.04	5.52	7.09
0.50	4.16	6.14	9.96	14.03	18.08
0.75	4.16	9.52	16.42	23.24	30.32
1.00	4.16	13.31	23.21	33.09	63.55

[a]f = 0.5, n = 5, b = 2, A = 50.

inframarginal units of R&D expenditures which is not present when absorption is costless and exogenous. The consequence is that producers' surplus may increase, driving total social welfare up, although equilibrium R&D expenditures are declining.

When γ is exogenous (i.e., $\beta = 0$), numerical analysis suggests that producer surplus, and equilibrium R&D, always decline with θ. However, even in this setting, Spence (1984) found that social surplus may actually increase with θ. A higher θ value leads to greater diffusion of firm R&D and, in some settings, this can result in greater levels of firm knowledge, although firm R&D, M, diminishes. The introduction of an endogenous absorptive capacity increases the likelihood of a positive association between spillovers and social surplus due to the observed positive relationship between producer surplus and θ, noted above. Table 3 in particular suggests that, under a wider range of conditions than suggested by Spence, increasing spillovers may actually improve market performance.

V. SUMMARY

Once incorporated into a model of cost-reducing technological change, the simple insight that appropriability is endogenous yields a striking result with respect to the relationship between spillovers and both R&D investment and social welfare. We find that spillovers may actually stimulate R&D investment and increase producers' and social surplus.

Spence (1984) had suggested that there exists a tradeoff between the negative incentive effects of spillovers and the greater efficiency with which an industry may conduct its R&D in the presence of spillovers. Introducing an endogenous absorptive capacity means, however, that spillovers no longer exercise one incentive effect. Rather, there are now two offsetting incentives, one associated with appropriability and the other associated with absorption. As a consequence, there is no longer a simple tradeoff between the effect of spillovers on the efficiency of inventive activity versus the effect of spillovers on private incentives.

Our general analysis and numerical example suggest the importance of absorptive capacity for technology policy. For example, in suggesting that spillovers may not impose the welfare costs with which they are typically associated, nor necessarily dampen private incentives to conduct R&D, the analysis indicates the need for more subtle, industry-specific analyses of the desirability of policy instruments designed to increase appropriability, such as patents.

ACKNOWLEDGMENTS

Cohen's research for this paper was supported by the National Science Foundation (PRA 83-10664). For their comments and suggestions we wish to thank Otto Davis, Mark Kamlet, Steven Klepper, Al Link, David Mowery, and the participants in the NBER Conference on Productivity and R&D Spillovers, especially Ariel Pakes and Peter Reiss, and the participants in the Yale Industrial Organization Seminar, especially Richard Levin, Richard Nelson, and Sidney Winter. We also thank Pamela Reyner and Maria Viskochil for typing assistance.

NOTES

1. We define spillovers in the present discussion to include any original knowledge generated in the research process that becomes publicly accessible, whether it be knowledge fully characterizing a new process or product innovation, or knowledge of a more intermediate sort.

2. Evenson and Kislev (1973) observe that the realization of technology transfer depends, in part, upon the recipients' own research efforts. In the context of the international transfer of agricultural technology, they demonstrate empirically that regions must conduct indigenous research to realize and accelerate the transfer of know-how. This point has been recognized in the context of manufacturing R&D by Allen (1977), Mowery (1983a, 1983b), and Gibbons and Johnston (1974). Mowery (1983a) demonstrates this point in his historical study of three large independent research organizations. He shows that, during the period 1900 to 1940, private contract research served as a complement to, rather than substitute for, in-house corporate research facilities. To identify both their technological needs and subsequently to assimilate externally generated technological knowledge—even that which is customized as is the case with contract research—firms required an in-house R&D capability.

3. Using the Yale survey data on industry appropriability and technological opportunity conditions, and the FTC's Line of Business Program data, we found a number of industries in which relatively high R&D intensity coincides with high spillovers. Taking imitation lags as a proxy for spillovers, we found four industries characterized by the modal imitation lag of 3 years or less and relatively high industry R&D intensity (R&D divided by sales) of greater than 3.5%. These include semiconductors, electron tubes, engineering and scientific instruments, and optical instruments and lenses. We thank Professors Richard Levin, Alvin Klevorick, Richard Nelson, and Sidney Winter for making the Yale survey data available to us.

4. If β is determined, in part, by the pace of technical advance, β could be viewed as being endogenous with respect to industry R&D. However, making β an increasing function of industry R&D would only magnify the effects characterized below. In-

creasing the importance of own R&D for absorptive capacity would tend to increase own R&D, which in turn, would lead to a higher value of β and a further increase in own R&D. Thus, for the sake of simplicity, we consider β to be exogenous.

5. Therefore, as β approaches 0, absorptive capacity is less responsive to the level of own R&D and γ_i approaches 1. Thus, a β of zero is equivalent to the setting in which absorptive capacity is not endogenous and $\gamma \equiv 1$.

6. This assumes that the Nash equilibrium is stable.

7. The complete derivative, $\partial M^*/\partial\theta$, equals $R_\theta/[a+(n-1)b]$, where $a \equiv \partial^2\Pi^i/\partial M_i\partial M_i$ and $b \equiv \partial^2\Pi^i/\partial M_i\partial M_j$. In a n-firm symmetric equilibrium, the stability condition for the Nash equilibrium implies that $a + (n-1)b < 0$ (Dixit, 1986).

8. The reaction function is downward sloping when $\Pi^i_{M_iM_j} < 0$. A sufficient condition for this to hold is that $\Pi^i_{z_jz_j} + \Pi^i_{z_iz_j} + (n-2)\,\Pi^i_{z_jz_k} < 0$.

9. The interaction of an endogenous absorptive capacity, γ, and spillovers, θ, yields another interesting result. Let us assume that the appropriability disincentive effect outweighs the absorption incentive effect such that we obtain the standard result that equilibrium R&D diminishes with θ. This result implies, however, that although θ is increasing, γ will be declining as long as $\gamma_M > 0$. Thus, the interaction of an endogenous absorptive capacity and θ means that even where the negative appropriability effect dominates, its effect is attenuated relative to a world where a firm's absorptive capacity is not a function of its own R&D. Even where spillovers have a negative net effect on incentives, they matter less.

10. Under these conditions, taking the derivative of Eq. (3.2) with respect to β yields the following expression.

$$R_{\beta\theta} = (n-1)\left\{M_j\gamma_{M\gamma}\Pi^i_{z_i} + \gamma_M\frac{\partial M^*}{\partial\beta}(\Pi^i_{z_i} + \Pi^i_{z_j}) + \gamma_\beta\Pi^i_{z_j}\right\}.$$

If we assume that $|\Pi^i_{z_i}| > |\Pi^i_{z_j}|$, which we can show to hold in the context of the example, then this expression is unambiguously positive.

11. To explore the effect of β, we differentiate Eq. (3.1) by β yielding.

$$\begin{aligned}\text{sign}\left\{\frac{\partial M^*}{\partial\beta}\right\} = \text{sign}\ &\theta(n-1)\{\Pi^i_{z_i}\gamma_{M\beta}M + \gamma_\beta\Pi^i_{z_j}\\ &+ \gamma[\Pi^i_{z_jz_j} + \Pi^i_{z_jz_i} + (n-2)\Pi^i_{z_jz_k}] + \gamma_\beta M[(\Pi^i_{z_iz_i}\\ &+ (n-1)\Pi^i_{z_iz_j})[1 + \gamma_M\theta(n-1)M]\}.\end{aligned}$$

If we assume that the second-order effects of knowledge on profits are the same as that which generates the traditional negative sign of $\partial M^*/\partial\theta$ when $\gamma \equiv 1$, then we can sign the derivative. In this case equilibrium R&D will increase with β, i.e., $\partial M^*/\partial\beta > 0$.

12. We use the same functional forms and base parameter value as in Spence (1984).

13. Given the demand equation, we can rewrite price as: $P = (x/A)^{-1/b}$. Therefore, setting marginal revenue equal to marginal cost yields $P(-x_i/bx + 1) = c_i$. This, in turn, implies that $x_i/x = b(1 - c_i/P)$. Note that this derivation corrects an error in Spence (1984), footnote 11.

14. See Bartle (1976, pp. 212–227).

15. A monopolist, rather than a number of smaller firms, maximizes social welfare because we have assumed constant marginal costs of production and constant rather than diminishing returns to scale in the generation of knowledge when θ and γ equal 1.

16. The reader should note that both within and across the tables presented the value of the first-best surplus does not change. The first-best, by definition, is not a function of θ, β, or T. Thus, in addition to being a benchmark, the first-best surplus acts as a numeraire with respect to the values associated with the market equilibrium.

REFERENCES

Allen, Thomas, *Managing the Flow of Technology,* Cambridge: MIT Press, 1977.

Arrow, Kenneth, "Economic Welfare and the Allocation of Resources for Invention." In Richard Nelson, ed., *The Rate and Direction of Inventive Activity,* Princeton: Princeton University Press, 1962.

Bartle, Robert, *The Elements of Real Analysis,* New York: Wiley, 1976.

Dixit, Avinash, "Comparative Statics for Oligopoly." *International Economic Review* 27(1986):107–122.

Evenson, Robert and Yoav Kislev, "Research and Productivity in Wheat and Maize." *Journal of Political Economy* 81(1973):1309–1329.

Gibbons, M. and R. Johnston, "The Roles of Science in Technological Innovation." *Research Policy* 3(1974):220–242.

Mowery, David, "The Relationship between Intrafirm and Contractual Forms of Industrial Research in American Manufacturing, 1900–1940." *Explorations in Economic History* 20(1983a):351–374.

Mowery, David, "Economic Theory and Government Technology Policy." *Policy Sciences* 16(1983b):27–43.

Nelson, Richard, "The Simple Economics of Basic Research." *Journal of Political Economy* 67(1959):297–306.

Spence, A. Michael, "Cost Reduction, Competition, and Industry Performance." *Econometrica* 52(1984):101–121.

COOPERATIVE RESEARCH AND INNOVATIVE ACTIVITY

Kathryn L. Combs

I. INTRODUCTION

It has long been recognized that the divergence of individual from collective returns to innovative activity lends itself to some form of corrective government policy.[1] Since 1646, when a Boston court granted the first patent in America, the United States has continued to grant monopoly patent rights to inventors in an attempt to stimulate private innovation. Much more recently, however, the United States has followed the lead of other countries by enacting a type of innovation policy that encourages cooperation in research and development (R&D) between firms.[2] In particular, Congress has passed the National Cooperative Research Act of 1984 (NCRA) and the Justice Department has clarified antitrust policy by issuing new Guidelines on Re-

Advances in Applied Micro-Economics, Volume 5, pages 47–67.

ISBN: 0-89232-797-9

search Joint Ventures. These and other related actions take a more permissive stance on cooperative R&D ventures.[3]

In theory, economic justification for policies encouraging cooperative R&D may exist on several grounds. Consider cooperating firms, for instance, which agree to cooperate in R&D activities but are competitive in sales.[4] Suppose further that discoveries made within the group are shared freely among members, but are protected from outsiders. The greater is the public-good nature of innovation, the lower is the incentive to conduct R&D. However, within a cooperative group, there is an offsetting, positive incentive to conduct R&D if the group is able to (1) internalize positive externalities in R&D, (2) realize economies of scale in R&D, (3) reduce wasteful duplication of R&D efforts, and/or (4) exploit potential interfirm R&D synergies or complementarities.[5]

This paper develops a game-theoretic model of R&D with uncertain returns and uses it to determine the degree of cooperation that would maximize social welfare, in comparison with that which would arise without government intervention.[6] One focus of this analysis will be to find conditions under which firms will choose to cooperate at all, if allowed. Other game-theoretic models of cooperative R&D include Katz (1986) and Ordover and Willig (1985). Katz examines the R&D activity in an industry having a fixed number of firms, where cooperating firms can collectively influence the amount of research to be conducted. He models R&D as a production-cost-reducing investment with known returns, in an environment where cooperation can internalize positive R&D externalities. In contrast, Ordover and Willig look at firms that make R&D investments (again with known returns) where interim synergies or economies of scale in R&D affect cooperation and innovation. They also allow for duplication of R&D efforts to be reduced between cooperating firms. Ordover and Willig limit themselves, however, to analysis of only two of the firms in the industry, thereby ignoring the strategic interaction between a representative noncooperating and cooperating firm.

Section II sets up a model of cooperative innovation that has similarities to Tandon (1983) (who follows Nelson, 1961), Brander and Spencer (1983), and D'Aspremont et al. (1983). The model includes a game among a number of potential entrants in which each noncooperating and cooperating player must succeed in its R&D activities in order to enter the product market. R&D activities include a random draw from a pool of research projects. Since some of these projects fail, R&D is an investment with uncertain returns. Cooperation in this model reduces wasteful duplication of R&D effort; this is both a social and private benefit of cooperation. However, if a cooperating group of firms is successful, all members of the group will enter the market and compete in some fashion. Thus, the more cooperation in R&D, the greater is the potential product market competition; this is the private opportunity cost (but another possible social benefit) of cooperation.

Each potential entrant decides the amount of its research, production quantities, and whether to cooperate, under Nash-type equilibrium assumptions. Sections III and IV define and discuss equilibrium in research expenditures and cooperation decisions, respectively. Section V computes equilibria for a simple example of three firms, a homogeneous good market with linear demand, and constant marginal cost. In this example, when there is no limit to the number of firms that can cooperate, the entire industry will cooperate when the probability of success in innovation is relatively high. No firms, however, will cooperate when the probability of success is relatively low, and only some will cooperate for an intermediate range of probability values.

Section VI defines the socially optimal degree of cooperation, constrained by firms' private choices of R&D expenditures and product output, computes it under varying parameter values for the example described in Section V, and compares it to the equilibrium degree of cooperation for each set of parameters. For parameter values reflecting a relatively low probability of success in R&D, it is socially optimal for some firms to cooperate; only for larger probabilities of success is it optimal for all firms to cooperate. For the parameter values examined in the context of the Section V example, total expected industry profit decreases but expected consumer surplus increases as the proportion of firms that cooperate increases. For larger probabilities of success, the consumer surplus effect dominates, resulting in the socially optimal degree of cooperation to include all firms. The final section summarizes the model's results and comments on its relevance to current cooperative R&D policy issues.

II. A MODEL OF RESEARCH AND DEVELOPMENT COOPERATION

Consider a product market that has n identical potential entrants but no incumbent. The actual number of entrants, n_e, where $n_e \leq n$, is a random variable that will be determined by potential entrants' levels of R&D investment and the extent of their cooperation in R&D activities.

Following Grossman and Shapiro (1986), define a research joint venture (RJV) as an organization jointly controlled by at least two "parents" (potential entrants) whose primary purpose is to engage in R&D. (The R&D can be conducted at separate facilities or at a central location.) The payoff to entry is the profit (gross of R&D expenditures) that a firm will earn in the product market; it will vary with the total number of actual entrants.

As in Katz (1986), the firm's problem spans several periods ("stages"). In stage one, the membership stage, firms decide whether to join the RJV. Assume (as does Katz) that there is only one RJV in the industry. In stage two, the R&D stage, firms conduct R&D.[7] The result of each firm's research endeavors is revealed immediately. All successful firms then enter the product market.[8] In stage three, the production stage, the successful firms compete in the product market, establishing a single-period equilibrium. Figure 1 shows a diagram of the problem's timing. In order to find a subgame-perfect Nash equilibrium, backward induction is used, i.e., the three-stage problem is solved recursively.

The R&D stage of a firm's activities is dividied into two distinct research components. A firm outside the RJV assigns equipment and scientists (the variable component) to a particular line of research (the fixed component). The probability of R&D success is affected by both components. The variable component of the research process involves the firm choosing a nonnegative amount, b, to spend on equipment, scientists, etc. The probability of success in the variable component of R&D, i.e., the probability that the equipment works, the scientists are appropriate matches for the job, etc., is f(b), where

$$f(b) = 1 - e^{-\lambda b}, \qquad b \geq 0, \lambda > 0.$$

The fixed component of the research process entails random selection of a research project, i.e., the selection of a particular line of research. Specifically, assume that each firm is able to select and conduct one of m research projects at zero cost ($m \geq n$), but that additional projects are infinitely costly. (In a sense, there is a physical capacity constraint.) Furthermore, assume that a firm outside the RJV selects its project randomly with replacement from a pool that contains one "good" and $m - 1$ "bad" research projects. Only the "good" project leads to an innovation. Thus, a firm outside the RJV will draw the one "good" project with probability $1/m$. Assuming that success in the

Figure 1.

Stage one

Potential entrants form the cooperative entity.

Stage two

(a)

Potential entrants conduct research.

(b)

Each potential entrant finds out if its R&D has been successful.

Stage three

Successful potential entrants enter product market, produce and sell.

Unsuccessful potential entrants drop out.

variable research component and success in the fixed research component are independent random variables and indexing a typical firm outside the RJV by j, then its joint probability of success in both parts of R&D, denoted by P_j, is

$$P_j = \frac{f(b_j)}{m}$$

An RJV will be modeled as a contract between firms whereby each member firm agrees to conduct its R&D program so as to avoid duplicating another member's research project. The contract also stipulates that each member will be required to spend an equal amount on research, which will be decided on and perfectly enforced by the RJV management itself. Finally, any discovery made by an RJV member will be available, without additional charge, for use by any other firm.[9] Under this contract, then, each member draws a research project without replacement from the m projects that are available. Since an RJV of size s will select a total of s distinct projects, the probability that it draws the good project is s/m. Letting P_{rjv} denote the RJV's overall probability of success in R&D and B denote each member firm's expenditure on variable research, assume

$$P_{rjv} = \frac{sf(B)}{m}$$

Note that $P_j \in [0, 1/m)$ and $P_{rjv} \in [0, s/m)$. Furthermore, P_j (P_{rjv}) increases as the outside (inside) firm spends more on its research, b (B), and increases if it has fewer projects, m, to choose from. If all firms join one RJV, and if there are exactly as many firms as there are projects ($s = n = m$), then P_{rjv} can be made arbitrarily close to one as the per-firm expenditure on research is made arbitrarily large. By entering into the RJV contract, then, a firm may have the opportunity to increase its chance of success of entering the product market. Note, however, that the presence of uncertainty (absent in Katz and Ordover and Willig) generates a very important benefit of staying *outside* the RJV. Regardless of the positive amount of R&D it does, an outside firm will always face a positive probability of becoming a monopolist in the product market, since there is some chance that all the other firms, including the RJV, will fail.

Using P(k, N) to denote the probability that success occurs for k out of N of the $n - s$ firms that are outside the RJV, then the probability that a particular outside firm, j, is successful and exactly k other outside firms are successful is $P_jP(k, n - s - 1)$, for $k \leq (n - s - 1)$, assuming the two events are independent. Likewise, the probability that a particular firm inside the RJV is successful and exactly k outside firms are successful is $P_{rjv}P(k, n - s)$, for $k \leq (n - s)$, assuming the two events are independent.[10]

Assume that both an unsuccessful outside firm and a firm in an unsuccessful RJV earn nothing. Use $R(n_e)$ to denote the actual benefits to R&D for any successful firm when there are n_e entrants. Denote an RJV member's expected benefits to R&D as $\pi^I(s,\mathbf{B})$, where "I" stands for "insider." **B** is a vector of length $n - s + 1$ with one entry corresponding to the level of research expenditures of a representative member of the RJV, and $n - s$ entries corresponding to the research expenditures of each outside firm. π^I can be expressed as

$$\pi^{I}(s, \mathbf{B}) = \sum_{k=0}^{n-s} P_{rjv}P(k, n - s)R(s + k)$$

V^{I} will be used to denote the expected net returns to R&D, defined as the expected benefits to R&D less R&D expenditures.

$$V^{I}(s, \mathbf{B}) = \pi^{I}(s, \mathbf{B}) - B,$$

where B is the first element of **B**. For an outside firm j, expected benefits to R&D and expected net returns to R&D are, respectively,

$$\pi_j^{O}(s, \mathbf{B}) = \sum_{k=0}^{n-s-1} P_{rjv}P_jP(k, n - s - 1)R(s + k + 1) + \sum_{k=0}^{n-s-1} (1 - P_{rjv})P_jP(k, n - s - 1)R(k + 1)$$

and

$$V_j^{O}(s, \mathbf{B}) = \pi_j^{O}(s, \mathbf{B}) - b_j,$$

where b_j is the (j + 1)th element of **B**. If s = 1, the payoffs of the outside and inside firms will be observationally equivalent.

Note that V^{I} (for an inside firm) and V^{O} (for an outside firm) are the expected payoffs to the stage one decision about whether to cooperate, and depend on the number of firms that decide to cooperate (determined in stage one), the amount of R&D done by each firm (determined in stage two), and the function R, which is the reduced form of actual product market profits (earned in stage three if successful). The functional form of R, of course, depends on the product market structural and behavioral assumptions. Stage three is not modeled explicitly in this paper except for the special case in section V, where a Cournot–Nash equilibrium in a homogeneous product market is assumed.[11] For this reason, the next section assumes the equilibrium in the production stage has been determined, with the per-firm equilibrium payoff summarized in R.

III. EQUILIBRIUM IN THE R&D STAGE

A. The Agents' Problems

Given the size of the RJV, s, the decision problem of each firm outside the RJV is to maximize expected net returns to R&D with respect to own R&D expenditures, given other firms' decisions. Specifically, firm j maximizes $V_j^O(s,\mathbf{B})$ with respect to b_j, subject to $b_j \geq 0$. The first-order, necessary condition for an interior solution to this problem is

$$\frac{\partial[\pi_j^O(s, \mathbf{B})]}{\partial b_j} = 1.$$

This holds for the n − s firms outside the RJV. Note that the term on the left-hand side of this equation is the expected marginal private benefit of a unit of R&D, and is set equal to one, the marginal cost of R&D. Since P_j is strictly concave in b_j, and is the only term in π_j^O that depends on b_j, then V_j^O is strictly concave in b_j. Thus, the first-order condition is both necessary and sufficient for a maximum.

The RJV's problem in this stage is to maximize the sum of members' expected net returns to R&D with respect to per-member R&D expenditure, subject to R&D expenditure being identical across members, and given the size of the RJV. This problem is equivalent, given the functional form of P_{rjv}, to the maximization of a representative member's expected net returns with respect to the average level of insiders' R&D. Specifically, the RJV maximizes $V^I(s,\mathbf{B})$ with respect to B, subject to B ≥ 0. The first-order, necessary condition for an interior solution to this problem is

$$\frac{\partial[\pi^I(s, \mathbf{B})]}{\partial B} = 1.$$

The left-hand side of this first-order condition is the expected marginal benefit to an RJV member of increasing its R&D by one unit, provided its fellow members do the same; again this is set equal to the marginal cost of R&D. Since P_{rjv} is strictly concave in B, V^I is strictly concave in B. Thus, the first-order condition is both necessary and sufficient for a maximum.

Lemma 1. If all firms are maximizing expected returns given s, then

$$\text{(a) } \pi^I(s, \mathbf{B}) = \frac{f(B)}{f'(B)} \qquad \text{for } n \geq s \geq 1,$$

and

$$\text{(b) } \pi_j^O(s, \mathbf{B}) = \frac{f(b_j)}{f'(b_j)} \qquad \text{for } (n - 1) \geq s \geq 1.$$

Proof. (a) and (b) follow directly from the first-order conditions:

$$1 = \frac{\partial[\pi^I(s, \mathbf{B})]}{\partial B} = f'(B)\frac{\pi^I(s, \mathbf{B})}{f(B)}$$

and

$$1 = \frac{\partial[\pi_j^O(s, \mathbf{B})]}{\partial b_j} = f'(b_j)\frac{\pi_j^O(s, \mathbf{B})}{f(b_j)}.$$

B. The Nash-Equilibrium Amount of Research

Recall that, as part of the research contract, all firms inside the RJV spend equal amounts on research. This section will consider a Nash equilibrium where, in addition, all outside firms spend equal amounts on variable research. Formally, let $\mathbf{B^*}$ denote this equilibrium, where $\mathbf{B^*} = (B^*, b^*, \ldots, b^*)$, an $(n - s + 1)$ vector with one entry B^* denoting the equilibrium level of inside firm research expenditure and $n - s$ entries of b^* denoting outside firm research expenditures. This reduces the $n - s + 1$ first-order conditions to a set of two equations—one for the representative outside firm and one for the representative inside firm—in two unknowns, B^* and b^*. If $s < n$, then $\mathbf{B^*}$ solves both equations. If there are no outside firms, then $s = n$ and $\mathbf{B^*} = (B^*)$ where B^* solves the first-order condition for the inside firm. Note that symmetry of the outside firms in equilibrium implies that the number of successful outside firms follows a binomial distribution. Specifically, for N outside firms,

$$P(k, N) = \binom{N}{k}[f(b)/m]^k\{1 - [f(b)/m]\}^{N-k} \qquad \text{for } k \leq N.$$

For the case of three potential entrants, a homogeneous product market and a Cournot–Nash equilibrium in this market, **B*** is calculated under various assumptions on parameter values and sizes of the RJV. These results are reported in Sections V and VI.

IV. EQUILIBRIUM IN THE MEMBERSHIP STAGE

Having determined a set of equilibrium decision rules for **B** as a function of RJV size, a subgame-perfect equilibrium for the entire three-stage problem can now be determined. Two types of RJV-size equilibria are discussed. The first allows for free entry (and exit) of individual firms into (and out of) the RJV. The second allows for free exit but also for the RJV to be able to prevent further entry of other firms.[12]

A. Free Entry and Exit Equilibrium

The type of RJV-size equilibrium defined below was formally introduced by the stable cartel literature (e.g., D'Aspremont et al., 1983) and used subsequently by Katz (1986).

Definition. An RJV with s members is said to be *internally stable* if $n \geq s \geq 2$ and $V^I[s,\mathbf{B}^*(s)] \geq V^O[s - 1,\mathbf{B}^*(s - 1)]$.

Definition. An RJV with s members is said to be *externally stable* if $1 \leq s \leq (n - 1)$ and $V^O[s,\mathbf{B}^*(s)] \geq V^I[s + 1,\mathbf{B}^*(s + 1)]$.

That is, no single member has an incentive to leave an internally stable RJV, and no single outside firm has an incentive to enter an externally stable RJV. An RJV of size $s = 1$ will always be considered to be internally stable, whereas one of size $s = n$ will always be considered to be externally stable. Both types of stability depend on the knowledge of an individual firm that its decision affects the extent of market cooperation and thereby the expected number of product market entrants.[13]

Definition. An RJV that is both internally and externally stable is said to be *stable*.

A stable RJV can be interpreted as a Nash noncooperative equilibrium of the game where each of n players chooses from two strategies—to join or not to join the RJV. Under these strategies, the arrangement of s firms inside and n − s outside is a Nash noncooperative equilibrium if and only if every player's membership decision is privately optimal given the membership decisions of all other players. That is, in an equilibrium, there is internal stability because no member in the s-firm RJV can increase its expected net returns by leaving, and external stability because no firm outside the s-firm RJV can increase its expected net returns by entering.

Proposition 1. There exists a stable RJV of size s^*, $s^* \in \{1, \ldots, n\}$ for finite n.

Proof (follows D'Aspremont et al.). Starting with an RJV of size $s = 1$, check to see whether it is externally stable. If it is, then $s^* = 1$ (since this size is already internally stable as discussed above). If not, then $V^I(2) > V^O(1)$, which in turn implies that an RJV of size $s = 2$ is internally stable. If it is also externally stable, then $s^* = 2$. If not, then $V^I(3) > V^O(2)$, which implies that an RJV of size $s = 3$ is internally stable. Again, if this is externally stable, $s^* = 3$. If not, proceed through all the possible values of s and stop on finding a stable size. If no RJVs from sizes 1 through $n - 1$ are stable, then $V^I(n) > V^O(n - 1)$ due to the external instability of an RJV of size $n - 1$. This implies that an RJV with all n members is internally stable. As assumed above, an n-firm RJV is externally stable. Thus, if no RJVs ranging from sizes 1 through $n - 1$ are stable, then an n-firm RJV must be stable. Hence, there is at least one stable RJV of size $s^* \in \{1, \ldots, n\}$.

One property of a stable RJV is that each firm does a (locally) maximum amount of research, as shown in Proposition 2.

Proposition 2. (a) The variable research done by a firm in a stable RJV is never less than that done by this firm if it were to exit the RJV, i.e., if s^* is a stable RJV size, then for $n \geq s^* \geq 2$,

$$B^*(s^*) \geq b^*(s^* - 1).$$

(b) The variable research done by a firm outside a stable RJV is never less than that done by this firm if it were to enter the RJV, i.e., for $(n - 1) \geq s \geq 1$,

$$b(s^*) \geq B^*(s^* + 1).$$

Proof. (a) is proved by combining Lemma 1 with the condition for internal stability. s* must, by definition, satisfy

$$V^I[s^*,\mathbf{B}^*(s^*)] \geq V^O[s^* - 1,\mathbf{B}^*(s^* - 1)].$$

By Lemma 1, this implies

$$\frac{f[B^*(s^*)]}{f'[B^*(s^*)]} - B^*(s^*) \geq \frac{f[b^*(s^*-1)]}{f'[b^*(s^*-1)]} - b^*(s^*-1).$$

Since

$$\frac{f(B)}{f'(B)} - B = \frac{(e^{\lambda B}-1)}{\lambda} - B,$$

$[f(B)/f'(B)] - B$ is increasing in B for all nonnegative values of B. Thus, $B^*(s^*) \geq b^*(s^* - 1)$.

(b) is likewise proved by combining Lemma 1 with the condition for external stability.

B. Equilibrium with Entry-Blocking Allowed

Consider an RJV rule whereby current members must vote to accept new members. Since all RJV members are identical in this model, then if it is in one member's interest to bar a potential member from joining, it will also be in the other members' interests. Imposing this constraint on a stable RJV yields the following definition of an entry-blocking equilibrium in RJV size. Let s_{max} be defined as

$$\max_s V^I[s, \mathbf{B}^*(s)] = V^I[s_{max}, \mathbf{B}^*(s_{max})],$$

and let $S_{max} \equiv \{s \mid s = s_{max}\}$. That is, S_{max} is the set of all RJV sizes that maximizes the expected payoff of an inside firm, and S^*, where $S^* \equiv \{s \mid s = s^*\}$, is the set of all stable RJV sizes.

Definition. s** is an *entry-blocking equilibrium RJV size* if

(a) (i) $\min(s| \; s \in S_{max}) \leq \max(s| \; s \in S^*)$, and

(ii) $s^{**} \in S_{max}$, and
(iii) $s^{**} \leq \max(s|\ s \in S^*)$
(iv) s^{**} is the size of an internally stable RJV;

or

(b) (i) $\min(s|\ s \in S_{max}) > \max(s|\ s \in S^*)$, and
(ii) $s^{**} \in S^*$.

To illustrate this type of equilibrium, consider the existence of a unique stable RJV size (s^*) and a unique size that maximizes an inside firm's expected payoff (s_{max}). In this case, if s_{max} exceeds s^* [condition (b)(i)], s_{max} would never be attained if freedom of exit is allowed, since s_{max} is not internally stable. Here, the stable size will dominate, so that the entry-blocking equilibrium size is s^*. On the other hand, if s_{max} is less than s^* [condition (a)(i)], and if entry-blocking is allowed, then an RJV with s_{max} members will not permit the additional $s^* - s_{max}$ firms to join. Here, the size in the interest of the RJV members will dominate, so that $s^{**} < s^*$.

Proposition 3. There exists an entry-blocking equilibrium RJV size, s^{**}, $s^{**} \in \{1, \ldots, n\}$, for finite n.

Proof. Since V^I is real-valued and finite for each value of s, and since there are a finite number of values of s, the set S_{max} is nonempty, and there is a minimum over this set. There also exists a finite, and by Proposition 2, positive number of stable RJVs, and hence, a maximum size among these. In the proof of Proposition 2, it was also shown that all RJVs of size less than a stable RJV are internally stable. Thus, if $\min(s|\ s \in S_{max}) \leq \max(s|\ s \in S^*)$, an s^{**} will be found by selecting a value, $s \in S_{max}$, that does not exceed $\max(s|\ s \in S^*)$ and that is internally stable. If $\min(s|\ s \in S_{max}) > \max(s|\ s \in S^*)$, s^{**} will be found by selecting a value, $s \in S^*$.

Both the stable and entry-blocking RJV equilibrium sizes are computed for an example in the following section.

V. AN EXAMPLE

The values of the research variables b^* and B^* can be found analytically when there are three potential entrants, since this case involves solving for the root of a third-degree polynomial.[14] The parameters of interest in this problem are m (the number of available research projects)—or s/m (the number of RJV members per project)—λ (the research parameter that is positively related to the firm's probability of success), and demand and cost parameters. Consider an example that assumes demand to be of the form P = A − Q, where Q is industry output in a homogeneous product market. Assume further that marginal and average production costs are assumed to be a constant, c, for each actual entrant. (A − c) is normalized to be one. A Cournot–Nash equilibrium in this product market is examined, in keeping with the spirit of the NCRA, which prohibits cooperation in production decisions. This equilibrium assumption can be shown to yield an ex post equilibrium profit (the entrant's product market payoff) of $(A - c)^2/(n_e + 1)^2 = (n_e + 1)^{-2}$. Values of the endogenous variables have been found by solving the three-stage problem recursively, and are thus a function of the parameters λ and m. Table 1 reports the equilibrium values of s for this example for nine λ, m pairs.

Given the number of firms and research projects, an increase in the stable RJV size can be induced by large enough increases in the probability parameter λ. An exception to this occurs when firms face a relatively large number of projects as compared with the number of firms, since this places a relatively small upper bound on the probability of RJV success. For example, when there are six projects, no RJV is observed to form regardless of the value of λ, but when the number of projects is reduced to five, cooperation occurs. Similarly, given the number of firms and the value of λ, the stable RJV size increases as the number of research projects decreases. This pattern

Table 1. Stable (and Entry-Blocking Equilibrium) Sizes of the RJV, n = 3

	λ					
m	*10*	*20*	*28*	*56*	*145*	*200*
3	[a]	1	2	3	3	3
		(1)	(2)	(2)	(2)	(2)
4	[a]	[a]	1	2	3	3
			(1)	(2)	(2)	(2)
5	[a]	[a]	1	1	2	3
			(1)	(1)	(2)	(2)
6	[a]	[a]	[a]	1	1	1
				(1)	(1)	(1)

[a]There is no equilibrium with positive B and b for these parameter values.

does not occur, though, for relatively small values of λ. For example, in the case of three projects, when $\lambda = 20$, no RJV forms whereas for $\lambda = 28$, an RJV of size two forms.

The entry-blocking equilibrium RJV size follows the same general pattern as does the stable size, except that the entry-blocking size never rises above two firms. For example, if the stable RJV consists of three firms, one of these will be blocked from joining if the blocking rule is in effect. Here, the opportunity cost of allowing another firm to join (that is, the reduction in ex post product market profits) must be prohibitively high for the current RJV members.

VI. SOCIALLY OPTIMAL COOPERATION

A social planning problem is set up that defines welfare as the sum of expected net returns [i.e., $sV^I(\mathbf{B}^*,s) + (n - s)V^O(\mathbf{B}^*,s)$] and expected consumer surplus. The objective of the planner is to choose the size of the RJV, s, that will maximize welfare constrained by the firms' private choices of research expenditures and production levels in the product market.[15] This size will be called the socially optimal RJV size or socially optimal degree of cooperation.

For the three firm case described in Section V, expected industry net returns (as total profits), expected consumer surplus (as consumer surplus), and research expenditures are computed for each of 16 (λ, m) pairs (four of which are reported in the Appendix as cases 1–4), total profits fall and consumer surplus rises as the number of firms in the RJV rises. Given the number of firms and projects, for high values of the probability parameter λ, consumer surplus increases as more firms cooperate. This is because a dollar of research expenditure will produce a greater number of product market entrants and thus a lower product price if it is spent within a cooperative group. However, for very low values of λ, consumer surplus at first increases but eventually decreases in RJV size. To understand why this occurs, recall that for small values of λ, where there is barely an incentive to conduct R&D, firms will not willingly form an RJV. Presumably the costs of joining—i.e., of sacrificing full appropriability of research results—are too great for low values of λ, compared to the benefits of joining—i.e., of increasing research productivity. Perhaps then, if forced to join under these conditions, a member firm's incentive to do R&D would fall.

Aggregate expected net returns to R&D, on the other hand, consistently fall in RJV size. Each outside firm's expected net returns displays a similar pattern, whereas for large λ, each inside firm's expected net returns are highest in a two-member RJV. For smaller λ values, however, each inside firm's expected net returns decrease consistently as more members join. Overall, for relatively high values of λ, the consumer surplus effect dominates, causing welfare to be maximized when there is industry-wide cooperation. But for lower values of λ, lesser degrees of cooperation are optimal. For example, as shown in Table 2, when there are four projects, a two-member RJV is optimal but an industry-wide RJV is optimal when $\lambda \geq 56$.

In the example, increased cooperation usually serves to increase the expected number of product market entrants, a measure of research output. As suggested by Katz, this should be expected when a high degree of R&D sharing is feasible. However, Katz (1986), Grossman and Shapiro (1986), and Ordover and Willig (1985) discuss other environments and conditions under which cooperation reduces research output. For example, Grossman and Shapiro bring up the possibility that when results are patented, cooperating firms might choose to cross license only among themselves and not to other potential competitors as they might in the absence of an RJV. In this paper, however, since the nature of cooperation is to reduce the duplication of R&D within an industry and to increase sharing of innovations, if more cooperation leads to a lower number of expected entrants (i.e., when λ is low), firms choose not to cooperate in equilibrium.

VII. SUMMARY

This paper examines the behavior of potential product market entrants and determines the extent of their cooperation in research activities.

Table 2. Socially Optimal Sizes of the RJV, n = 3

	λ					
m	10	20	28	56	145	200
3	*a*	3	3	3	3	3
4	*a*	*a*	2	3	3	3
5	*a*	*a*	*a*	3	3	3
6	*a*	*a*	*a*	3	3	3
7	*a*	*a*	*a*	3	3	3

[a] There is no equilibrium with positive B and b, for these parameter values. Thus, it is impossible to compute expected total profit and consumer surplus for these parameter values, in order to determine the socially optimal RJV size.

There is endogenous formation of a cooperative research entity whose members share research strategies and innovations. The research environment is uncertain, and there are no spillovers of research results except among cooperating firms. Success in research in this environment means entry into a new product market.

A three-firm example of the model developed in this paper yields the following results:

1. The greater the degree of R&D cooperation in equilibrium, the greater is the potential probability of success of R&D. In addition, although firms may respond to higher potential probabilities of success by lowering their actual R&D expenditures (a measure of research input), the expected number of innovators (a measure of research output) will always increase.
2. Provided the potential probability of success is high, an exogenous increase in potential success will cause expected consumer surplus to increase but expected aggregate profit (total expected net returns to R&D) to decrease.
3. For all parameter values examined, social welfare is higher when there is free entry into the cooperative group. Moreover, permitting a form of research cooperation in which there are membership restrictions will yield higher welfare than prohibiting all forms of research cooperation.
4. Cooperative research groups whose main purpose is to facilitate sharing of R&D information and innovations will likely form only when gains to joining are high. If the probability of success in R&D is low in the absence of a cooperative group, it may be difficult to induce firms to join a group, let alone to induce a single firm to conduct R&D.[16] Hence, close attention should be paid to claims that cooperation may be necessary to induce R&D.
5. R&D information and innovation sharing are socially beneficial aspects of cooperative research groups, which should be weighed against other negative or anticompetitive aspects of these groups.[17]

Future work will use numerical methods to compute the equilibrium and optimal degree of research cooperation in the case of more than three potential entrants. Since the number of potential entrants is a proxy for market concentration, these computations will be useful in determining the effect of market power on the amount of R&D cooperation.

APPENDIX

Equilibrium Values of Research, Total Profit, and Consumer Surplus: Three Potential Entrants

Variable	*Number of RJV members* 1	2	3
	Case 1: m = 3, λ = 20		
B*		0.017	0.011
b*	0.019	0.018	
Total profits	0.013	0.010	0.004
Consumer surplus	0.039	0.055	0.056
	Case 2: m = 3, λ = 28		
B*		0.024	0.020
b*	0.024	0.020	
Total profits	0.030	0.027	0.020
Consumer surplus	0.058	0.087	0.121
	Case 3: m = 3, λ = 56		
B*		0.024	0.022
b*	0.022	0.019	
Total profits	0.068	0.067	0.067
Consumer surplus	0.085	0.129	0.201
	Case 4: m = 4, λ = 28		
B*		0.014	0.010
b*	0.016	0.015	
Total profits	0.013	0.010	0.004
Consumer surplus	0.034	0.047	0.050

ACKNOWLEDGMENTS

This work has been supported in part by California State University Affirmative Action Faculty Development Grants and a Sloan Foundation Grant. I would like to thank Herbert Mohring, Robert Porter, Albert Link, Kerry Smith, and Stacey Schreft for their helpful suggestions.

NOTES

1. For a discussion of innovation policy, see Kamien and Schwartz (1982).
2. Japan, for example, has for many years actively encouraged cooperative research. This is described by Doane (1984) and Fusfeld (1986). Fusfeld also describes several cooperative research entities in Europe.
3. The NCRA (PL 98-462) roughly defines a "joint research and development

venture" as an arrangement between two or more parties under which their R&D programs are to some degree determined and conducted together. It stipulates that such agreements, which have received prior approval from the Justice Department and the FTC, are not per se illegal, but rather are to be judged with a rule of reason if they come under antitrust action. In addition, the liability of the joint R&D venture is limited to actual damages sustained, as opposed to the treble damages that apply for most violations of the antitrust laws. Link and Bauer (1989) describe ventures which have received federal approval for their research activities.

15 U.S.C. Section 638(d)(2)(1982) exempts a cooperative research group of small businesses from federal antitrust enforcement by statute, if the group has previously been approved by the Small Business Administration and the Department of Justice. Also, the Department of Commerce, under 15 U.S.C. 1512 and 3710, provides assistance for the establishment of Industrial Technology Partnerships.

4. In order to receive protection under the NCRA, cooperating firms are allowed to cooperate only in their R&D activities and are prohibited from cooperating in the product market.

5. An example of a positive externality in R&D would be the positive effect a published research article would have on other research in the same field. For a more detailed description of this and the other possible economies of cooperative R&D, see Grossman and Shapiro (1986).

6. Seminal game-theoretic studies of innovation include Reinganum (1981), Lee and Wilde (1980), and Dasgupta and Stiglitz (1980), to name a few. See Kamien and Schwartz (1982, Chapter 5) for additional references through 1980.

7. Katz (1986) includes an additional stage between stages one and two, which he calls the agreement stage, in which "member firms choose the R&D cost-sharing and R&D output-sharing rules that characterize the agreement." Since the model presented here will assume a fixed contractual form for the RJV, this stage is unnecessary and is omitted.

8. Entry of all successful firms is reasonable under the assumption that innovations are kept as trade secrets rather than patented. In fact, Levin et al. (1987) find that R&D managers tend to view secrecy as "somewhat more effective than patents in protecting [process innovations]" from being duplicated.

9. Equal access to innovations may seem to make sense only when all firms make the same contribution to R&D, assumed here to be a contract stipulation (see Section III,A). Some RJVs do have a set membership fee. Some, however, base these fees on sales of the participants, even though there is equal sharing of innovations. In fact, there is a wide variety of cost- and innovation-sharing setups that may be worth exploring in the context of this model. Katz (1986) examines some of these in a nonstochastic environment.

10. These independence assumptions amount to an assumption of there being no positive spillovers or public good aspects of R&D between firms (except between firms within an RJV). This is a special case of Katz (1986). In an empirical study, Scott (1988) finds no evidence that cooperative R&D is conducted in FTC 4-digit industry categories in which there have been spillover problems.

11. Cartel behavior in the product market could just as easily be assumed. Even so, R declines in n_e, since as members join the cartel, monopoly profit is split between more firms.

12. This blocking rule is in effect at Microelectronics and Computer Technology

Corporation (MCC). Such a rule would have been prohibited in an earlier proposed version of the NCRA, in which limits on membership were not allowed.

13. If there were a continuum of potential entrants, this effect would be inconsequential.

14. More than three potential entrants require either analytic solution techniques for the case of a fourth degree polynomial or approximation of the root for a higher ordered polynomial.

15. This planning problem will likely yield a level of welfare less than that which would arise if the planner could directly control R&D.

16. Grossman and Shapiro (1986) in fact mention that members of cooperative research groups usually have large R&D budgets.

17. See, for example, Katz (1986), Ordover and Willig (1985), and Grossman and Shapiro (1986).

REFERENCES

Brander, James A. and Barbara J. Spencer, "Strategic Commitment with R&D: The Symmetric Case." *Bell Journal of Economics* 14(Spring 1983):225–235.

Dasgupta, Partha and Joseph E. Stiglitz, "Uncertainty, Industrial Structure and the Speed of R&D." *Bell Journal of Economics* 11(Winter 1980):1–28.

D'Aspremont, Claude, Alexis Jacquemin, Jean Jaskold Gabszewicz and John A. Weymark, "On the Stability of Collusive Price Leadership." *Canadian Journal of Economics* 16(February 1983):17–25.

Doane, Donna L., "Two Essays on Technological Innovation: Innovation and Economic Stagnation and Interfirm Cooperation for Innovation in Japan." Ph.D. dissertation, Yale University, December 1984.

Fusfeld, Herbert I., *The Technical Enterprise*. New York: Ballinger Publishing Company, 1986.

Grossman, Gene M. and Carl Shapiro, "Research Joint Ventures: An Antitrust Analysis." *Journal of Law, Economics, and Organization* 2(Fall 1986):315–337.

Kamien, Morton I. and Nancy L. Schwartz, *Market Structure and Innovation*. Cambridge: Cambridge University Press, 1982.

Katz, Michael L., "An Analysis of Cooperative Research and Development." *The Rand Journal of Economics* 17(Winter 1986):527–543.

Lee, Tom and Louis L. Wilde, "Market Structure and Innovation: A Reformulation." *Quarterly Journal of Economics* 94(March 1980):429–436.

Levin, Richard C., Alvin K. Klevorick, Richard R. Nelson and Sidney G. Winter, "Survey Research on R&D Appropriability and Technological Opportunity Part I: Appropriability." *Brookings Papers on Economic Activity* (Number 3 1987).

Link, Albert N. and Laura L. Bauer, *Cooperative Research in U.S. Manufacturing*, Lexington, Massachusetts: Lexington Books, 1989.

Nelson, Richard R., "Uncertainty, Learning, and the Economics of Parallel Research and Development Efforts." *Review of Economics and Statistics* 43(November 1961):351–364.

Ordover, Janusz A. and Robert D. Willig, "Antitrust for High Technology Industries: Assessing Research Joint Ventures and Mergers." *Journal of Law and Economics* 28(May 1985):311–333.

Reinganum, Jennifer F., "Dynamic Games of Innovation." *Journal of Economic Theory* 25(1981):21–41.

Scott, John T., "Diversification versus Cooperation in R&D Investment." *Managerial and Decision Economics* 9(1988): 173–186.

Tandon, Pankaj, "Rivalry and the Excessive Allocation of Resources to Research." *Bell Journal of Economics* 14(Spring 1983):152–165.

INNOVATIVE ACTIVITY, PRODUCTIVITY GROWTH, AND FIRM PERFORMANCE:

ARE LABOR UNIONS A SPUR OR A DETERRENT?

Barry T. Hirsch

I. INTRODUCTION

Factors limiting the appropriability of returns from innovative activity and capital investment are likely to affect the level and mix of investment and, in turn, have an impact on productivity levels and growth. Much previous research has focused on product market structure and other factors affecting the appropriability of the returns from R&D and patents.[1] Only recently has attention has been given to the potentially important role of labor unions on various dimensions of economic performance. Neglect of unionism's potential role is surprising. U.S. labor law provides unions with varying degrees of monopoly power in

Advances in Applied Micro-Economics, Volume 5, pages 69–104.

ISBN: 0-89232-797-9

the factor market, thus allowing union and nonunion labor to appropriate some share of firm quasi-rents. Unions typically have significant effects on the level, dispersion, and wage–fringe mix of labor compensation, as well as affecting productivity and governance structures in the workplace.[2] Hence, it should not be surprising if the investment behavior and economic performance of unionized companies differ significantly from those of nonunion companies.

This paper examines the effects of labor unions on the investment behavior and economic performance of U.S. firms during the 1970s, with particular emphasis given to union effects on R&D investment, capital investment, and productivity. A model of union rent seeking is presented in which a portion of firm quasi-rents is appropriated by labor. The implications of union rent seeking are then examined, with emphasis given to a delineation between "direct" and "indirect" union effects on investment behavior, productivity, and productivity growth. Empirical evidence is based on a unique firm-level data sample representing the activities of U.S. manufacturing firms during the 1970s.

Substantial differences in investment behavior and economic performance between union and nonunion forms are found. Unionized companies invest significantly less in both R&D and physical capital than do similar nonunion firms. The union impact on these investments is both direct, resulting from union appropriation of investment returns, and indirect, resulting from lower profitability, which in turn raises the cost of funds. Unions are likewise found to impact negatively on firm productivity and productivity growth. These latter effects occur directly through union effects in the workplace, and indirectly through union effects on R&D and capital investment. These findings lead to two major conclusions: first, union effects on long-run firm performance are substantial and should not be ignored in studies examining investment behavior, technological change, and productivity growth; and second, the relatively poor performance of unionized companies during the 1970s helps to explain increased management resistance to union organizing and the declining importance of collective bargaining in the U.S.[3]

Section II of this paper presents the union rent-seeking framework employed in this study, focusing in particular on the impact of collective bargaining on firm investment decisions. In Section III, the data are described and descriptive evidence on firm performance variables is provided for companies with varying levels of union coverage. Section IV provides discussion of econometric specification and presents evidence, in turn, of union effects on R&D expenditures, capital investment, productivity levels, and productivity growth. Section V offers an interpretation, and qualification, of the paper's major findings. A summary follows in Section VI.

II. UNION RENT SEEKING, INVESTMENT, AND ECONOMIC PERFORMANCE

A. Static Models and the Bargaining Process

Labor unions and management bargain over the level and mix of pecuniary and nonpecuniary compensation, work conditions, and workplace governance structures. Management is assumed to maximize the value of the firm (the discounted stream of future earnings). The union maximand is less clear.[4] It will use its bargaining power to acquire present and future contract provisions providing compensation–employment combinations for its members, more highly valued than those available in a competitive labor market. As discussed below, each party has a degree of monopoly or monopsony power, thus making short- and long-run bargaining outcomes indeterminate a priori. The parties engage in repeated bargaining (typically, every 3 years) and arrive at either cooperative (i.e., jointly maximizing) or noncooperative bargaining outcomes. It will be argued that in either case, company profits, investment decisions, productivity, and productivity growth will likely differ between union and nonunion firms.

Labor union monopoly power derives from a combination of U.S. labor law and the potential costs that a union can impose on a firm through a strike or other variation in labor input. In bargaining units where a union has won recognition under National Labor Relations Board auspices, it is the sole representative of workers in negotiations with management. Management must bargain in "good faith" with the union, but it is not required to arrive at a contractual agreement. Because it is costly for a firm not to reach an agreement or to substitute a nonunion work force, the union has some degree of monopoly power in the labor market. Union bargaining strength is of course limited by the level and elasticity of the labor demand curve (although settlements need not be on the demand curve) or, more specifically, by the substitution capabilities of consumers and management and by the legal rules and enforcement surrounding the NLRB union representation process. Firm monopsony power results primarily from the fixed costs to workers of job change and the fact that employees possess firm-specific skills not easily transferred to other firms. One can make similar arguments about industry-specific skills that are difficult for workers to transfer in the event of industry-wide employment downturns.

Much of the literature on bargaining outcomes has employed a single-period model and contrasted the properties of settlements on the labor demand curve with Pareto-superior settlements off the labor demand curve. The conventional bargaining model predicts outcomes on the labor demand curve following *sequential* wage and employment determination. The union is constrained by the labor demand curve (i.e., it faces a wage–employment tradeoff) and "selects" a wage above the competitive wage that maximizes union rents, commonly defined as $(w_u - w_c)L$, where w_u is the union wage, w_c is the (unobserved) competitive wage, and L is employment. The firm is free to vary employment at the union wage, and maximizes profits by selecting the employment level on its labor demand curve corresponding to w_u.

Bargaining outcomes on the labor demand curve, however, are generally not Pareto-optimal. There exist outcomes in wage–employment space to the right of the labor demand curve, at a lower wage and higher employment level than at the union's obtainable outcome on the demand curve, preferred by both the union and firm; that is, corresponding to higher union utility and firm profit. The range of "efficient" bargaining outcomes is defined by a contract curve, derived from the tangencies between the union's indifference curves and the firm's isoprofit curves. The contract curve can in general take on a positive or negative slope, but in the unique "strong efficiency" case (Brown and Ashenfelter, 1986) it is vertical at points above w_c in wage–employment space. Bargaining outcomes on a vertical contract curve would imply the use of a factor mix *identical* to the (short-run) competitive case. In essence, the union and firm agree to maximize the joint value of the enterprise, comprised of the sum of firm profits and union rents, and subsequently bargain over the division of the surplus between profits and wages (Abowd, 1987).

The existence of preferred bargaining outcomes off the labor demand curve does not ensure that such outcomes are obtainable. In order to achieve such an outcome there must be explicit or implicit contracting that allows for simultaneous bargaining over wages *and* employment. Stated alternatively, there must be some mechanism that forces the firm to have a greater employment level than designated by the demand curve. Otherwise, following contract agreement on the wage, the firm would select an employment level to maximize profits, thereby obtaining an outcome on the labor demand curve. While labor contracts containing explicit employment requirements are rare, stable long-run repetitive bargaining and union work rules may allow the obtaining of efficient outcomes by preventing the firm from engaging in opportunistic behavior. Extant empirical evidence, albeit limited, rejects the hypothesis of bargaining outcomes on a labor demand curve, but it is not necessarily supportive of the hypothesis of settlements on a vertical contract curve (Hirsch and Addison, 1986; Farber, 1986).

The primary limitation of the conventional on-the-demand curve and off-the-demand curve models is that they are static single-period models applied in situations where repetitive bargaining, reputational "capital," and evolved protocols (Reder and Neumann, 1980) are essential elements of the bargaining process. While the off-the-demand curve model relies on the existence of repeated bargaining to ensure that the firm does not behave opportunistically (i.e., hire at an employment level on the demand curve once the wage is determined), the strong efficiency result described above holds only in the short run. Joint profits and union rents are maximized, *given* the level of the capital stock. In the long run, union rent seeking will be distortionary if firms respond by altering their investment in tangible and intangible capital. It is this possibility to which we now turn.

B. Union Rent Seeking and Dynamic Bargaining Models

Recent papers have provided diverse theoretical models of the union bargaining process in a dynamic setting.[5] Here, an intuitive discussion of a game-theoretic model, referred to here as a union rent-seeking model, is provided. Outlined first will be the nature of bargaining with noncooperative outcomes. Examined next will be the effects of bargaining with cooperative outcomes. The union rent-seeking framework outlined in this paper relies on several assumptions: the firm has, or would have in the absence of a union, long-lived intangible or physical capital providing quasi-rents[6]; the firm cannot costlessly substitute nonunion for union labor (or plants); and the time horizon over which the union evaluates its utility is shorter than the horizon over which firm owners evaluate earnings (or, similarly, the union discounts more highly than the firm future returns).[7]

Each of these assumptions is reasonable. Once innovative capital or physical capital (often emanating from past R&D) is in place, its productive life typically exceeds the life of a union contract. The union strike threat, made possible by legal bargaining rights granted to unions and to workers' possession of firm-specific skills, makes it costly for firms to substitute nonunion for union labor. The union is also likely to have a limited time horizon. Whereas owners will in general have an unlimited time horizon since ownership shares can be transferred (albeit the future may be highly discounted), union members are unable to sell or transfer their positions in the union.

Consider first the case of a noncooperative bargaining outcome. Once long-lived capital is in place, the union will appropriate or tax some share of the quasi-rents deriving from that capital. As long as the union maintains a credible strike threat and the firm can recover its variable costs, the firm will "voluntarily" share with the union its returns on capital rather than severely curtail production. The firm is likely to face higher union "tax" rates on innovative and physical capital the more firm specific is the capital and the longer is its productive life. In response to the union tax, the firm will reduce its investment in long-lived capital until the postunion marginal rate of return is equal to the opportunity costs of funds (the union places a wedge between the social and private rates of return on capital). Investment in all forms of vulnerable capital will decrease; the limiting case is that the firm will cease investment and eventually shut down its union operations. Alternatively, the firm may always maintain some inefficient capital (or plants) to mitigate union wage demands, since the firm would respond to high wages by shutting down low productivity plants, thus decreasing union employment (see Baldwin, 1983).[8]

As long as bargaining occurs for a limited number of bargaining rounds, union appropriation of firm quasi-rents and a reduction in investment activity will occur. A union could announce a relatively low future wage demand in order to encourage the firm to invest in long-lived capital. But the union's commitment would be neither credible nor binding beyond the contract period, since once the capital is in place the union would increase its wage demands in the final bargaining period. Knowing this, the firm would not commit to a nonunion investment level.[9] In short, as long as there are a limited number of bargaining periods, noncooperative bargaining outcomes are likely to obtain.

Collective bargaining, however, is generally characterized by infinitely repeated bargaining, the exception being where a firm is expected to shut down operations.[10] Repeated bargaining implies that current behavior by both the firm and union will affect their reputation and credibility in future bargaining rounds. Because the scope for opportunistic behavior is limited, cooperative bargaining outcomes are more likely to obtain. A cooperative outcome is defined here as one that maximizes the joint value of the firm and union; that is, the sum of the firm's market value (the present value of future earnings to shareholders) and the present value of union members' rents [this joint value is referred to by Abowd (1987) as the value of the enterprise].

Does the possibility of cooperative outcomes from repeated union–management bargaining imply that union representation has no distortionary effects on output, price, or factor usage? This is the case in the short run; the firm and union maximize the size of the pie, given the existing capital stock, and bargain over the distribution of returns to labor and to shareholders.[11] In the long run, however, union rent seeking will be distortionary (relative to an otherwise similar nonunion environment); in particular, it is likely to lead to reduced investment in long-lived relation-specific capital.[12]

The reason for underinvestment in specific fixed-cost capital is the limited time horizon over which a democratically controlled labor union evaluates its future returns, coupled with the nontransferability or incomplete property rights union workers have in union membership. The union responds to the preferences of members with median preferences, often relatively senior members with a relatively short expected remaining tenure at the firm. Moreover, senior workers may make relatively high wage demands if they face relatively low probabilities of permanent (seniority-based) layoff and perceive little threat to their pension payments (government pension guarantees, although perhaps warranted on other grounds, presumably worsen union myopia). Largely unweighted in the union calculus are preferences of relatively junior members or of unobserved workers who could be future union members were the union's compensation demands lower. Thus, the union will weight highly current rents and discount heavily potential future rents. Although efficient (cooperative) contracting maximizes the sum of owner and union member "wealth," rational union myopia will result in lower investment than is obtained in a nonunion firm, shifting returns more heavily toward the present and away from the (highly discounted) future. And apart from the partial transfer of stock ownership to the union, there are few mechanisms by which to make union goals more fully incentive-compatible with those of the firm.[13]

The union rent-seeking model predicts that collective bargaining coverage fundamentally changes investment decisions because the firm responds to a rationally myopic union by decreasing investment in vulnerable capital. Contrary to the prediction of the conventional on-the-demand curve model, firms facing a rent-seeking union *may* decrease both the capital level and the capital–labor ratio. In the case of heterogeneous capital, the firm will decrease investment most in long-lived relation-specific capital whose returns are most easily appropriated, while either increasing or decreasing investment in capital whose returns are less easily appropriable. Even the prediction that unionized firms will invest relatively more than nonunion firms in labor-saving capital need not follow. If the union can retain its preinvestment strike threat with a reduced work force (say, through the ability to shut down a plant), then the returns from labor-saving capital are no less appropriable than those from factor-neutral investment. Indeed, the union may demand higher per employee compensation and/or employment guarantees if the firm embarks on a labor-saving investment strategy. Of course, if the union strike threat and bargaining power is in part a function of the size of its work force, then the prediction that unionized firms' investment will be labor saving follows more readily.

The returns from investment in R&D and non-R&D innovative activity may accrue over a shorter time span than returns from physical capital, but such capital is still relatively long lived and appropriable (Connolly et al., 1986). Or, the knowledge about products or processes emanating from R&D projects may lead to investment in physical capital whose returns in turn face a high union tax rate. That is, the decision to lower future investment in physical capital may decrease current investment in R&D. For these reasons, unionized firms are less likely to invest in innovative activity than are similar nonunion firms. This decrease in innovation is likely to be most notable for relatively factor-neutral product or process innovation, whereas labor-saving process innovation may be less affected, since the substitution effect of a wage increase may increase the relative importance of labor-saving innovation.[14]

Firms are often reluctant to patent and license innovative processes resulting from R&D and other investment in innovation, because the process by which firms patent and sell licenses is costly, risky, and often revealing of trade secrets. Innovations that can be licensed are less likely to be subjected to the union strike threat and rent seeking, however, because the returns from patentable innovations do not depend on continued plant operations. Hence, unions may be less able to capture returns associated with patentable innovations, and union firms should have a higher propensity to patent, given levels of innovative activity.

Finally, if union rent seeking results in decreased investment in tangible and intangible capital, an implication is that unionized firms will be less productive, face slower productivity and sales growth than otherwise similar nonunion firms, and, relatedly, are less likely to survive in the long run. Output is a function of random components, input quantity, input quality, and the organization and coordination of production and managerial processes. Union rent seeking operates *indirectly* to reduce measured productivity (i.e., value added per worker) or productivity growth through reduced investment in R&D and other forms of capital. Whether or not unions have *direct* effects, that is, whether union firms have different productivity levels or growth rates than nonunion firms, holding constant stocks (or changes in stocks) of R&D and physical capital, is an important yet distinct question to be addressed below.

From our model of union rent seeking, wherein unions tax the quasi-rents that make up the normal returns to long-lived tangible and intangible capital, several empirical regularities are expected to appear in the data. First, union firms should experience lower rates of profit than otherwise similar nonunion firms.[15] And even in the event of cooperative or efficient long-run contracting between firms and relatively myopic unions, the union tax on profits is likely to be distortionary and lower investment in capital whose returns are most vulnerable to union appropriation. We expect to observe lower investment by union firms in physical capital and R&D, as well as the possibility of lower capital-to-labor ratios and a higher propensity to patent, given levels of innovative activity. Lower investment in long-lived tangible and intangible capital will subsequently retard productivity and productivity growth. The possibility that unions directly affect productivity and productivity growth, independent of their effects on R&D and capital investment, also will be examined.

III. DATA AND DESCRIPTIVE EVIDENCE

The data set employed in this paper is based on information from 315 publicly traded Fortune 1000 firms operating in the U.S. manufacturing sector in the 1970s for which information both on firm-level union coverage and financial data from Standard and Poor's Compustat files are available. Annual Compustat data for 1970 through 1980 are used; union coverage data are available only for 1972. Missing data for some variables result in the exclusion of some "firm-years" from various analyses.

An important empirical contribution of this paper is the use of firm-level, rather than industry-level, data on union coverage. Previous firm-level studies of market value or investment behavior (Salinger, 1984; Connolly et al., 1986; Hirsch and Connolly, 1987; Bronars and Deere, 1986) have had to match three-digit industry-level union data to individual firm observations. Hence, these studies have not been able to account for the considerable intraindustry variation in unionization, and may have entangled to a significant degree union and industry effects on market value and investment. The firm-level union data employed here are for a single year, 1972, and were obtained from a 1972 Conference Board Survey.[16] The primary union data measure the percentage of production and maintenance workers covered by a collective bargaining agreement. Because we are interested in the extent of unionization within the entire firm and firms vary in the proportion of their work force comprised of production workers, this coverage ratio is multiplied by the estimated proportion of production workers in the firm. This conversion is based on the assumption that there exists zero coverage among nonproduction workers; coverage among such workers causes the total firm coverage estimates to be understated. Mean union coverage for our sample of firms in 1972 is 43.6% of the total work force, as compared to 58.9% of production and maintenance workers.[17]

The second primary data set, constructed at the National Bureau of Economic Research and Harvard University, matches Compustat company information with U.S. patents data from the Office of Technology Assessment and Forecasting.[18] The initial universe was all publicly traded firms in the manufacturing sector that were listed on any of four Compustat files (Industrial, Over the Counter, Research, or Full Coverage files) in 1976. Information from years prior to and following 1976 is included to provide an unbalanced panel data set with a maximum 1904 firms in 1976 and fewer in other years, 315 for which union coverage information is available in the Conference Board Survey. Company 10-K reports filed with the Securities and Exchange Commission provide the source for much of the information on Compustat. This data set contains relatively complete information on firm market values, earnings, gross and net plant, the book value of debt, R&D investment, and patents (filed and granted). Less complete data are available for advertising expenditures and labor compensation. Industry data are matched to the firm at the two-, three-, or four-digit level, based on Compustat's SIC-code variable designating the firm's principal industry. Industry data on shipments, capital intensity, the ratio of production to total employees, and investment are obtained from the Bureau of Industrial Economics Industrial Profile and Capital Stock Data Base tapes consolidating data from the Annual Survey of Manufactures. Data on industry concentration (adjusted for imports and regional concentration), as well as import penetration, are available for 1972 and 1977 from Weiss and Pascoe (1986).

Prior to estimation of the investment, productivity, and productivity growth models, it is useful to examine differences in key firm-level economic performance variables by firms' union status. In Table 1, we

Table 1. Variable Means by Union Category, 1970–1980[a]

	All Firms		*Low union*		*Medium union*		*High union*	
Variable	*n*	*Mean*	*n*	*Mean*	*n*	*Mean*	*n*	*Mean*
COV	3410	0.436	1112	0.084	1193	0.471	1105	0.751
q	3260	1.076	1079	1.518	1130	0.908	1051	0.804
π_k	3257	0.076	1078	0.090	1127	0.072	1052	0.066
R&D/S	2407	0.021	805	0.030	913	0.017	689	0.016
PAT/S	2902	0.045	942	0.055	1055	0.049	905	0.030
INV/S	3289	0.061	1084	0.067	1143	0.061	1062	0.055
ADV/S	1928	0.021	675	0.031	663	0.018	590	0.014
K/S	3262	0.717	1079	0.652	1130	0.723	1053	0.777
ln(VA/L)	3274	3.015	1082	3.076	1140	2.990	1052	2.979
ρ_t	2002	0.014	671	0.026	696	0.009	635	0.006
DEBT/EQUITY	3249	0.503	1075	0.543	1129	0.455	1045	0.516
CR4	3410	0.397	1112	0.413	1193	0.369	1105	0.410
I-IMPORT	3410	0.071	1112	0.071	1193	0.060	1105	0.083
I-GROWTH	3410	3.096	1112	4.320	1193	3.052	1105	1.912

[a]Low union (COV < 0.28); medium union ($0.28 \leq$ COV < 0.63); high union (COV ≥ 0.63).

COV	Proportion of firm's workers covered by a collective bargaining agreement.
q	Market value of firm divided by replacement cost of tangible assets (measured by value of net inflation-adjusted capital stock).
π_k	Gross rate of return to capital; gross cash flows divided by the value of the gross inflation-adjusted capital stock.
R&D/S	Annual R&D expenditures divided by sales.
PAT/S	Patent stock (calculated based on number of patents granted and a 30% depreciation rate) divided by sales.
INV/S	Annual investment expenditures divided by sales.
ADV/S	Annual advertising expenditures divided by sales.
K/S	Net inflation-adjusted capital stock divided by sales.
DEBT/EQUITY	Value of long-term debt adjusted for age structure, divided by equity value of firm.
ln(VA/L)	Natural log of value added per employee, in millions of 1972 dollars. (See Appendix and footnote 21.)
ρ_t	Partial productivity growth, calculated as the average annual 4-year growth rate in value added, minus the average annual growth rate in employment times labor's share of total costs (See Appendix and footnote 21.)
CR4	Four-firm concentration ratio in firm's primary four-digit industry
I-IMPORT	Percentage of imports in firm's primary four-digit industry
I-GROWTH	Average percentage growth rate in real industry shipments over the previous 4 years in firm's primary four-digit industry.

present means and standard deviations for variables of interest, separately for the entire sample over the 1970–1980 period (growth rates are for 1970–1974 through 1976–1980), and for the 315 firms (for a maximum of 11 years) divided into approximately equal-sized groups of low (n = 103), medium (n = 110), and high (n = 102) union coverage levels, COV ("low" is defined as COV < 0.28, "medium" as $0.28 \leq$ COV < 0.63, and "high" as COV ≥ 0.63). Within the low union sample, 31 of the firms have zero coverage and 65 have less than 10% coverage. These 96 firms are defined as "nonunion" in subsequent regression analyses. Because of missing data, particularly for years after 1976 as firms "leave" the sample due to mergers, going private, or dissolutions, total sample sizes in Table 1 are less than 11 times 315 (or 7 times 315 for the growth rates). Variable definitions are provided in the footnote to Table 1.

A number of interesting patterns are evident from these descriptive statistics. The low union sample of firms has an average coverage of 8.4%, as compared to 47.1 and 75.1% for the medium and high union samples, respectively. The existence of union rent seeking is suggested by the finding that as firm union coverage increases, profitability is substantially lower, whether measured by Tobin's q or π_k.[19] Market valuation of the firm (as measured by q) drops particularly sharply as one moves from low to middle union coverage, suggesting that even moderate levels of unionization significantly reduce investors' expectations of future shareholder earnings.

Capital intensity, as measured by the capital stock per worker, K/S, increases moderately with union coverage. Firms with higher coverage, however, have lower capital *investment* intensities—the ratio of capital investment to sales (INV/S) decreasing as one moves from low to high coverage firms. R&D investment intensity (R&D/S) is also found to decrease as union coverage increases, differences being particularly large between the low union and medium/high union categories.[20] New patents per dollar of (deflated) sales (PAT/S) also declines with union coverage, although here the difference is largest between the high union and other two union groups. We find a U-shape relationship between firms' debt–equity ratios, DEBT/EQUITY, and union category, the debt–equity ratios being higher in both the low and high union samples than in the middle union sample. Just over half of the sample report advertising expenditures, but among these firms, advertising intensity (ADV/S) decreases sharply as we move from low to high union coverage (a similar pattern is evident if nonreporting firms are assumed to have zero advertising).

Labor productivity, measured by the logarithm of value added per worker, is about 8% lower among medium/high union firms than among companies with low union coverage.[21] "Partial" productivity growth (Griliches, 1986), measured by the average annual 4-year growth rate in value added, minus the growth rate in employment times labor's share, is substantially higher among the low union companies, about 2.6% annually as compared to less than 1% among medium/high companies. And in results not shown, average growth rates in employment, capital, and R&D all decrease with respect to union coverage.

Differences in industry concentration, CR4, and industry import penetration, I-IMPORT, exhibit less clear-cut patterns with respect to firms' union coverage. Industry sales growth, I-GROWTH, however, decreases sharply as we move from the low to high union category, indicating that union firms are located within four-digit industries with significantly slower growth. The sizable differences seen above between the economic performance of companies with low and high levels of union coverage demonstrate the need for careful empirical analysis. In the remainder of the paper, we seek to identify the extent to which differences in investment behavior, productivity, and productivity growth can be attributed to differences in union coverage.

IV. EMPIRICAL SPECIFICATION AND RESULTS

This section presents empirical analysis examining the impact of unionization on firm investment behavior, innovative activity, productivity, and productivity growth. We first examine firm investment in R&D and physical capital, distinguishing between direct and indirect impacts of union coverage on investment behavior. Next, differences in productivity levels and productivity growth between union and nonunion firms are examined. Detailed variable definitions are provided in the Appendix; a further description of variables is in the text.

A. Union Coverage, Innovative Activity, and Capital Investment

The union rent-seeking model predicts differences between the investment behavior of union and nonunion firms. Primary attention is given here to differences with respect to investments in physical capital and R&D, the latter being a proxy for innovative activity. Because we are interested in how unionism affects current investment behavior, we focus on investment flows or additions to the stock of physical or R&D capital (capital stocks are controlled for on the right-hand side of equations). Investment intensity equations take the simple form:

$$I_{it} = \Sigma\ \beta_{Ik}X_{Ikit} + \psi_I UN + e_{Iit} \qquad (1)$$

where I_{it} represents the natural logarithm of investment in physical capital or R&D by firm i in year t, I indexes investment vectors, and e_{Iit} is a random error term with zero mean and constant variance. X_I is a vector of k + 1 firm- and industry-specific variables, including a constant ($X_0 = 1$), that affect investment, while β_{Ik} is the coefficient vector attaching to X. In this and subsequent regression models, union coverage status, UN, enters separately (i.e., not in interaction with other variables) as a categorical union/nonunion variable, equal to zero if union coverage is less than 10% and equal to one if coverage is at least 10%. Experimentation indicated that most union effects occur at relatively low coverage levels, but do not necessarily increase with increasing coverage (see, also, Clark, 1984). Conclusions are similar when continuous union coverage or multiple categorical variables are used.

Included in X_I are such variables as contemporaneous profitability (measured by the rate of return on capital), firm size, capital intensity, R&D and/or capital stock variables, industry concentration, industry sales growth, industry import penetration, and industry and year dummies. The coefficient ψ_I measures the *direct* partial effect of union coverage on investment. The total union effect will also include *indirect* effects on investment deriving from lower earnings in union firms. Auxiliary profit equations are estimated in order to estimate the magnitude of these indirect union effects on investment behavior.

Table 2 presents regression results for R&D and capital investment equations. The dependent variable in the R&D equations is the logarithm of real annual investment expenditures on R&D, ln(R&D). Specifications are presented with and without inclusion of industry dummies. As control variables, we include current profitability (measured by the rate of return on capital), an R&D stock variable, the log of real sales, the log of the capital stock, industry concentration, industry sales growth, industry import penetration, and year dummies. The R&D investment equations are reported for the sample of R&D-active firms reporting positive R&D expenditures (n = 2382), and for a larger sample where nonreporting firms for which patent data are available

Table 2. R&D and Capital Investment Equations—Regression Results[a]

	Dependent variable					
	ln(R&D)		*ln(R&D)^{est}*		*ln(INV)*	
Variable	*(1)*	*(2)*	*(3)*	*(4)*	*(5)*	*(6)*
UN	−0.140	−0.100	−0.102	−0.088	−0.102	−0.102
	(4.47)	(2.94)	(3.65)	(2.90)	(4.24)	(3.88)
π_k	2.723	2.283	2.200	1.764	5.767	5.720
	(8.60)	(7.42)	(7.85)	(6.45)	(23.32)	(23.29)
ln(L)	0.273	0.215	0.190	0.213	−0.030	0.075
	(10.95)	(7.09)	(9.26)	(8.55)	(1.71)	(3.42)
ln(K)	0.116	0.325	0.088	0.197	—	—
	(5.67)	(11.29)	(5.14)	(8.48)		
R&D-STK^{est}(−1)	0.672	0.519	0.745	0.592	—	—
	(55.70)	(38.40)	(69.81)	(48.23)		
R&D-STK^{est}	—	—	—	—	0.020	0.014
					(2.05)	(1.16)
ln(K)(−1)	—	—	—	—	1.102	1.000
					(74.36)	(48.28)
CR4	−0.047	−0.259	0.071	−0.210	0.145	0.058
	(0.64)	(2.85)	(1.11)	(2.68)	(2.62)	(0.85)
I-GROWTH	0.012	0.010	0.013	0.011	0.013	0.007
	(5.18)	(3.97)	(5.87)	(4.94)	(6.67)	(3.72)
I-IMPORT	0.287	0.095	0.347	0.224	−0.277	−0.401
	(1.63)	(0.50)	(2.16)	(1.27)	(1.97)	(2.53)
IND	No	Yes	No	Yes	No	Yes
YEAR	Yes	Yes	Yes	Yes	Yes	Yes
$\bar{R}^2$	0.877	0.897	0.865	0.884	0.900	0.911
n	2382	2382	3001	3001	3142	3142

[a]|t| in parentheses.

are assigned predicted values of R&D stocks and investment expenditure (n = 3001).[22]

Primary interest here centers on the coefficients associated with firm union status, measuring the direct union effect, and π, allowing estimation of an indirect effect. Estimates of the *direct* union effect on R&D investment indicate that unionized firms have R&D investment 9–10% lower than otherwise similar nonunion firms, after accounting for other firm and industry determinants of R&D. Estimates from the two samples are very similar. Estimates of the direct effect of unionism understate unionism's total effect, however, because union rent seeking also decreases investment indirectly owing to lower firm earnings that impinge upon all investment decisions. In an auxiliary profit equation (where profitability is measured by the rate of return on capital,

π), the partial effect of union coverage on π is estimated to be $\partial\pi/\partial\text{UN} = -0.018$. Hence the *total* effect of unionism on R&D investment is:

$$\begin{aligned} \text{dln R\&D/dUN} &= \partial\text{ln R\&D}/\partial\text{UN} + (\partial\text{ln R\&D}/\partial\pi)(\partial\pi/\partial\text{UN}) \\ &= -0.088 + (1.764 \times -0.018) = -0.120 \end{aligned} \quad (2)$$

where $\partial\text{ln R\&D}/\partial\text{UN}$ and $\partial\text{ln R\&D}/\partial\pi$ are obtained from the coefficients on UN and π in Table 2, specification (4), and the estimate of $\partial\pi/\partial\text{UN}$ is obtained from the UN coefficient in a profitability regression, not shown.[23] Thus, the estimates imply that unionized firms will have R&D investment about 11% lower than similar nonunion firms (percentage effects are approximated by $[e^{\lambda} - 1]100$, where λ is the estimated logarithmic differential). Approximately three-quarters of the effect is a direct union effect, while a quarter of the effect occurs indirectly via union effects on firm earnings.

Union rent seeking is expected to affect tangible capital investment in a manner similar to R&D investment. Moreover, capital investment is an important mechanism by which technological change is effected. Capital investment is both complementary to investment in innovative activity, and has an important impact on subsequent productivity levels and growth. Table 2, columns (5) and (6), presents regression results from the estimation of capital investment equations where the log of annual real investment expenditures, ln(INV), is the dependent variable. Unionization is negatively and significantly related to capital investment, decreasing investment directly (through its tax on the gross rate of return to investment), and indirectly through the decrease in earnings that provide a source of relatively low-cost financing. We estimate the total effect of unions on annual capital investment as

$$\begin{aligned} \text{dln INV/dUN} &= \partial\text{ln INV}/\partial\text{UN} + (\partial\text{ln INV}/\partial\pi)(\partial\pi/\partial\text{UN}) \\ &= -0.102 + (5.720 \times -0.018) = -0.205 \end{aligned} \quad (3)$$

where $\partial\text{ln INV}/\partial\text{UN}$ and $\partial\text{ln INV}/\partial\pi$ are obtained from the coefficients on UN and q in Table 4, specification (6), and the estimate of $\partial\pi/\partial\text{UN}$ is obtained as previously. The estimates imply that unionized firms will have capital investment about 18.5% lower than nonunion firms. Approximately half of the effect is a direct union effect, while the remaining half is an indirect union effect deriving from the decrease in current firm earnings.

The evidence presented in this section provides strong evidence that union rent seeking has significant real effects on firm investment behavior. Cooperative bargaining outcomes between unions and firms potentially can be reached, implying no real allocative effects, *given* existing stocks of tangible and intangible capital. The relatively shorter time horizon adopted by union rank-and-file than among the firm's shareholders, however, implies reduced investment in long-lived fixed-cost capital even where cooperative outcomes obtain. Noncooperative bargaining outcomes typically imply even larger reductions in investment. The finding that unionized firms invest significantly less in R&D and physical capital than do nonunion firms implies that union firms and sectors will grow more slowly over time than their nonunion counterparts. Lower investment may also have an impact on long-run levels of productivity and productivity growth among unionized firms. We next turn to this topic.

B. Unions, Productivity, and Productivity Growth

Unions may have positive or negative direct effects on levels or changes in productivity, holding constant labor and nonlabor inputs. In addition, unionization will have an indirect impact on productivity levels and growth to the extent that it affects investment in tangible and intangible capital inputs. The traditional view of unions by economists portrays unions as a labor market distortion directly retarding productivity and growth. Negative union effects result from union work rules, limitations on management discretion and flexibility in promotions and job assignments, and decreased individual worker incentives due to limitations on merit-based wage dispersion.

Recent interest in union effects in the workplace was sparked by Freeman and Medoff's collective voice/institutional response (CV/IR) view of unions (Freeman, 1976; Freeman and Medoff, 1984). This view emphasizes the potential positive role of unions on economic performance in work environments characterized by long-run attachment of workers and firms, typically owing to large investment in firm-specific on-the-job training, worker complementarities in production (i.e., reliance on teamwork in production and training), and significant workplace "public" or nondivisible goods (e.g., job safety, personnel policies, hours of operation).[24] It is argued that reliance on individual bargaining and entry/exit behavior as the primary instruments for worker voice is inefficient in such an environment. Unions provide a potential mechanism for correcting this "market failure," because a collective voice representing median or average workers may more accurately represent the preferences of the work force and decrease turnover. Worker cooperation and morale may be improved from the adoption of more formalized governance structure and grievance procedures, by lessening wage dispersion through use of standardized wages and strict reliance on seniority, and from restrictions on management's ability to take unilateral actions without consideration of worker preferences.

Cooperative labor–management relations are necessary for unions to have positive productivity effects, hence the institutional response component of the CV/IR view. Given scant attention in the CV/IR literature is the possibility that nonunion firms may provide formalized governance structures that serve as instruments of worker voice, while not being encumbered by the higher costs or other negative effects of unions. Recent evidence that large nonunion establishments have highly formalized governance structures and provide mechanisms for worker input, while avoiding many of the costs associated with unions, suggests that unions are not always a necessary condition for establishing effective voice (Foulkes, 1980; Kochan et al., 1986). Indeed, increased use of "positive labor relations" by firms in nonunion plants, wherein workers are provided with many of the advantages of unionization, can be seen as a response to the threat of union organizing.

The empirical literature examining union effects on productivity typically follows Brown and Medoff (1978) in employing some variant of the Cobb–Douglas production function

$$Q = AK^{\alpha}(L_n + cL_u)^{1-\alpha}, \tag{4}$$

where Q is output, L_u and L_n are union and nonunion labor respectively, K is capital, A is a constant of proportionality, and α and $(1 - \alpha)$ are the output elasticities with respect to capital and labor, respectively. The parameter c measures productivity differences between union and nonunion labor. A $c > 1$ implies union labor is more productive, in line with the CV/IR view; a $c < 1$ implies union labor is less productive, in line with the traditional view. Brown and Medoff show that Eq. (4) can be approximated by the following (ignoring the error term),

$$\ln(Q/L) = \ln A + \alpha \ln(K/L) + (1 - \alpha)(c - 1)P, \tag{5}$$

where P represents union density (L_u/L).

Equations (4) and (5) assume constant returns to scale, an assumption that may be relaxed by including a ln L variable as a measure of establishment size. The productivity differential of unionized establishments is estimated by the composite coefficient on P. If it is assumed that the union productivity effect solely reflects the differential efficiency of *labor* inputs, the union labor productivity effect is calculated by dividing the coefficient on P by $(1 - \alpha)$. Note also that estimation of (5) is similar to estimation of a total factor productivity (TFP) equation; $c > 1$ implies that unions have higher TFP. That is, subtracting $\alpha \ln(K/L)$ from both sides of (5),

$$\mathrm{TFP} = \ln Q - \alpha \ln K - (1 - \alpha) \ln L = \ln A + (1 - \alpha)(c - 1)P. \tag{6}$$

More recently, the debate over union effects on productivity has shifted to union effects on productivity growth. Hirsch and Link (1984) show that changes in total factor productivity, ρ, derived by differencing the Brown–Medoff model above, is a function of changes in union density, ΔP. Following the productivity growth literature emphasizing the role of R&D on growth, Hirsch and Link employ a Cobb–Douglas function that includes a third factor, technical capital (T). Their estimating equation (ignoring control variables) is

$$\rho = \theta + \Phi(dT/dt)/Q + (1 - \alpha)(c - 1)\Delta P, \tag{7}$$

where θ is the rate of disembodied growth; Φ is $\partial Q/\partial T$, the marginal product of technical capital, dT/dt approximates net investment into stock T, and $(dT/dt)/Q$ is proxied as R&D investment per unit of sales. A positive coefficient on ΔP implies $c > 1$ and would support the CV/IR view. Estimating the production function in difference form (i.e., a simple form of a fixed effects model) has the advantage of netting out unmeasured or omitted determinants of productivity whose omission from single cross-section estimates may bias coefficients, but has the disadvantage that measures of changes in unionization are rarely available over suitably long time periods. In their empirical work, Hirsch and Link include both a level of unionism variable, P, and a change in unionism variable, ΔP, for two-digit manufacturing industries.

Several limitations attach to the production function test (Addison and Hirsch, 1989). First, the use of value added as the output measure confounds price and quantity effects, since part of the measured union productivity differential may result from higher prices in unionized sectors. Quantity can be measured in physical units in industry-specific studies, but union effects vary so widely across economic environments that it is difficult to generalize from industry-specific studies. A related possibility is that the union coefficient in the production function crudely tracks the union–nonunion wage differential. An additional limitation is the overly restrictive assumption of the Cobb–Douglas functional form and of neutral, disembodied technology. Data deficiencies provide still further limitations. In the aggregate studies, union and nonunion sectors are assumed to have identical production functions ($\alpha_u = \alpha_n$). The reliability of the production function test also depends on the ability to control for important inputs in the production process other than union status and quantities of labor and capital. Specifically, union and nonunion establishments may differ systematically in the quality of unmeasured organizational factors (e.g., managerial supervision and the quality of labor relations) such that "firm effects" are not independent of union status.

Perhaps the most serious criticism of the union productivity test is that of selectivity. Union firms facing higher wage rates must be more productive if they are to survive in the very long run. Hence, the productivity effect is not being measured across a representative sample of firms; rather, only those union firms that have survived by increasing productivity sufficiently to offset higher union wages are observed. Measurement of union productivity differentials among surviving firms thus biases upward the estimated productivity effect of unions on a representative firm. The importance of the limitations outlined above varies significantly with the particular study or application. Addison and Hirsch (1989) interpret the extant evidence and conclude that no compelling case exists for a statistically or quantitatively significant union productivity effect in general, positive or negative. In this paper, it is union effects on both productivity levels and productivity growth that are of interest.

In order to examine union effects on productivity, the following variant of the Brown–Medoff Cobb–Douglas production function [Eq. (5)] is estimated:

$$\ln(VA/L)_{it} = \Sigma\, \beta_{Vk} X_{Vkit} + \alpha \ln(K/L)_{it} + (1 - \alpha)(c - 1)UN_i + e_{Vit}, \tag{8}$$

where subscript V signifies vectors attaching to Eq. (8). The log of value added per employee in firm i and year t, $\ln(VA/L)_{it}$, is a function of the log of the capital–labor ratio, $\ln(K/L)$, and firm-level union coverage, UN. The vector X_{Vk} includes the log of labor, $\ln(L)$; the log of the R&D

stock, ln(R&D-STK); and year and industry dummies. These two vectors of dummies are important because labor productivity varies considerably across industries and over time, and unionization is not randomly distributed across industries. A positive (negative) coefficient on UN implies that union establishments are more (less) productive than similar nonunion establishments, that is, that $c > 1$ ($c < 1$).

Estimates from Eq. (8) are presented in Table 3, for specifications with and without inclusion of industry dummies, and separately for the sample with direct R&D stock measurement and for the larger sample including R&D stock estimates for some firms. The coefficient on firm union coverage status is negative and significant in all specifications. Estimates from both samples indicate that unionized companies have approximately 8% lower productivity than nonunion companies with identically measured inputs. The estimated union effect is significantly more negative when industry dummies are excluded (consistent with the Brown–Medoff finding that unions are highly organized in less productive industries). These negative estimates are notable, particularly since many of the econometric biases inherent in the Brown–Medoff methodology, as discussed above, lead to *upward* biased estimates of the union effect.[25]

In results not presented, the union–productivity relationship was examined further by interacting UN with the other right-hand side variables (but not the year and industry dummies). The lower productivity of unionized firms is found to be associated with significantly lower output elasticities with respect to physical and R&D capital. The

Table 3. Productivity Equations—Regression Results[a]

Variable	*(1)*	*(2)*	*(3)*	*(4)*
UN	−0.140	−0.083	−0.130	−0.085
	(10.91)	(6.35)	(11.31)	(7.24)
ln(K/L)	0.238	0.191	0.259	0.255
	(26.74)	(15.84)	(35.78)	(27.34)
R&D-STK	0.120	0.078	—	—
	(21.22)	(11.66)		
R&D-STK^{est}	—	—	0.106	0.052
			(22.52)	(9.11)
ln(L)	−0.137	−0.103	−0.112	−0.069
	(18.02)	(12.75)	(18.48)	(11.01)
IND	No	Yes	No	Yes
YEAR	Yes	Yes	Yes	Yes
$\bar{R}^2$	0.442	0.595	0.448	0.575
n	2304	2304	3146	3146

[a]Dependent Variable is ln(VA/L). $|t|$ in parentheses.

explanation for these differences is not entirely clear. Lower output elasticities with respect to physical capital and R&D are consistent, however, with the rent-seeking model presented earlier (in particular, see Baldwin, 1983), in which union companies invest in "second-best" tangible and intangible capital to mitigate union wage demands. Union firms also are more likely to be in mature industries with older and less productive capital stocks. Although the capital and R&D variables are age-adjusted stock measures, these adjustments may not fully account for quality differences in the capital stock.

Finally, it should be noted that there are indirect as well as direct effects of unions on productivity. Both physical and R&D capital increase output and, as seen in the previous section, unionized firms invest less than nonunion firms in both types of capital. Hence, union firms in our sample have lower value added per worker not only because of direct union effects in the workplace, but also because tangible and intangible capital stocks are lower than they would be in the absence of collective bargaining coverage. An estimate of unionism's total effect on productivity would require that we estimate union effects on employment and the capital–labor ratio.[26] The partial indirect effect of unionism on productivity due to lower R&D investment can be crudely approximated, however. If high union firms have R&D capital stocks 12% smaller than otherwise similar low union firms [due to steady-state R&D investment expenditures 12% lower, as seen in Eq. (2)], than a union firm would have a labor productivity an additional 0.6 to 0.9% less than a nonunion firm (based on coefficients on R&D-STK of 0.052 and 0.078). This indirect effect of unionism on labor productivity, thus, appears to be relatively small in magnitude.

The effects of unionization on productivity growth are examined using a variant of Eq. (7). Rather than compute changes in total factor productivity, "partial" productivity growth rates (Griliches, 1986) are calculated as the growth rate of deflated value added, minus the growth rate of employment times labor's share of total cost. The growth rate of capital is included on the right-hand side of the equation. Such a specification is appealing in data sets where capital's share is difficult to estimate accurately, and it allows for a straightforward estimation of unionism's indirect effects on productivity growth via changes in capital and R&D investment. Thus, the productivity growth equation takes the following general form:

$$\rho_{it} = \Sigma\, \beta_{\rho k} X_{\rho kit} + \phi UN_i + e_{\rho it}, \tag{9}$$

where subscript ρ signifies vectors attaching to Eq. (9), and ρ_{it} is productivity growth, as just defined, by firm i over period t (here representing average annual 4-year growth rates for 1970–1974 through 1976–1980, measured by the difference in log values, divided by four). The vector X_ρ includes average annual growth rates in the capital stock, the R&D stock, and employment over period t; firm size (measured by the average number of employees over the period); average industry growth rates, import shares, and energy cost shares; and year and industry dummies. The direct effect of unions on productivity growth is approximated by the coefficient on UN; indirect effects will take place via union effects on capital and R&D investment. Because we measure unionization only at a single point in time, we are unable to relate changes in productivity to changes in union coverage.

Table 4 presents regression results for the productivity growth equations, with and without inclusion of industry level variables and dummies. Annual partial productivity growth, ρ, averaged 1.4% among our sample of company-years. Productivity growth is positively

Table 4. Productivity Growth Equations—Regression Results[a]

Variable	*(1)*	*(2)*	*(3)*
UN	−0.021	−0.013	−0.006
	(8.98)	(5.39)	(2.27)
d ln(K)	0.075	0.111	0.154
	(3.72)	(5.66)	(7.95)
d ln(L)	0.224	0.189	0.181
	(10.75)	(9.32)	(9.26)
d R&D-STK^{est}	0.029	0.025	0.020
	(3.42)	(3.02)	(2.55)
$\overline{\text{R\&D-STK}}^{est}$	0.002	0.001	0.003
	(3.49)	(1.07)	(2.10)
$\overline{\text{ENERGY/VA}}$	—	−0.162	−0.039
		(9.32)	(1.35)
$\overline{\ln(L)}$	—	−0.0003	−0.0017
		(0.26)	(1.21)
$\overline{\text{I-GROWTH}}$	—	0.0016	0.0009
		(7.96)	(4.17)
$\overline{\text{I-IMPORT}}$	—	0.027	−0.025
		(1.90)	(1.60)
IND	No	No	Yes
YEAR	Yes	Yes	Yes
$\bar{R}^2$	0.278	0.335	0.402
n	1932	1932	1932

[a]Dependent variable is annual 4-year growth rate, ρ_{70-74} through ρ_{76-80}. $|t|$ in parentheses.

and significantly related to the growth rates of physical capital, employment, and R&D. In regression models without industry variables, ρ is *substantially* lower among union firms.[27] Point estimates of the UN coefficient suggest that union companies realized productivity growth 2.1 percentage points lower than nonunion companies, far exceeding the growth rate's sample mean.

Once industry-level variables and two-digit dummies are included, however, the estimated direct union effect on productivity growth is reduced sharply. The union coefficient changes from −0.021 to −0.013 when industry-level variables are added, and to −0.006 with the further addition of industry dummies. Our results strongly suggest that much of the negative relationship found in previous studies between productivity growth and unionization primarily captures industry-level effects. Union firms are realizing significantly slower productivity growth than nonunion firms; however, slower growth may not result primarily from direct effects of unions in the workplace. Rather, highly unionized firms are more likely to be in industries with high energy costs, slower sales growth, and in broad (two-digit) industry categories with slow growth.[28] The magnitude of the estimated direct union effect is hardly trivial, however; the coefficient of −0.006 implies that high union firms have productivity growth 0.6 percentage points slower than similar nonunion firms, relative to a mean growth rate of 1.4%.

In addition to the direct union effects on productivity growth examined above, union coverage may have an indirect effect of lowering productivity growth by decreasing new investment in physical capital, R&D, and other forms of innovative activity. For example, unions decrease productivity growth rates by lowering the steady-state level of R&D stocks, although calculations of this effect based on parameter estimates from Eqs. (2) and (9) suggest the magnitude of this effect is quite small. (Note that union firms with lower R&D expenditures and stocks need not have differential growth rates in their stocks.)

V. QUALIFICATIONS AND INTERPRETATION

The evidence presented in this paper provides compelling evidence that there are large and significant differences in economic performance between union and nonunion firms. What is not clear from extant evidence is the degree to which unionization is the causal force in these empirical relationships, and the exact routes through which union organizing and bargaining power affect firm (and industry) performance. We have proffered a model of union rent seeking through which union effects on profitability, investment behavior, and productivity growth are closely related and can be analyzed in a unified framework. Empirical evidence is broadly supportive of this framework. Yet, numerous reservations attach to this evidence and it should be interpreted not as conclusive but, rather, as tentative and suggestive support for the rent-seeking model.

Although space does not allow detailed examination of theoretical or econometric qualifications attaching to the analysis, several reservations and concerns warrant discussion. The most serious caveats (although hardly specific to this study) are the endogeneity of unionism and simultaneous determination of key variables in the model, the error structure of the time-series cross-section estimation, selectivity bias engendered by an inability to observe nonsurviving firms, the difficulty in separating firm-level and industry-level union effects, and the appropriateness of using R&D as a proxy for innovative activity.

Firm-level union coverage is treated as an exogenous variable in this paper, even though it is certainly the case that unionization is not randomly distributed across firms and industries. It would be technically feasible to account for the endogeneity of key variables or to estimate a full system of simultaneous equations (or, in a more limited fashion, to test for exogeneity using Hausman-type specification tests). Given the limitations of available data and theory, however, we have little confidence in such efforts. We have no firm-level information that would help us estimate a reduced form union equation, although industry-level variables (at the three-digit level) are available on work force characteristics. And while all equations could be trivially overidentified by excluding selected variables or through the estimation of nonlinear relationships (or through the use of stocks in one equation and flows in another), selection of instruments would be largely arbitrary since reasonable arguments can be made that almost any variable affecting, say, R&D expenditure, would also affect profitability or capital investment.

These remarks are not intended to argue that simultaneity bias is not important but, rather, that superficial treatment of simultaneity is unlikely to be helpful. That being said, we are confident that the qualitative relationships found in this paper are not a statistical artifact or the result of simultaneity bias. In fact, biases that we can identify suggest that union effects on economic performance may be underestimated. Unions are more likely to be successful in organizing firms with the largest potential profits or quasi-rents; hence, the negative union coefficient in the rate of return equations may *understate* the true negative impact of unions on earnings (Voos and Mishel, 1986; Hirsch and Connolly, 1987). By extension, we may then be underestimating the indirect effect that unions have on R&D and new capital investment through their effect on earnings.

A bias in the opposite direction results from simultaneity between R&D and earnings, each having a positive effect on the other. Hence, the coefficient on π in the R&D investment equation may be biased upward and, by extension, the indirect effect of unions on R&D may be estimated with bias (it is conceivable that these biases roughly offset each other). Regardless of the relative sizes of these opposing biases on unions' indirect effect on investment, the conclusion that unions have a direct negative impact on investment continues to hold, since union coefficients in the investment equations were negative and significant, regardless of the inclusion of π. Moreover, simultaneity bias between capital and unionization (unions are more likely to organize in capital-intensive industries), likely results in an underestimate of the negative effect of unions on capital investment.

An econometric problem inherent in estimation of panel data is that error terms are serially correlated across time for given firms. Thus, the standard errors presented in the paper are biased downward. Alternative pooled estimation methods were not used here. Separate estimation of all models by year eliminates serial correlation, but sharply reduces sample size. Results from yearly regressions produced moderate to substantial year-to-year variability in the union coefficients, with much larger standard errors attached to these coefficients. An alternative method would be the estimation of two-way fixed-effects models including dummy variables for each firm as well as year. Unfortunately, inclusion of firm dummy variables would introduce perfect collinearity with the union variable since firm unionization does not vary across time in these data.

Further qualification of our results stems from the inherent selection bias engendered by the fact that only firms that survive unionization are observed. If unions impact negatively on profits, investment, and growth, those firms able to partially offset union effects through higher productivity or special firm-advantages are more likely to survive than the average firm that becomes unionized (and, as discussed above, successful firms are more likely to become organized). For this reason, estimated negative effects of unions on profits, investment, productivity, and productivity growth are likely to *understate* average union effects, since firms most adversely affected by unions are least likely to have survived and be included in any sample of firms.

A final statistical caveat concerns the difficulty in distinguishing between union and industry effects. Highly unionized firms are more likely to be in less profitable, slower growing industries with lower rates of new investment and productivity growth. Regression results presented in this paper include specifications with and without two-digit industry dummies and, typically, estimated union effects decrease following accounting for industry differences. In order not to overstate the effect of unions on economic performance, conclusions expressed in the paper are based on regression results from specifications with dummies included. We may be understating unionism's true effects by including dummies, however, since some industry differences in performance are likely to result from differences in industry-level union coverage.[29] The presence of both firm- and industry-level union coverage data potentially can enable us to distinguish among these effects, but such analysis awaits future study.

A rather different concern is that expenditures on R&D and estimated R&D stocks may be inadequate proxies for the much broader category of investment—innovative activity—for which we would like to make inferences. While evidence in this area is limited, that which exists suggests that the union effects we have uncovered apply to innovative activity broadly, and not just to R&D. In work not shown in this paper, use of patent stock data instead of R&D (i.e., an output rather than an input measure of innovative activity) produced highly similar inferences about union effects. In other studies, Hirsch and Link (1987) analyze survey data from a sample of small- and medium-sized firms and they find that unionized firms rank product innovative activity as being significantly less important in their strategy and performance than do similar nonunion firms. Also, Acs and Audretsch (1987) find that both small- and large-firm innovations (defined based on measured outcomes independently of R&D or patents) have been significantly lower in more highly unionized industries.

Finally, it should be noted that inferences about union effects on economy-wide efficiency cannot be drawn directly from our evidence. Even though unions significantly distort resource allocation at the firm level, their economy-wide effect may be less significant. For example, lower new capital investment among unionized firms may be offset by higher capital investment elsewhere in the economy. If resources could costlessly flow to their highest valued use, there would be little effect of unions on economy-wide efficiency. But unions could not then have the significant long-run effects on firm profitability and other aspects of performance that have been observed. Given that unions have some degree of monopoly bargaining power, and shifting of resources from union to nonunion environments occurs slowly, union distortions at the firm level necessarily translate into some degree of inefficiency economy-wide.

VI. SUMMARY

This paper has provided evidence in broad support of the union rent-seeking model. Building on previous theoretical work, a repeated bargaining model is presented wherein both cooperative and noncooperative outcomes result in lower levels of R&D and capital investment among union companies than among similar nonunion companies. A key assumption of these models is that the time horizon for a union is shorter than investors' horizon over which some forms of long-lived capital are evaluated. Unions appropriate some portion of the quasi-rents that make up the normal return to long-lived capital. Firms rationally reduce their investment in vulnerable forms of physical and innovation capital, due both to the union "tax" on investment returns, and because current firm earnings, which provide a relatively lower cost source of funding, are reduced. Decreased investment in physical and innovation capital subsequently has an impact on productivity and rates of productivity growth. These "indirect" effects of unions on productivity and productivity growth are distinct from any "direct" effects unions may have on productivity (or technical efficiency) in the workplace.

Empirical evidence on the union rent-seeking model is based on an unbalanced 1970 to 1980 panel of 315 firms for which firm-level union coverage data are available for 1972. Examined are union effects on profitability, investment behavior, productivity, and productivity growth. Evidence of large and significant differences in the economic performance of union and nonunion firms is found. Unionized companies are found to have lower investment in R&D and capital investment than their nonunion counterparts. The union effect on investment is comprised of two components—a direct effect resulting from the union tax or appropriation of quasi-rents emanating from long-lived capital, and an indirect effect due to more costly financing owing to lower earnings. Indirect effects appear to be important, accounting for about one-quarter of the total union effect on R&D investment and half of the effect on capital investment.

The direct and indirect effects of unions on productivity and productivity growth are then examined. Previous estimates of union effects on productivity have varied considerably. For this sample of firms, unionization is associated with about 8% lower productivity, given levels of inputs. Output in unionized firms is even lower if one considers the indirect effect of unions in lowering the long-run stocks of physical capital and R&D, although these indirect effects appear relatively modest. Finally, attention is focused on the effects of unions on productivity growth rates from 1970–1974 through 1976–1980. Union firms exhibit substantially slower productivity growth over this period, but most of this slower growth results from highly unionized firms being in four-digit industry groups with slower sales (demand) growth and higher energy costs, or in broad two-digit industry groups with slower productivity growth. Even after controlling for these industry and firm effects, however, union companies are found to have exhibited slower growth than nonunion companies. We are unable to reliably estimate the indirect effects of unionization on productivity growth.

The intent of this paper has been to draw attention to the potentially important role that labor unions have on the economic performance of firms. Recent theoretical and empirical research strongly suggests that unionization has had a substantial impact on firm profitability, investment behavior, innovative activity, productivity, and productivity growth during the 1970s. Yet the relationship between collective bargaining and firm performance still has received only limited attention from researchers. To date, both the magnitude of union effects and the precise routes through which unions impact economic performance are not well understood. Further study is clearly warranted, although substantial improvement in our understanding of what unions do will depend crucially on the development of improved data sets.[30]

Such efforts should prove fruitful. Private-sector unionism has declined sharply in recent years and nonunion work environments have increasingly become the norm for much of the work force and in most sectors of the economy. Indeed, this transformation in U.S. industrial relations may be in part a response to the relatively poor economic performance of union companies. Future research can improve not only our knowledge of unionism's impact on firm performance, but also our understanding of the complex relationship between the appropriability of investment returns, innovative activity, and subsequent productivity growth.

APPENDIX: DEFINITIONS OF VARIABLES INCLUDED IN REGRESSION MODELS

Variable	Definition
UN	Dummy variable equal to 1 if proportion of firm's workers covered by a collective bargaining agreement in 1972 is greater than or equal to 0.10, and 0 otherwise.
π_k	Gross rate of return on capital; gross cash flows divided by the value of the net inflation-adjusted capital stock (Cummins et al., 1985).
ℓn(R&D)	Natural log of R&D expenditures in 1972 dollars. Deflator shown in Cummins et al. (1985).
R&D-STK	Natural log of R&D stock in millions of 1972 dollars; calculated based on 15% depreciation rate.
R&D-STK(−1)	Natural log of (R&D stock minus annual expenditures), in millions of 1972 dollars.
ℓn(INV)	Natural log of annual investment, in millions of 1972 dollars.
ℓn(K)	Natural log of net inflation-adjusted capital stock in millions of 1972 dollars (Cummins et al., 1985).
ℓn(K)(−1)	Natural log of (capital stock minus annual investment), in 1972 dollars.
ℓn(L)	Natural log of employment, in thousands.
ℓn(K/L)	Natural log of net capital stock per employee, in millions of 1972 dollars.
ℓn(VA/L)	Natural log of value added per employee, in millions of 1972 dollars. Value added estimated by (sales − cost of goods + labor costs). Where labor cost not available, it is approximated by [employees × (average industry compensation)(1 + 0.25COV)]. See footnote 21.
$\rho_{70-74/76-80}$	Partial productivity growth, calculated as the average annual growth rates in value added during 1970–1974 through 1976–1980, minus average annual growth rates in employment times labor's share of total costs (see above).
CR4	Four-firm concentration ratio in firm's primary four-digit industry, adjusted for regional markets and imports, available for 1972 and 1977. Pre-1972 data assigned 1972 values; post-1977 data assigned 1977 values; 1973–1976 data assigned values based on linear interpolation.
I-IMPORT	Percentage of imports in firm's primary four-digit industry, defined as [IMPORTS/(SHIPMENTS+IMPORTS−EXPORTS)], available for 1972 and 1977. Pre-1972 data assigned 1972 values; post-1977 data assigned 1977 values; 1973–1976 data assigned values based on linear interpolation.
I-GROWTH	Average percentage growth rate in real industry shipments over the previous four years in firm's primary four-digit industry. Shipments deflated by industry-specific price indices.
ENERGY/VA	The proportion of energy costs to value added in the firm's primary four-digit industry.

ACKNOWLEDGMENTS

Research support from the W.E. Upjohn Institute for Employment Research is gratefully acknowledged. Al Link and Kerry Smith provided helpful comments on an earlier draft of the paper.

NOTES

1. Among others, see the articles in Griliches (1984) and, more recently, Levin et al. (1987).

2. For comprehensive reviews of the literature on union effects, see Freeman and Medoff (1984), Hirsch and Addison (1986), and Addison and Hirsch (1989). Lewis (1986) focuses exclusively on estimation of union wage effects, while Kochan et al. (1986) describe the recent transformation in U.S. industrial relations. For a recent analysis of U.S. labor law, see Flanagan (1987).

3. For a recent dialogue on union decline, see Freeman (1988) and Reder (1988).

4. There are, in fact, multiple parties to the bargaining process: management, shareholders, union leadership, and the rank-and-file. It is generally assumed that management (the agent) attempts to maximize shareholders' (principals') wealth. It is also reasonable to assume that union leaders (or agents) accurately represent the interests of the rank-and-file (principals), with union goals being most influenced by members with preferences close to the median. Incentive compatibility between principals and agents effectively reduces the number of bargaining parties to two—the union and the firm.

5. See Baldwin (1983), Grout (1984), Bronars and Deere (1986, 1987), van der Ploeg (1987), Tauman and Weiss (1987), Crawford (1988), and, relatedly, Lawrence and Lawrence (1985). Empirical evidence bearing directly on these models is provided in Connolly et al. (1986) and Bronars and Deere (1986, 1987).

6. Stated alternatively, capital has fixed costs and is relationship specific. Once in place, returns to that capital exceeding its opportunity costs provide quasi-rents; these quasi-rents provide what are largely normal returns to prior R&D and capital investment.

7. We do not consider in this paper the possibility of opportunistic behavior leading firms to appropriate *worker* rents. Firms may appropriate worker rents associated with firm-specific skills by paying wages lower than lifetime marginal products, reneging on pension promises, and the like. Healthy firms are unlikely to do so, however, because the loss in reputation capital will make it more difficult (costly) to attract and retain future workers. Declining firms may be more likely to engage in opportunistic behavior. For discussion of possible firm appropriation of the returns to firm-specific training, see Williamson et al. (1975), Klein et al. (1978), and Crawford (1988).

8. The implicit assumption in Baldwin's model is that the contract wage is similar across all union plants and the firm is free to vary employment. Hence, union wage demands based on productivity in a firm's efficient plants would lead to layoffs or shutdowns at the firm's inefficient plants.

9. The union could make its wage commitment credible by offering a "bond" or "hostage" that it agrees to forfeit in the event it reneges on its promise. The bond must be held by a third party, since if it were held by the firm (say, in the form of promised pension payments), the firm would have incentive to default on the bond and could not make a credible commitment to the union (such commitments are credible in the case of infinitely repeated bargaining). Bonds held by third parties are not observed in practice.

10. Note the somewhat surprising conclusion that union wage demands (and the union–nonunion wage differential) may increase in a *declining* industry with long-

lived specific capital. For similar arguments along these lines, see the analysis of the U.S. steel industry by Lawrence and Lawrence (1985).

11. This is the strong efficiency case (Brown and Ashenfelter, 1986) referred to previously. Strong efficiency implies that the firm's employment level is a function of the opportunity cost wage, and not the "own" wage as implied by settlements on the labor demand curve. This prediction has formed the basis for several empirical tests of on-the-demand curve versus off-the-demand curve bargaining models.

12. Crawford (1988) argues that governing long-term relations with short-term contracts will in general lead to inefficient contracts and underinvestment in relation-specific fixed-cost capital. The argument in this paper is more fundamental: even if efficient (jointly maximizing) contract settlements are obtained, there will be lower investment by union than by similar nonunion companies.

13. Profit sharing, based on current accounting profits rather than stock value, does not make union members more future oriented (although it may increase labor productivity).

14. For evidence that R&D "Granger causes" capital investment, but investment does not Granger cause R&D, see Lach and Schankerman (1987). Most company-financed R&D expenditures are for product innovations (Link and Tassey, 1987). Of course, product innovations by companies selling intermediate products make up the major source of process innovations to purchasers.

15. Unions are also likely to capture profits associated with market power in product markets. For a detailed examination of this issue, an analysis of specification of profit models measuring union effects, and references, see Hirsch and Connolly (1987).

16. The union data were kindly provided by David C. Hershfield, who developed the figures from data collected in a 1972 survey by the Conference Board.

17. These figures compare to union *coverage* figures for manufacturing for 1968–1972, calculated from the BLS Expenditures for Employee Compensation (EEC) surveys, of 46% of the total work force and 61% of production employees; and estimates of union *membership,* calculated from the 1973–1975 May Current Population Surveys, of 37 and 49%, respectively (Freeman and Medoff, 1979). Differences among these measures results in part from the secular decline in private sector unionization during this period.

18. Discussion and documentation for the data set, named the R&D Master File, are provided in Bound et al. (1984), Cummins et al. (1985), and Body and Jaffe (no date). The data were kindly provided by Zvi Griliches.

19. Rates of return on sales exhibit a similar, although less marked, pattern. As expected, rates of return on *equity* are approximately equal across classes (since equity values adjust to differences in expected earnings)—21.3, 20.4, and 20.0 for the low, middle, and high union categories, respectively.

20. Average R&D/S is computed only for firms reporting positive R&D; nonreporting firms are excluded. For early years in our sample, many nonreporting firms are in fact R&D active. For most years, however, nonreporting firms typically are not R&D active. A identical pattern with respect to union coverage is evident when nonreporting firms are assumed to have zero R&D investment. See Bound et al. (1984) for a detailed discussion of nonreporting of R&D.

21. Value added is measured with error owing to the absence of data in Compustat on the cost of materials. The Compustat item "cost of goods" measures materials and

production costs, including all labor costs. In order to calculate value added, firm labor costs must be added back in. But only about 40% of the firms in our sample had direct measures of labor compensation and pension costs. For the remaining firms, labor costs were estimated by multiplying firm employment times average industry compensation, the later being inflated by 0.25 times COV in order to reflect the higher labor costs in union firms (were this not done there would have been spurious negative correlation between unionism and estimated value added). The 0.25 COV adjustment factor was arrived at through experimentation on the sample of firm-years with actual labor and pension costs. For these firms, mean measurement error (defined as the difference between "actual" value added and "estimated" value added) was uncorrelated with union coverage. Thus, measurement error in value added should not result in coefficient bias in subsequent productivity level or productivity growth equations.

22. Constructed for estimation in this paper were predicted R&D expenditure and stock variables equal to the actual values for those firms with reported positive values, and equal to predicted values for companies with zero or unreported values, but with patent stock information. Predicted R&D variables are calculated based on coefficient estimates from auxiliary regressions of R&D on the patent stock, patent stock squared, patent stock cubed, and year and industry dummies. The log of the R&D stock regression had a sample size of 2417 and an R^2 of 0.73. The log of annual real R&D expenditure regression had a sample size of 1949 and an R^2 of 0.68.

23. Full regression results from the profit equation are available on request. Similar results are obtained if the market valuation measure, Tobin's q, is used as the profits measure. The profitability equation included variables measuring the R&D stock divided by sales, firm size, capital intensity, industry growth, industry concentration, import intensity, and industry and year dummies. The estimated union effect on profit is smaller (i.e., less negative) when the sample was restricted to include only firms with reported R&D expenditures (and thus calculable R&D stocks).

24. Williamson et al. (1975) discuss a similar workplace environment, which they characterize as one of "ideosyncratic exchange." Interestingly, they do not explicitly discuss unions, whereas Freeman and Medoff, by contrast, give little attention to the possibility of a nonunion solution to the public goods problem. Surveys of the productivity literature, with interpretation, are provided in Freeman and Medoff (1984), Hirsch and Addison (1986), and Addison and Hirsch (1989).

25. Unlike industry-level analyses, firm-level analysis may impart little upward bias to value added due to the price effects of union wage increases, since individual firms are unlikely to be able to pass through cost increases to consumers. Union firms' inability to pass through cost increases is evinced most directly by their significantly lower profit rates.

26. On theoretical grounds, unionism unambiguously reduces employment. Bronars and Deere (1987) provide explicit evidence showing that firms respond to union representation elections by lowering employment.

27. When the equation is estimated for the smaller sample with complete R&D stock information, the R&D coefficient is larger, but results with respect to union coverage are not affected.

28. Slower growth at the two-digit industry level may be related in part to industry-wide unionization. Unfortunately, the data are not rich enough to distinguish clearly between firm-level and industry-level union effects.

29. Of course, it might also be argued that the two-digit level is too broad a

category for industry dummies and that our firm-level union coverage variable is really capturing industry-specific differences in performance *within* two-digit industry categories.

30. The author is currently assembling a large data set with firm-level union coverage information.

REFERENCES

Abowd, John M., "Collective Bargaining and the Division of the Value of the Enterprise." National Bureau of Economic Research Working Paper No. 2137, January, 1987.

Acs, Zoltan J. and David B. Audretsch, "Innovation in Large and Small Firms." *Economics Letters* 23(1987):109–112.

Addison, John T. and Barry T. Hirsch, "Union Effects on Productivity, Profits, and Growth: Has the Long Run Arrived?" *Journal of Labor Economics* 7(January 1989):72–105.

Baldwin, Carliss Y., "Productivity and Labor Unions: An Application of the Theory of Self-Enforcing Contracts." *Journal of Business* 56(April 1983):155–185.

Body, David and Adam Jaffe, "Documentation for Data Set SPV." Mimeographed, National Bureau of Economic Research, no date.

Bound, John, Clint Cummins, Zvi Griliches, Bronwyn H. Hall and Adam Jaffe, "Who Does R&D and Who Patents?" In Zvi Griliches (ed.), *R&D, Patents, and Productivity*. Chicago: University of Chicago Press, 1984.

Bronars, Stephen G. and Donald R. Deere, "The Real and Financial Decisions of Unionized Firms in a Dynamic Setting." Mimeographed. University of California, Santa Barbara and Texas A&M, May 1986.

Bronars, Stephen G. and Donald R. Deere, "Union Threats, Unionization, and Firm Behavior: A Decision Event Study." Mimeographed. University of California, Santa Barbara and Texas A&M, September 1987.

Brown, Charles and James Medoff, "Trade Unions in the Production Process." *Journal of Political Economy* 86(June 1978):355–378.

Brown, James N. and Orley Ashenfelter, "Testing the Efficiency of Employment Contracts." *Journal of Political Economy* 94(June 1986, supplement):S40–S87.

Clark, Kim B., "Unionization and Firm Performance: The Impact on Profits, Growth, and Productivity." *American Economic Review* 74(December 1984):893–919.

Connolly, Robert A., Barry T. Hirsch and Mark Hirschey, "Union Rent Seeking, Intangible Capital and Market Value of the Firm." *Review of Economics and Statistics* 68(November 1986):567–577.

Crawford, Vincent, "Long-Term Relationships Governed by Short-Term Contracts." *American Economic Review* 78(June 1988):485–499.

Cummins, Clint, Bronwyn H. Hall, Elizabeth S. Laderman and Joy Mundy, *The R&D Master File: Documentation,* Mimeographed, National Bureau of Economic Research, September 1985.

Farber, Henry S., "The Analysis of Union Behavior." In Orley Ashenfelter and Richard Layard (eds.), *Handbook of Labor Economics, Volume II*. Amsterdam: North-Holland, 1986.

Flanagan, Robert J., *Labor Relations and the Litigation Explosion*. Washington: Brookings Institution, 1987.

Foulkes, Fred K., *Personnel Policies in Large Nonunion Companies*. Englewood Cliffs, N.J.: Prentice Hall, 1980.

Freeman, Richard B., "Individual Mobility and Union Voice in the Labor Market." *American Economic Review Papers and Proceedings* 66(May 1976):361–368.

Freeman, Richard B., "Contraction and Expansion: The Divergence of Private Sector and Public Sector Unionism in the United States." *Journal of Economic Perspectives* 2(Spring 1988):63–88.

Freeman, Richard B. and James L. Medoff, "New Estimates of Private Sector Unionism in the United States." *Industrial and Labor Relations Review* 32(January 1979):143–174.

Freeman, Richard B. and James L. Medoff, *What Do Unions Do?* New York: Basic Books, 1984.

Griliches, Zvi (ed.), *R&D, Patents, and Productivity*. Chicago: University of Chicago Press, 1984.

Griliches, Zvi, "Productivity, R&D, and Basic Research at the Firm Level in the 1970's." *American Economic Review* 76(March 1986):141–154.

Grout, Paul A., "Investment and Wages in the Absence of Binding Contracts: A Nash Bargaining Approach." *Econometrica* 52(March 1984):449–460.

Hirsch, Barry T. and John T. Addison, *The Economic Analysis of Unions: New Approaches and Evidence*. Boston: Allen & Unwin, 1986.

Hirsch, Barry T. and Robert A. Connolly, "Do Unions Capture Monopoly Profits?" *Industrial and Labor Relations Review* 41(October 1987):118–136.

Hirsch, Barry T. and Albert N. Link, "Unions, Productivity, and Productivity Growth." *Journal of Labor Research* 5(Winter 1984):29–37.

Hirsch, Barry T. and Albert N. Link, "Labor Union Effects on Innovative Activity." *Journal of Labor Research* 8(Fall 1987):323–332.

Klein, Benjamin, Robert G. Crawford, and Armen A. Alchian, "Vertical Integration, Appropriable Rents, and the Competitive Contracting Process." *Journal of Law and Economics* 21(October 1978):297–326.

Kochan, Thomas A., Harry C. Katz and Robert B. McKersie, *The Transformation of American Industrial Relations*. New York: Basic Books, 1986.

Lach, Saul and Mark Schankerman, "The Interaction between Capital Investment and R&D in Science-Based Firms." National Bureau of Economic Research Working Paper No. 2377, September 1987.

Lawrence, Colin and Robert Z. Lawrence, "Manufacturing Wage Dispersion: An End Game Interpretation." *Brookings Papers on Economic Activity* (1:1985):47–106.

Levin, Richard C., Alvin K. Klevorick, Richard R. Nelson and Sidney G. Winter, "Appropriating the Returns from Industrial Research and Development." *Brookings Papers on Economic Activity* (3:1987):783–820.

Lewis, H. Gregg, *Union Relative Wage Effects: A Survey*. Chicago: University of Chicago Press, 1986.

Link, Albert N. and Gregory Tassey, *Strategies for Technology-Based Competition: Meeting the New Global Challenge*. Lexington, MA.: Lexington Books, 1987.

Reder, Melvin W., "The Rise and Fall of Unions: The Public Sector and the Private." *Journal of Economic Perspectives* 2(Spring 1988):89–110.

Reder, Melvin W. and George R. Neumann, "Conflict and Contract: The Case of Strikes." *Journal of Political Economy* 88(October 1980):867–886.

Salinger, Michael A., "Tobin's q, Unionization, and the Concentration-Profits Relationship." *Rand Journal of Economics* 15(Summer 1984):159–170.

Tauman, Y. and Y. Weiss, "Labor Unions and the Adoption of New Technology." *Journal of Labor Economics* 5(October 1987):477–501.

van der Ploeg, F., "Trade Unions, Investment, and Employment: A Non-cooperative Approach." *European Economic Review* 31(October 1987):1465–1492.

Voos, Paula B. and Lawrence R. Mishel, "The Union Impact on Profits: Evidence from Industry Price-Cost Margin Data." *Journal of Labor Economics* 4(January 1986):105–133.

Weiss, Leonard W. and George A. Pascoe, Jr., "Adjusted Concentration Ratios in Manufacturing, 1972 and 1977." Statistical Report of the Bureau of Economics to the Federal Trade Commission, June 1986.

Williamson, Oliver E., Michael L. Wachter, and Jeffrey E. Harris, "Understanding the Employment Relation: The Analysis of Ideosyncratic Exchange." *Bell Journal of Economics* 6(Spring 1975):250–n

TECHNICAL STANDARDS AND TECHNOLOGICAL CHANGE IN THE TELECOMMUNICATIONS INDUSTRY

Sanford V. Berg

I. INTRODUCTION

While OPEC and the energy crisis symbolize the economic forces of change in the United States during the 1970s, the AT&T divestiture and the associated telecommunications revolution may well be chronicled as the major economic developments of the 1980s. Innovations in the telecommunications industry have given rise to a number of major technological developments, especially in signal delivery systems.[1] Components of such complex technological systems require compatibility (interface) standards for the attachment of basic equipment and the use of inputs. However, with telecommunications opened to new entry for voice, video, and digital transmission, and with the traditional links between the provision of local telephone service and

Advances in Applied Micro-Economics, Volume 5, pages 105–127.

ISBN: 0-89232-797-9

other services cut, the potential for incompatibilities is serious. Thus, telecommunications deregulation, along with changes in radio spectrum management and the development of new services, raises questions about the relationship between technical standards and economic performance.[2]

We know that competition and innovation will both be affected by the standards-setting process and the technical protocols that may emerge from the process. In some cases, de facto compatibility may enhance innovation at the expense of price competition; in others standardization can promote some entry, but exclude potentially attractive technologies from the market. Because it is difficult to determine a priori which types of standards and which standards specification processes are socially beneficial and which are not, a better understanding of the trade-offs among compatibility, competition, and technological advance seems imperative for well-directed policy in the future.

The purpose of this paper is to illustrate how technological innovations have affected private initiatives and public policies in the area of setting standards. The three case studies provide some insights as to whether we are devoting too many or too few resources to the standards specification process in telecommunications. In addition, the discussions of videotex protocols, computer interfaces, and networking standards illustrate how technological opportunities interact with institutional structures for the resolution of standards issues.

The first case study examines teletext and videotex systems. These systems enable enhanced transactions services, such as home shopping and banking. Compared with government authorities in Europe and Japan, the U.S. Federal Communications Commission has not taken an interventionist role in the standards-specification process for this technology. Such "benign neglect" may (or may not) have been a good strategy, given the strengths and limitations of private competitive (and cooperative) activities in this market.

The second case study, technical standards affecting computer interfaces and operating systems, provides additional historical insights regarding how industry performance is affected by government refraining from mandating compatibility standards. In rapidly changing technological fields, premature standardization (imposed from outside the industry) could dampen incentives to innovate, even though such standards would provide a focal point that reduced uncertainty for both suppliers and demanders.

The third case study describes how networking standards are evolving, particularly in the context of international markets. Here, the interconnection of computers reflects even more complicated compatibility issues than those raised by videotex and by different computer operating systems. However, here the development of networking protocols raises the possibility of linking computers that may have very different operating systems. Thus, technological advances in networking protocols illustrate how standards specification can resolve technical incompatibilities without requiring standardization among all components of the system.

After presenting these telecommunications case studies in Section II, the next section discusses several lessons that emerge from these studies. The focus is on the joint roles of innovation and standardization in the context of network technologies. Network technologies are characterized by increasing returns in production or use and a substantial amount of technical interrelatedness among (durable) system components. As defined by David and Bunn (1988), "gateway technologies [permit] the technical interconnection of system-components that would otherwise remain isolated" (p. 3). Such technologies achieve ex post technical compatibility in the absence of standardization.

David and Bunn analyze the pivotal role of the "rotary converter" in the context of electricity networks. The device, patented by Bradley in 1887, was used to transform direct electrical current into alternating current (and vice versa). The converter had dramatic effects on the subsequent development of electricity systems: although it served a technically neutral function, allowing passage in either of two directions, the gateway technology had a nonneutral impact on the alternative technologies—leading to the ultimate adoption of alternating current for electricity generation and transmission. The telecommunications and computer networking issues discussed here are still in the process of being resolved, so we cannot fully evaluate industry performance.

Section III turns to the impacts of key participants and "third-party" entrants who develop gateway technologies in new industries. Some important lessons have emerged from historical experiences. For example, induced innovations can reduce competitive pressure for improvements in incompatible systems that are sponsored by rival firms (as happened with Edison General Electric and Westinghouse). In addition, the creation of gateway technologies (or protocols) can reduce incentives for standardization.

After reviewing lessons from recent telecommunications experiences, the paper concludes with several policy recommendations. In general, the case for mandating standards is weakest where the particular technology has diverse uses (as do both communications and computer systems) and where technologies are undergoing rapid change. Nevertheless, government action that establishes a "focal point" can promote efficiency, especially when no technology is clearly preferred by the ultimate demanders.

II. CASE STUDIES FROM TELECOMMUNICATIONS

The relationship between standards specification processes and innovation is complex, whether the process involves competition, cooperation, or coercion. The slow penetration of videotex in the United States stems from both delays in the standardization of technical protocols and from the extensive substitutes available in this economy. Rapid growth in computer usage and technology occurred without significant government intervention, despite incompatibilities among competing operating systems. Finally, networking standards further illustrate how difficult it is to identify clearly preferable standards for sharing resources over computer networks. First, let us examine each type of system to see the role of standards in promoting innovation.

A. Competition in Teletext and Videotex

Teletext and videotex technologies involve the provision of additional services via television signals. Both technologies involve a host computer, a communication linkage system, data bases, and home terminals. In a teletext system, viewers receive frames, while in the videotex system, users interact with data bases. Competing signal transmission technologies include broadcast TV (from ground or satellite), telephone, and cable. Similarly, receiver/adaptors range from simple television attachments to complex home computers. These two technologies illustrate the demand interdependencies that complicate the standards determination process. Furthermore, they reveal how a government agency, the FCC in this case, can affect the development of the relevant standards.

Some analysts see these technological systems dramatically altering market transactions, as in shopping and banking by terminal. However, market penetration has been relatively slow in the United States, with the demand for the product and various services associated with it being not well understood. Is the standards process a bottleneck for market penetration? Some analysts maintain that the issues are more economic than technical: even with compatibility standards, the markets just may not exist, given the competition from overlapping services. Developments in Britain and Japan illustrate conflicting perceptions of the ultimate market for such network services, which have led to different systems (involving different protocol/information requirements).

Other nations that have experienced successful market penetration of similar technologies have usually relied on major government commitments. For example, the British Prestel system is a major operational system similar to teletext, although the standards (or protocols) used for that system differ dramatically from those proposed in the United States (Tyler, 1976). The two systems differ in terms in error detection, redundancy, hardware dependence, memory usage, and image complexity. For example, the coding scheme (and required information) determines the decoding required by the terminal (system overhead) and whether the conceptual content of the information is retained. Since production costs and customer valuation will both depend on which standards are adopted (and whether competitive systems are incompatible), the debate over which standards to adopt has potentially significant resource allocation impacts. For example, premature standardization on a simplistic teletext system might jeopardize later acceptance of a more sophisticated videotex.

The question is what (if any) teletext or videotex system will ultimately prevail in the United States. Similar questions are asked by manufacturers of component technologies in all countries. For these two technologies, the FCC has adopted a policy of leaving the selection of protocols to voluntary cooperation and market forces. AT&T has offered NAPLPS (North American Presentation-Level Protocol Syntax—derived from the French Antiope and Canadian Telidon protocols) as the standard for interactive systems. IBM–Sears–CBS formed a joint venture in videotex that is expected to support NAPLPS. Although IBM's prior entry in videotex was Prestel-oriented (for the European market), CBS was instrumental in the compromises yielding North American Broadcast Teletex standards (NABTS) compatible with NAPLPS. Since IBM and AT&T will be battling for position in this new industry, implementation issues associated with the technical standard may play a role in the viability of the new industry.[3]

Note that because Europe and Japan are developing potentially incompatible standards, international considerations are important for videotex. The European Postal and Telecommunications Council has several levels of standards, from alphamosaic (a technique using small squares) to alphageometric and alphaphotographic (covering the bit-plane). The Japanese CAPTAINS system has a bit-plane standard (partly because of the complexity of Japanese characters). There are many levels within each system and great cost (and quality) variance. Although the protocols differ for the European and North American standards, the latter seems to be winning out. The problem of international standards is underscored by the fact that multinational firms must compete in several markets.

However, standards are not the only factors affecting the size of a market. Regulatory decisions in early 1983 determined some technical features of teletext transmission and its treatment as a subcarrier service. The FCC established the portions of the vertical blanking interval that would carry teletext signals. It also ruled that cable systems would *not* be required to retransmit teletext in conjunction with regular video signals. As a consequence of this decision, broadcasters cannot guarantee advertisers a large home audience. In the case of interactive systems, the corporate market for videotex is likely to be most important in the short run. However, the opportunities for residential applications are substantial if regulatory decisions are conducive to the creation of a large enough market.

Note also that competing standards need not result in fragmented markets and a smaller aggregate demand if incompatible standards can be reconciled via a gateway technology such as a universal chip decoder. Already, suppliers are offering translator integrated circuits that allow the North American protocol (NAPLPS) to interface with the Prestel system. Thus, achieving unanimous agreement on a standard is not crucial if low-cost translators are available. This development suggests that standards committees in areas susceptible to integrated circuitry might do well to specify *families* of standards, so basic equipment manufacturers could move forward and third-party interface manufacturers could focus on their gateway technologies.

In the past, the FCC tended to select a *single* standard when confronted with competing protocols and associated technologies (as with standards for color TV in 1950, which were reversed in 1953). Under the FCC's current deregulatory stance, factors in the competitive marketplace have been allowed to dominate the process. Consider the FCC's decision on Zenith's TV stereo transmission system (supported by the Electronic Industries Association). Broadcasters and cable operators favored a *decision* on stereo TV (rather than letting a winner emerge via the marketplace). Intervention by the FCC has some justification: the scarce radio spectrum requires either private ownership or public allocation to avoid broadcast externalities. Nevertheless, the FCC did not mandate a standard. It did "protect" (bless) the industry-preferred Zenith standard, but allowed others to develop. Hence, the FCC accepted a "focal point" technology. The same basic issue confronted the FCC for stereo AM radio, where it again decided to let competitive (incompatible) systems operate (see Berg, 1987).

In the United States, regulatory emphasis on market forces is somewhat controversial. For example, Sterling (1982) has expressed concern with this approach. He sees the dramatic increases in claims on the spectrum as possibly requiring greater FCC regulation and tighter frequency-preserving standards. This view is not inconsistent with FCC policy: once the performance parameters are set, let the market select technical protocols. In the process, standards associations may be key players, but the emphasis would be on voluntary cooperation rather than coercion. Such an approach presumes that negotiation costs are small relative to the group benefits and that competitive relationships will not be unduly disrupted.

The choice of the appropriate institutional mechanism for promoting compatibility is a complicated one. The bottom line is that the choice between imperfect competition and imperfect regulation must be based on historical experience rather than theory which is divorced from real-world constraints. Longley's (1968) review of how the FCC shifted the FM broadcasting band in 1945 suggests that the technical factors (signal propagation interference) were less important than political and economic factors (one-half a million FM receivers were made obsolete to obtain another low band channel for the infant television industry).

However, even when economic considerations clearly dominate the FCC debate, ultimate decisions need not promote resource allocation improvements. Webbink (1969), in his evaluation of the 1962 All-Channel Television Receiver Law, concluded that the attempt to promote UHF television lead to significant inefficiencies. Recent FCC decisions on stereo AM, teletext, and other issues represent experiments in letting new technologies face the market rather than government agencies. The current emphasis on market forces and consensus standards represents a major shift in FCC policy. Unfortunately, theory by itself is not an adequate guide for evaluating the legitimacy of this shift. Since we have no theory of imperfect governments, we need a case-by-case review of how the government tends to intervene in comparable circumstances. For an excellent start on such an enterprise, see Besen and Johnson (1986) for a comparison of U.S. experiences in eight technologies: AM stereo, TV stereo, teletext/videotex, color TV,

TV program scrambling, direct broadcast satellites, high definition TV, and cellular radio. See Crane (1979), Pelkmans/Benten (1987), and Collins (1987) for international issues.

B. Computer Interfaces and Operating Systems

The computer industry provides yet a second example of how standards, costs, and demands interact. For example, rules and conventions describe how data should be formatted so that when a terminal receives information, processing and display functions can proceed smoothly. As more specific requirements are incorporated into a standard (as with NAPLPS), the "compliance" costs rise for some firms (unless gains from variety-reduction and scale economies overcome the costs of add-ons). For example, complicated protocols require certain system overhead, which constrains other system capabilities. Apple's MacIntosh system differs from IBM's system, although gateway technologies are emerging that allow the former to emulate the latter. Thus, manufacturers and consumers face trade-offs when making production and purchase decisions.

To illustrate the range of issues that arises in computer standards, consider the RS-232C interface (a term familiar to microcomputer enthusiasts).[4] The technical title of the standard is "Interface Between Data Terminal Equipment and Data Circuit-Terminating Equipment Employing Serial Binary Interface." Although widely accepted, the RS-232C standard for communicating between terminals and printers has some limitations that technical groups are now trying to sort out. Yet without such a standard, compatibility among microcomputer components would be severely limited.[5]

The case of microcomputers illustrates how pioneers, producing the first product with wide distribution, usually set technical interface standards. For example, the number of pins on connectors in microcomputer systems was originally set in the mid-1970s by Altair, the first hobbiest microcomputer. The Altair system for making electrical connections over a group of common lines ultimately became the industry standard (in modified form) and was given a generic name to prevent confusion (and to ensure that no company had a special advantage). Its S-100 bus (now the IEEE 696 bus) became the norm.

Furthermore, in the case of the IEEE 696 bus, the standard not only determined the number of pins, but the function of each pin (and data transfer protocols). The technical features of particular protocols (discussed by Garetz, 1983) are beyond the scope of this paper. Suffice it to note that this kind of standard has downward compatibility (in that all the pins do not have to be used) and even upward compatibility (some pins are reserved for future assignment and others are available to manufacturers for specific applications). In this sense, a standard is like a potentially private good whose ownership assignment is handled via technical committees. Just as the radio spectrum is a scarce good whose allocation affects the wealth of firms, assignment of functions to pins (or specification of protocols) can give advantages to one firm. Furthermore, compatibility might be achieved not through standardization, but through interfaces incorporating translator chips, jerry-rigging signal protocols, "fooling" the system, etc. Thus, standard *specification* may be as important as standard selection, to the extent that the former completely articulates characteristics that would be needed for an interface (gateway technology).

Not all computer standards are hardware-specific, but they generally have implications for hardware design. Brock (1975) has presented case studies of two attempts to develop standards in the computer industry: COBOL (Common Business Oriented Language) and ASCII (American Standard Code for Information Interchange). The motivation for the first effort was to facilitate the exchange of programs across different computer systems. The second effort involved lowering the cost of exchanging data among systems. Both illustrate the problems associated with trying to standardize during technologically dynamic phases of the industry's history.

Computer users with business applications had an interest in the development of a language that would not be machine-dependent, so the same programs could be run on different computer systems. In the late 1950s, the rise in programming costs relative to computing and memory costs put a premium on program compatibility. With the Department of Defense taking the lead, a Conference of Data Systems Languages (CODASYL) met in 1959. RCA and Univac saw this effort as strengthening their positions vis-à-vis IBM, while the dominant firm announced that it would not support COBOL, the new language. As a major buyer, the Government Services Administration pressed for COBOL in the early 1960s. In 1968, the American National Standards Institute (ANSI) approved a national standard COBOL, but variants remained. Nevertheless, the efforts of CODASYL illustrate how user groups (and key buyers) can influence compatibility.

The effort in the area of data exchange also began in 1959 and again was slowed by the opposition of IBM. Data exchange is affected by coding schemes, in which characters and decimals numbers are represented by binary numbers. These representations were closely linked to machine designs, so the manufacturers had vested interests in particular schemes. IBM, in particular, preferred its EBCDIC code for its series 360 machines. Earlier IBM machines had used a six-bit binary number representation; the EBCDIC system was consistent with the earlier one. The American Standards Association supported ASCII, which involved a sorting sequence partially incompatible with the earlier IBM system. Additional hardware or software would be needed to achieve compatibility. IBM voted against ASCII in 1962, and EBCDIC continued to be the de facto industry standard. However, in this case, Control Data and Honeywell also opposed ASCII.

Finally, in 1968, President Johnson issued a memorandum establishing ASCII as a federal standard for federal purchases (including its use in magnetic tape formats). However, IBM pushed to confine ASCII to an interchange code, so it would not be required as an internal code. IBM succeeded in this effort, and continued to market non-ASCII (and even non-EBCDIC!) systems. Whether this behavior reflected the costs of variety reduction or strategic behavior by a dominant firm is unclear.

An even more fragmented situation has emerged in the area of actual operating systems for mainframe computers and their microcounterparts. Standards for operating systems of microcomputers (associated with the various 8-, 16-, and 32-bit processors) have emerged via the competitive marketplace. The lack of standardization among microcomputer operating systems and the existence of many versions of the BASIC language reflect a similar set of strategic considerations for firms. In some situations, the cost of "giving up" a standard (such as an idiosyncratic language) may be very high for a firm, since the unique features of the machine may not be accessible through "traditional" BASIC. Agreement on lower-level protocols for signals is one thing, agreement to limit your product is another. The evolution of the microcomputer industry is described by Hergert (1987), who documents the role of IBM in setting de facto standards with its PC. He sees reduced consumer search costs as a major benefit of compatibility within a series of product lines, while noting other dimensions of the standards question: retraining costs that arise when standards or software changes, network externalities (Katz and Shapiro, 1985), switching costs (Farrell and Saloner, 1985), inventory costs (for distributors), and meeting particular preference patterns. According to Hergert, "the IBM standard can be generalized to include the floppy disk format, keyboard layout, printer interface, video display, cables, hard disk format, modems, memory chips, and other components of the system" (pp. 77–78).

As has already been noted, different generations of operating systems also have resulted in incompatibilities over time, so that some software designed for the PC cannot be run on the IBM AT. Thus, compatibility can be a matter of degree, rather than an all-or-nothing variable (Berg, 1988). When IBM PC clones cut dramatically into IBM's market share, the decision to shift to new standards in PS/2 represents a resumption of IBM's strategy to shake up the market when its product becomes a relatively undifferentiated commodity.

Presumably, one of the motivations behind much R&D in computers is to alter production trade-offs and reduce the cost disadvantage of nonstandardization. Yet the demand disadvantage may still be present, if consumers perceive high costs to obtaining compatibility. Such problems lead some firms to consider the collective determination of standards. For example, Gabel (1987) describes the efforts of 10 European computer manufacturers to create open standards based on the "UNIX" operating system—in opposition to IBM's proprietary standards. Given the links between home computers and likely videotex and networking demand, we need to ask whether the government should have tried to play a greater role in promoting a single standard.

Debates over standards for microcomputers need to recognize that compatibility may not be a highly valued objective when the nature of the new product is relatively unstable compared to when products are in more mature phase of the product life cycle. When the technology is relatively stable, compatibility may have a lower cost (in terms of opportunities foregone). In some cases, standards are obsolete even when they are announced. For example, the MSX standard offered by the Japanese for 8-bit home computers emerged at a relatively late date. The need for such a standard had already been superseded by technologically more advanced microcomputers. Thus, the question to be asked is whether a "Czar of Microcomputing" really could have done a more masterful job than has emerged via the competitive marketplace.

C. Networking Standards

Another issue has arisen in the context of technological opportunities in networking, from local to transnational. Again the roles of dominant firms, regulators, and politics become intertwined. The problem is how to balance compatibility among components against flexibility that facilitates continued innovation. There are two kinds of networks raising compatibility issues: local area networks (LANs) for computers and integrated services digital networks (ISDN) for telecommunications. Both types of networks will be major factors affecting computer applications in industry over the next decade.

Examples of Local Area Networks abound on campuses, in corporate headquarters, and throughout production facilities. By interconnecting computers, input devices, output devices, and other peripherals, LANs permit data files and other information resources to be shared by many users. The standards issue is whether network architecture will permit different suppliers to serve the market. For example, simple interface devices may enable interconnection among products with high degrees of nonstandardization within a LAN.

As described by Young (1983), communications tasks can be broken down into various layers (or subtasks) ranging from the purely physical connection and data protocols, through network switching and data transport, to higher levels (message segmentation, commands, and actual applications—like on-line banking). The International Standards Organization has promoted the layered approach so complete system redesign will not be necessary as technological advances hit the various levels (and to weaken market power that might emerge at any particular level). The associated protocols can be modified to maintain compatibility.

Detailed consideration of the alternative proprietary systems would take us far afield. Suffice it to note that IBM, WANG, Xerox, and others offer or are developing proprietary LANs. Some of these now function, especially in retailing (grocery stores and chains). These stand in sharp contrast with proposed open networks based on voluntary consensus standards. The various systems vendors have essentially promulgated families of standards—and (according to Young) these are being ratified by standards organizations. For example, the Institute for Electrical and Electronic Engineers (IEEE) technical committees have members from user-groups and vendors, plus international representatives. Young concludes that the National Bureau of Standards has paved the way for much cooperation within the IEEE committees. In fact, an NBS demonstration of prototype office and factory automation networks (the latter involving General Motors) implement standards needed for multivendor networks. Young views the NBS as making significant contributions toward stimulating private investments in R&D: formal procedures are particularly important when the technology and preferences are not well understood. LAN interface chips that incorporate the IEEE standards for various network layers are coming onto the marketplace: the resulting compatibility ought to enhance competition and facilitate the achievement of economies.

Integrated services digital networks (ISDNs) use telephone lines, cables, optical fibers, microwave radios, and satellite links, to transfer data to distant points. The similarities with LANs are many, but ISDNs are international in scope and involve telecommunications carriers (usually owned by governments). ISDNs integrate traditionally analogue (telephone) systems with digital services in one digital network. As with Prestel vs NAPLPS, developing standards in an international context is a complicated process. Collins (1987) documents the areas of conflict and cooperation within the European community—noting that the benefits of cooperation tend to occur over a long time horizon, while the costs (and lost strategic advantages) are borne by suppliers immediately.

The primary technical group involved in standardization is the International Telegraph and Telephone Consultative Committee (CCITT), part of the International Telecommunication Union. The Department of State is the official U.S. representative, with technical inputs provided by numerous groups, including firms, the FCC, the Defense Communications Agency, IEEE, and ANSI. The technology itself is stable and fairly mature, so the development of a performance-oriented standard seems feasible. However, without existing systems to crystallize technical issues, the interest in standards has come mainly from carriers rather than equipment manufacturers. Perhaps this reflects an interest in moving enhanced services back into communications network functions.[6] Besides triggering equipment/network disputes, the emergence of new technological opportunities raises difficult coordination issues at the international level.

The Director of the CCITT has stressed the role of standardization in ensuring continuity—both for delivery technique and for the basic service itself (Burtz and Hummel, 1984). Yet the clash between innovation and continuity is clear, especially when the definition of "essential services" (vs enhanced services) is elastic. The problem is particularly troublesome, given the role of developing countries, whose votes are potentially important in international forums.

III. LESSONS TO BE LEARNED

Developments in the three related areas (videotex, computers, and networking) are consistent with Besen and Johnson's overview of lessons from standards experiences in broadcasting and recent theoretical analyses of technical compatibility standards. These relate to the circumstances under which formal standard setting is likely to be particularly important, how firms sometimes coalesce around "focal point" technologies, and the dangers of premature standardization. In addition, the authors emphasize the role of market demand as a determinant of the success of new technologies, the importance of specialized uses for standards adoption, the disproportionate influence of firms at concentrated stages of production, and how homogeneity of preferences (and nonproprietary technologies) promote agreements on standards.

Braunstein and White (1985) expand the gains to compatibility to include "portfolio savings" (where systems users desire to sample from many present and future services), avoidance of user-borne interface costs (including down-time for transshipment), basic equipment savings (no need for duplicate systems), and "repertory savings" (related to inputs like records, tapes, or software). They characterize the vertical linkages requiring compatibility, and show that the source of a technological change can influence how competitive markets (and dominant firms) coalesce around (or resist) particular standards. Berg (1989) derives the conditions for optimal standards in the context of the theory of public goods. Market augmentation is viewed as the main source of compatibility gains.

Clearly the shift away from regulatory mandates of technical standards has implications for new telecommunications services. With the AT&T divestiture, a major new player has entered the competitive arena and seven regional holding companies are beginning to explore the implications of new technologies for regulated local operations and for their unregulated subsidiaries. What once seemed to be an integrated industry has become three separate markets: customer premises equipment (CPE), local exchange transport, and interchange transport.

Dorros (1985) argues that interface standards and performance standards are essential for proper functioning of the telecommunications subindustries. The former define how equipment in the submarkets can be linked in terms of technical protocols (signal levels and channel structure), while the latter refer to how one allocates, say, maximum decibel loss, to subindustries so desired end-to-end performance is maintained. He is concerned that bilateral ad hoc standards may raise costs or even lead to market failure. Dorros is less concerned about network architecture standards (switching hierarchies or routing algorithms), equipment standards (for compatibility within a subindustry), and service standards (signal-to-noise ratios or bandwidth), yet a case can be made that inefficiencies can arise for these areas as well.

Policy makers need to obtain empirical evidence on how the cost of network reconfiguration is affected by various levels of standardization. Furthermore, the distributional impacts of these costs are not unimportant from the standpoint of policy development. In partial recognition that the glue is gone, the regional operating companies have formed the Exchange Carriers Standards Association. While such organizations may promote network compatibility, they potentially could limit competition—by excluding potential suppliers or limiting interfaces with competitive technologies.

As is noted in the final staff report of the Federal Trade Commission on *Standards and Certification* (April 1983),

> [Standards and certification] can produce significant societal benefits by aiding information flow, hastening technology transfer, and promoting efficiencies in production and distribution. Standards . . . are developed through organizations which bring together committees of persons knowledgeable in discrete product areas. . . [They] often form the basis for buyer-seller transactions in complex goods. (p. 12)

The FTC's main concerns were with anticompetitive impacts of excluding products, imposing unnecessary technical restrictions, diverting business from one producer to another, and hurting consumers. Most of the cases cited in the FTC study referred to non-technology-intensive products, where some form of certification was important to assess the market. But the FTC recognizes that many products are parts of complex systems, where the value of the basic equipment and associated inputs or attachments depends on compatibility among the components. In some cases, as with phonographs that can play records of 78, 45, or $33\frac{1}{3}$ rpm, the cost to handle several standards may be small. However, the coexistence of multiple standards often raises questions as to which formats will dominate the market in the future, as in the videocassette and videodisk industries. If some benefits to interchangeability are external to the individual firm, underprovision of compatibility may result.

Recent models have examined the consequences of rivalry, cooperation, and government mandated standards. If the private gains to collective action are substantial, some cooperative standards activity will result (despite spillovers). Not only are the costs of meetings relatively small, but gains occur in many areas, including market augmentation (if compatibility results), reduced input costs, and improved understanding of underlying nonproprietary technologies. Nelson (1982) and Bozeman et al. (1986) have stressed the last point by noting that firms have incentives for sharing information related to basic research. Of course, strategic considerations can delay standards development, especially if the basic technology is not stabilized and firms perceive different market potential for compatible products. Finally, antitrust concerns arise when cooperation pervades the industry.

Any model of the standards specification process needs to be able to accommodate the points raised in the case studies. For example, Brock's (1975) work on COBOL and codes for information interchange yielded two hypotheses:

> (1) Self-regulation [cooperation] is more likely to occur in situations where the regulations do not upset the competitive relationship among firms.
> (2) Self-regulation is more likely to occur if firms are somewhat balanced in size, causing the regulations to affect each firm equally.

Brock concluded that the computer industry differed from others which had successful experience with self-regulation. Product certification programs and safety regulations have tended to affect the perceptions of consumers toward the products of some industries as a whole. Thus, there are gains to all from cooperation (as the market expands). However, gateway technologies and compatibility standards for computers often affect the relationships among companies. Incentives to cooperate are dampened if firms perceive a zero-sum game. Furthermore, with IBM the dominant mainframe and microproducer, its standards tend to become de facto standards, which further reduces IBM's incentives to cooperate in the development of voluntary standards (since early disclosure would reduce IBM's lead times).

Hunt (1975) in his study of major appliances, developed additional hypotheses:

> (3) Self-regulation is more likely to occur where it can help improve industry sales and margins and/or where profit-reducing government regulation is believed to be probable if self-regulation is not undertaken.
> (4) The existence and power of an independent organization which can carry out the self regulation programs is positively related to the private demands for such a program. Further, the importance of such a staff increases as the number of participating firms and the number of policies under consideration increase, since these two factors affect decision-making costs. (Hunt, 1975, pp. 52–53)

The threat of government action was important for home appliances, since safety and certification were the main factors inviting government intervention. On the other hand, while the National Bureau of

Standards was outraged in 1969 by the introduction of the IBM System 3 (which was neither ASCII nor EBCDIC), apparently no other government agencies put pressure on IBM through procurement policies. Given the technological opportunities in computers, the perceived likelihood of "outside" intervention was probably low, leading to less concern for this factor.

Note that cost interdependencies can reinforce the demand augmentation gains from standardization. The literature on integrated circuits is replete with references to cost-savings as the major motivation behind the cooperative development of information protocols (or the acceptance of standards set by innovators). For example, Rosenberg and Steinmueller (1982) state, "[Integrated circuit] firms have been compelled to standardize designs and to agree on industry standards of connection and communications." They argue that multiple supply sources bring lower prices. Perhaps most important, with standards specified, systems designers can incorporate the component into the product even before delivery. They also point out that the exchange of electronic signals requires successful linkages between components produced by different subcontractors. Rosenberg and Steinmueller conclude, "Standardization and connection standards may seem purely technical details to the casual observer, but in fact they reflect the importance of achieving economics of scale" (p. 183).

Other economists have also stressed the role of standards in the industry:

> Accompanying the rapid pace of innovation in the integrated-circuit industry has been an intense competitiveness among firms. With each new round of product development, several firms typically vie to have their product design accepted by customers as the industry standard. As soon as a clear favorite emerges, a number of additional firms enter the race and adopt the standard design. Through price competition, the introduction of improvements on the standard design, and use of marketing and distribution strengths, these firms strive for a share of sales in the new product area. (Wilson et al., 1980, p. 77)

Soma (1976, p. 147) also accepts the view of Wilson et al. that standardization is required to attain economies of scale associated with input/output (communication signals), hardware (common communication linkages and paths), and software (languages and programs). Also, some buyers refuse to purchase chip designs made by only a single vendor since it makes them vulnerable to dislocations caused by a strike, fire, or business failure. Thus, cross-licensing and imitation are widespread in the microelectronics industry.[7]

IV. CONCLUDING REMARKS

The fundamental question is whether too much or too little is being done to promote compatibility and innovation in telecommunications. Suppliers and buyers each have incentives to take some initiative in the establishment of standards. Standards specification by producers opens up the possibility of foreclosing the market to potential entrants, especially if the standards prove to be unduly restrictive or dependent upon special patented procedures. Thus, the main FTC recommendation for standards organizations involved improved procedural practices so all affected parties could have their complaints and concerns addressed in a balanced and timely fashion.

Similar concerns arise if buyers cooperate in the specification of standards. Specification of performance criteria by buyers is, in effect, a form of market demand aggregation. Where previously there were a large number of diverse needs, a single market emerges. At issue is whether a particular buyer or producer is excluded without there being significant social benefits.

Whoever takes the initiative, the advantages are clear for potential producers and users of the product. For manufacturers, information-gathering cost are reduced, and the expected extent of the market demand is larger—thus reducing commercial risk. In the process of specifying functional characteristics of the product, prototypes may be developed under contract to potential producers, which results in a sharing of technical risks.

Of course, supplier and user associations are not the only groups capable of defining product standards. For particular industries, the role of the federal government in establishing de facto guidelines can be significant. As the single largest purchaser of many inputs for defense, for example, it can help define the acceptable characteristics of new inputs. Nevertheless, the losses from premature standardization could be substantial. This concern is presumably at the core of recent FCC decisions.

Beyond the traditional antitrust problems (which may not be great if adequate institutional precautions are taken), there is a fundamental problem with cooperative specification of standards, whether by producers or consumers. Even functional (rather than physical) standards almost always exclude (or delay) some technology from competing in the future; however, without standards specifications, no market may exist.

Thus, an element of technological forecasting is involved in the selection procedure; firms with vested interests in particular approaches may frustrate the selection of efficient guidelines. For example, Motorola is the dominant producer of land mobile radios. It has fought changes in FCC rules that would permit the introduction of new technologies. In addition, potentially fruitful avenues of research may be closed off by premature rigidification; potential entrants in the input-supply industry may be locked out of the competitive process. However, self-regulated standardization or certification programs may also be defended on the basis of economy gained through interchangeability and a reduction in entry barriers (through lower design costs). A "rule of reason" approach suggests that some limits on group action be imposed. Furthermore, agreements for the "free sharing of advances" may introduce disincentives to innovative activity since participants have lower incentives to "be first."

Although standards have emerged from complex input–output relationships in many industries, most of the examples used here arise in the context of information processing. Yet the historical example of railroad gauges best illustrates how compatibility problems arise and can impose costs on individual demanders and on suppliers. In Britain, being first with railroads involved some economic gains, but retention of multiple gauges may have been quite costly. The source of incompatibility is understandable: a firm tunneling through a mountain wanted narrow gauges, while another preferred wider gauges, in the pursuit of a more even ride. Decades later, after heavy investments in incompatible networks, shipments were still being unloaded from one train and reloaded onto another. Possibly, if modularity among containers had been more extensive, the efficiency consequences would have been minimal.

Today, electric pulses signaling 0's and 1's may be *so flexible* that *standardization* is unnecessary in many cases. However, standards *specification* may still require cooperation for defining families (layers) of protocols which best facilitate the subsequent development of gateway technologies. Thus, the cost of "transhipment" (via specialized chips) may be small even if production runs are low. Due to the nature of the underlying technology and to demand characteristics, this process seems to be occurring in videotex, computers, and networks without substantial coercion.

The issues described here are not going to be easily resolved, even analytically, let alone institutionally. However, given the implications of standardization for competition, innovation, and international trade, most would agree that the standards problem is one the most important, yet understudied, issues before us today.

ACKNOWLEDGMENTS

The perspectives presented here do not necessarily represent those of sponsoring organizations. While the author gratefully acknowledges comments by Irwin Dorros, E. Hummel, Charles L. Jackson, Kurt Kent, Al Link, Christopher H. Sterling, and an unidentified referee on earlier drafts of this material, the conclusions remain the author's responsibility.

NOTES

1. Besides innovations in computers, these developments include direct broadcast satellites, point to point microwave, two-way cable systems, low power television, teletext and videotext, narrowband land mobile radio, and cellular radio.

2. Standards serve a number of functions, including variety-reduction, information, quality, and compatibility (Link, 1983; Link and Tassey, 1987). Variety reduction standards limit the range of product characteristics, facilitating comparison shopping and allowing suppliers to achieve scale economies. Information standards included test and measurement methods for quantifying attributes of new technologies or products (Tassey, 1982b). Quality standards, such as the UL listings for electric appliances, set levels of product performance, including safety, reliability, and durability. Compatibility standards, which is the main topic of this paper, specify properties necessary for a product to be used with a complementary product or in an interdependent system.

3. See Hinden (1982) for an overview of technological developments and Neustadt (1982) for a comparison of proposed standards.

4. As Witten (1983) describes it, RS-232C has four parts: "electrical signal characteristics (voltages and interpretations as 0's and 1's), interface mechanical characteristics (plug size), functional description of signals (21 in number), and a list of standard subsets of signals for specific interface types."

5. Incompatibilities (and lack of modularity) can be designed into systems to insulate a product from rivals. Such a strategy can be fatal for a fringe producer. One reason given for Texas Instruments dropping out of the home microcomputer market was its failure to adopt industry standards. The TI machine used a patented feature in its own cartridges, so that third-party suppliers were discouraged from developing software. This strategic decision may have been fatal.

6. On the other hand, in a letter to the author, Irwin Dorros states: "The carriers' interests in ISDN standards stem from their strong desire to interface effectively with their customers in this era of divided responsibility for end-to-end service. Be assured that the carriers' differences with the FCC on the location of the interface is not based on their desire to move 'enhanced services back in the network', despite assertions by some. There is little economic incentive to do so. The carriers are interested in a *practical* interface with maximum decoupling of the network from CPE (Customer

Premises Equipment). The carriers believe this will stimulate the most innovative, timely, and the least cost deployment of ISDN. Further, it will ensure the benefits of ISDN to all telecommunications customers, large and small alike. Unfortunately, the FCC has viewed the matter as an equipment supply issue rather than an interface standards issue."

7. Rodgers (1981) describes information-exchange in Silicon Valley, as it relates to the development of our technologies. G. M. P. Swann (1987) analyzes the rapid growth in second-source activity in microprocessors. He views network externalities as an important feature of this market: limiting incentives for new design entry but enabling new entry by firms. For a fascinating characterization of similar issues in the early automobile industry, see Thompson (1954). He explored the linkages between mechanical technology and business structure, as he emphasized the role of the Society of Automative Engineers in developing interchangeability standards. As would be expected, smaller companies were the main supporters of intercompany technical standardization. In a more recent example, Link and Tassey (1987) examine numerically controlled machine tools in automated batch manufacturing.

REFERENCES

Berg, Sanford V., "Duopoly Compatibility Standards with Partial Cooperation and Standards Leadership." *Information Economics and Policy* 3(1988):35–53.

Berg, Sanford V., "Public Policy and Corporate Strategies in the AM Stereo Market." In H. Landis Gabel (ed.), *Product Standardization and Competitive Strategy*, pp. 149–170. Amsterdam: North-Holland, 1987.

Berg, Sanford V., "Technical Standards as Public Goods: Demand Incentive for Cooperative Behavior." *Public Finance Quarterly*, (January 1989): 29–54.

Besen, Stanley M. and Leland L. Johnson, *Compatibility Standards, Competition, and Innovation in the Broadcasting Industry*, RAND, R-3452-NSF, 1986.

Bozeman, Barry, Albert Link and Asghan Zardkoohi, "An Economic Analysis of R&D Joint Ventures." *Managerial and Decision Economics* 7(1986):263–266.

Braunstein, Yale M. and Lawrence J. White, "Setting Technical Compatibility Standards: An Economic Analysis." *Antitrust Bulletin* (Summer 1985): 337–355.

Brock, Gerald, "Competition Standards and Self-Regulation in the Computer Industry." In Richard E. Caves and Marc J. Roberts (eds.), *Regulating the Product: Quality and Variety*. Cambridge, MA: Ballinger, 1975.

Burtz, L. and E. Hummel, "Standard Setting in International Telecommunications." *Telecommunications Policy* (March 1984):3–6.

Collins, Hugh, "Conflict and Co-Operation in the Establishment of Telecommunications and Data Communications Standards in Europe." In H. Landis Gabel (ed.), *Product Standardization and Competitive Strategy*. Amsterdam: North-Holland, 1987.

Crane, Rhonda, *The Politics of International Standards: France and the Color TV War*. Norwood, N.J.: Ablex, 1979.

David, Paul A. and Julie Ann Bunn, "The Economics of Gateway Technologies and Network Evolution: Lessons from Electricity Supply History." *Information Economics and Policy*, 3(1988), 165–202.

Dorros, Irwin, "Standards, Innovation, and ISDN." *Public Utilities Fortnightly* (March 7, 1985):6–10, 47.

Farrell, Joseph von R. and Garth Saloner, "Standardization, Compatibility and Innovation." *Rand Journal of Economics* (Spring 1985):70–83.

Gabel, H. Landis, ed., *Product Standardization and Competitive Strategy*. Amsterdam: North-Holland, 1987.

Gabel, H. Landis, "Open Standards in the European Computer Industry." In H. Landis Gabel (ed.), *Product Standardization and Competitive Strategy*. Amsterdam: North-Holland, 1987.

Garetz, Mark, "The IEEE Standard for the S-100 Bus." *Byte* (February, 1983).

Hergert, Michael, "Technical Standards and Competition in the Microcomputer Industry." In H. Landis Gabel (ed.), *Product Standardization and Competitive Strategy*. Amsterdam: North-Holland, 1987.

Hinden, Harvey J., "Videotex Looks Brighter as Developments Mount." *Electronics* (August 25, 1982):89–100.

Hunt, Michael S., "Trade Associations and Self Regulation: Major Home Appliances." In Richard E. Caves and Marc J. Roberts (eds.), *Regulating the Product: Quality and Variety*. Cambridge, MA: Ballinger, 1975.

Johnson, Leland L. and Stanley M. Besen, "Compatibility Standards and Competition: Lessons from AM Stereo and TV Stereo." *Proceedings of the Fourteenth Annual Telecommunications Policy Research Conferences,* forthcoming.

Katz, Michael L. and Carl Shapiro, "Network Externalities, Competition, and Compatibility." *American Economic Review* (June 1985):424–440.

Link, Albert N., "Market Structure and Voluntary Product Standards." *Applied Economics* (June 1983).

Link, Albert N. and Gregory Tassey, "The Impact of Standards on Technology-Based Industries: The Case of Numerically Controlled Machine Tools in Automated Batch Manufacturing." In H. Landis Gabel (ed.), *Product Standardization and Competitive Strategy,* pp. 239–262. Amsterdam: North-Holland, 1987.

Longley, Lawrence D., "The FM Shift in 1945." *Journal of Broadcasting* (Fall 1968):353–365.

Nelson, Richard R., "The Role of Knowledge in R&D Efficiency." *Quarterly Journal of Economics* (August, 1982):453–470.

Pelkmans, Jacques and Rita Benten, "Standardization and Competitiveness: Private and Public Strategies in the EC Color TV Industry." In H. Landis Gabel (ed.), *Product Standardization and Competitive Strategy*. Amsterdam: North-Holland, 1987.

Rogers, E., "Technological Information-Exchange in High-Technology Industries in the Silicon Valley." In D. Sahal (ed.), *The Transfer and Utilization of Technological Knowledge*. Lexington, MA: D.C. Heath, 1981.

Rosenberg, Nathan and W. Edward Steinmueller, "The Economic Implications of the VLSI Revolution." In Nathan Rosenberg (ed.), *Inside the Black Box: Technology and Economics*. Cambridge University Press, 1982.

Soma, John T., *The Computer Industry: An Economic-Legal Analysis of Its Technology and Growth*. Lexington, MA: Lexington Books, 1976.

Sterling, Christopher H., "The FCC and Changing Technological Standards." *Journal of Communication* (Autumn 1982):137–147.

Swan, G. M. P., "Industry Standard Microprocessors and the Strategy of Second-

Source Production." In H. Landis Gabel (ed.), *Product Standardization and Competitive Strategy*. Amsterdam: North-Holland, 1987.

Tassey, Gregory, "Infratechnologies and the Role of Government." *Technological Forecasting and Social Change*, (21)(1982a):163–180.

Tassey, Gregory, "The Role of Government in Supporting Measurement Standards for High-Technology Industries." *Research Policy* (1982b):311–320.

Thompson, George V., "Intercompany Technical Standardization in the Early American Automobile Industry." *Journal of Economic History* (Winter 1954):1–20.

Tyler, M., "Videotex, Prestel, and Teletext: The Economics and Politics of Some Electronic Publishing Media." *Telecommunications Policy* 3(1)(1976):37–51.

Webbink, Douglas W., "The Impact of UHF Promotion: The All Channel Television Receiver Law." *Law and Contemporary Problems* (Summer 1969).

Wilson, Robert W., Peter K. Ashton and Thomas P. Egan, *Innovation, Competition, and Government Policy in the Semiconductor Industry*. Lexington, MA: Lexington Books, 1980.

Witten, Ian H., "Welcome to the Standards Jungle." *Byte* 8(2)(February 1983):146–178.

Young, John H., "Effect of Standards on Information Technology R&D: Local Area Networks and Integrated Services Digital Networks." Prepared for Office of Technology Assessment, November 25, 1983.

PART II

THE VALUATION OF RECREATION RESOURCES

INTRODUCTION:

RESEARCH ISSUES IN RECREATION BENEFIT ANALYSIS

V. Kerry Smith

Substantive empirical modeling of recreation demand began with Harold Hotelling's letter to the Director of the National Park Service in 1947 (Hotelling, 1949). In that letter, Hotelling outlined the travel cost approach to recreation demand, at least as it has been practiced using origin zone data (see Clawson and Knetsch, 1966). In the over 40 years since his suggestion, this literature has established itself as a prominent component of empirical research in resource and environmental economics. Indeed, in this decade, the travel cost recreation demand model has increased its prominence. Beginning with the Water Resource Council's standards in 1979, a requirement under Executive Order 12291 for benefit-cost analysis, and most recently the Department of Interior's regulations for performing natural resource assess-

Advances in Applied Micro-Economics, Volume 5, pages 131–137.

ISBN: 0-89232-797-9

ments (see Kopp and Smith, 1989), the travel cost model has played an increasingly important role in benefit measurement.

This section of Volume V contains four papers, each of which discusses a different aspect of the current literature in recreation demand modeling. All four papers represent the innovative frontier of this literature. The first paper by Kling and Weinberg addresses a methodological issue. It considers the performance of different empirical models for measuring the demand for outdoor recreation based on the properties of their corresponding estimates of consumer surplus values for quality changes. These authors postulate the "true" utility function for recreation services of different quality to follow a modified translog specification and then generate data from the utility maximizing behavior of a set of hypothetical households subject to this utility function and budget constraints. Errors are introduced in the solutions through one parameter (the first order term) in the utility function. These authors demonstrate how Monte Carlo methods can enhance our understanding of the techniques used in recreational demand analysis.

Three aspects of their design are important. First, because they selected a flexible functional form, the underlying model is capable of accommodating a wide range of preference patterns. Second, it is *not* the "true" model underlying any of the empirical models evaluated. Thus, all of the frameworks applied to their generated data should be regarded as approximations. Finally, they keep the basic decision structure simple and do not deal with other problems that are likely to exist in applying any of the models with real data. These issues include the treatment of time on site per trip, the modeling of the opportunity cost of travel (and on site) time, the definition of a recreation site and its substitutes, and the role of recreation related capital equipment (e.g., boats, recreational second homes, etc.), as well as other potential complications. This last design decision is both a strength and a weakness. It allows them to focus on the performance of random utility and more traditional models in the valuation of quality. However, it prevents them from evaluating whether the observed performance might be affected by these other issues.

While they seem to interpret their findings as somewhat discouraging in that the parameterization of the true utility function has important implications for performance of the final empirical models they studied, I view their paper in a different light. It tells me to look at the data first and to consider the likely importance of "corner solutions" in evaluating the behavior of individuals in the sample. If a large number of individuals choose not to use any particular site, the discrete choice models focusing on the trip occasion appear to do a better job than more conventional travel cost demand models that assume interior solutions (i.e., positive consumption levels for all goods). This is so even if we attempt to adjust for concentration of observations at zero with maximum likelihood estimators such as Tobit, which should not be surprising. After all, the behavioral model underlying the demand function does not account for corner solutions. It assumes interior solutions. Use of Tobit or another maximum likelihood technique to allow for concentration of observations at zero from a theoretical perspective is an ad hoc adjustment. It recognizes that more conventional distributional assumptions made *after the fact* are unlikely to be relevant for these types of problems, but it does not identify the fundamental issue(s) underlying the zeros in the first place. By contrast, the discrete choice model does just this. The random utility framework recognizes that people sometimes decide not to visit a recreation site during the time period analyzed. Thus, the model is more consistent with the behavior that appears to dominate in samples with large numbers of zeros. As the parameterization of the true utility function adjusts the composition of the sample so it includes fewer observations with zero trips, then the best framework shifts from one suited to corner solutions to a model that assumes interior solutions. The sample of optimal decisions is more consistent with trips being selected as integrated decisions. In this case, the random utility model would be inappropriate because it views the trips as independent decisions, when, in fact, the parameters of the utility function underlying the optimization model yield a larger set of coordinated decisions.

This work extends Cathy Kling's past contributions (1988a, 1988b) in using sampling experiments to evaluate economic models. Instead of focusing on properties of the demand function in evaluating strategies for estimating the characteristics of recreation demand, she proposes redirecting attention to the variable of interest—consumer surplus. This is an excellent strategy. Of course, good reasons still exist for considering more experiments and a wider range of models. Indeed, the early work of Guilkey, Lovell and Sickles (1983) in evaluating neoclassical cost functions offers a model for the kind of research design needed here. Kling and Weinberg have demonstrated that this more comprehensive strategy is likely to offer some real insight into the modeling judgments that must be made to describe recreation demand.

The second paper is also about judgments, but it attempts to learn from past literature. In another context, Yoshiaki Kaoru and I found several hundred travel cost demand studies undertaken since about 1970 (see Smith and Kaoru, 1990). How do we review this literature and evaluate its potential importance for policy purposes? As Walsh, Johnson and McKean indicate, this evaluation process is crucial to many management and allocation decisions of public agencies. Indeed, pioneering effort by the U.S. Forest Service, originally by Loomis and Sorg (1982), attempted to develop procedures for establishing comparability between estimates of the value of recreational resources for use in mandated planning for public lands. Walsh and his co-authors updated this summary and added substantively to the insights it provides. Combining travel cost and contingent valuation models allows us to explain the variations in estimates by the features of the studies, thus creating a systematic, statistical overview of existing knowledge. This overview can serve many purposes. One of the most important of these is to understand the exact implications of using a best-judgment estimate for each type of recreation resource. It also helps define new research needs.

Meta analysis or the statistical summaries of existing research findings has been used extensively in empirical research in psychology, education, and other social sciences. But it has seen only limited application in economics. The Walsh et al. work clearly demonstrates that meta analysis can help economists evaluate existing knowledge and determine whether estimates of the consumer surplus derived from particular recreational activities can be explained by the features of the resources and the modeling assumptions used. Such summaries are likely to enhance the benefit transfer process that ultimately must take place in policy related research.

Walsh et al. do not specifically discuss another aspect of their paper. Because they included both travel cost and contingent valuation results in their review, econometric models based on these data allow a broader evaluation of the consistency for indirect and direct approaches to benefit measurement by comparing results across studies. Moreover, their data permit this evaluation to be prepared while taking account of the differences in design assumptions of the direct and indirect approaches to benefit measurement. This issue was identified as an important point by Bishop and Heberlein (1979) and Smith, Desvousges and Fisher (1986) in their comparative evaluations of the two approaches to benefit measurement. By combining results across studies that include travel cost and contingent valuation results, the Walsh et al. study suggests an important direction for future research evaluating contingent valuation results.

The last two papers in the volume do this as well. The work by

Morey and Shaw applies Morey's (1981) earlier utility-based approach to modeling recreation demand. Following the Wales and Woodland (1983) framework for describing how the shares of recreation trips undertaken to different sites respond to the characteristics of those sites, Morey and Shaw provide an important addition to the literature on modeling the demand for recreation sites. They demonstrate that one need not consider all possible sites in a given region to model the demand for recreation in that region. Additionally, they show how the treatment of the consumer surplus measure (allowing for separable budgeting in the definition of consumer behavior) influences benefit measures for improvements in fishing quality from particular environmental policies. Both are important insights. From the perspective of future research, however, one of the most important issues raised in the paper is how to deal with recreation decisions in the presence of numerous alternative sites. Morey and Shaw's model addresses the issue by imposing prior restrictions on preferences. This takes the form of a particular functional specification for how site characteristics can influence the selection of a site, as well as decisions on how many times to use that site. If we accept their modeling structure, we don't need to include information on all the sites. The same, of course, is true of the more popular random utility framework using a logit formulation introduced by McFadden (1974). However, in this case, the independence of irrelevant alternatives and the requirement that we consider each trip decision as independent are important limitations to the modeling structure. Morey and Shaw offer us another alternative. A potential next step in this line of research would be to evaluate how sensitive the outcomes are to the site composition analyses conducted with their model.

Finally, we close this section with a paper on the importance of habit formation in the demand for recreation. As McConnell, Strand and Bockstael acknowledge, learning-by-doing found its first empirical application for demand analysis in outdoor recreation with the Davidson, Adams, Seneca (1966) paper. Since then, economists have found it more difficult (largely because of data limitations) to consider the temporal dimensions of demand. In their usual innovative style, McConnell, Strand and Bockstael have shown us the importance of the temporal dimensions of demand. They draw upon the literature developed for modeling savings and durable decisions to develop an interesting framework for considering how habits affect consumption choices over time. Their paper is likely to rekindle interest in this issue among recreation and nonrecreation environmental economists.

It is also important to recognize that these questions extend beyond consistent descriptions of individuals' recreation decisions during a particular season to the significant problem of valuing recreation sites as assets. In order to do so, we must understand the characteristics of individuals' demands over time and how experience and site conditions affect them.

Where is the research in this second part of Volume 5 likely to lead us? It offers new insights into the performance of estimators, how to summarize what we know about the benefits provided by recreation, new strategies for modeling household decisions in the presence of a large number of sites, and a framework for describing recreation decisions that have important temporal characteristics. In the process, I hope it also serves to highlight some issues that deserve further research. What is a site, and how important is its definition? Can we develop better insights into how to treat estimation as a strategy, including a return to more careful data inspection as part of model development? Moreover, by identifying the temporal features of recreation demand for consideration, this research designates the formation of habits as important to the recreation demand model used, not only to value sites as assets, but also to the use of those models in describing temporal responses to interruptions in recreation supply.

These papers illustrate a transformation in the character of applied work describing recreation demand decisions. In the early stages of the literature, applications largely "borrowed" models and methods adapted to serve other objectives in applied microeconomics, using them for describing recreation demand. While the existing applied micro-econometric literature remains an important source for modeling strategies and estimators with robust properties, the current generation of applications in recreation demand now has much to offer as a feedback or "reverse flow" to this general literature. This return comes largely in the form of methodological and practical insights into the performance of the models and specific insights into how they must be adapted for problems that involve interactions of time allocation and commodity choice decisions.

REFERENCES

Bishop, Richard C. and Thomas A. Heberlein. 1979. "Measuring Values of Extra-market Goods: Are Indirect Measures Biased?" *American Journal of Agricultural Economics* 61:926–30.

Clawson, Marion and Jack L. Knetsch. 1966. *Economics of Outdoor Recreation* (Baltimore: Johns Hopkins University).

Davidson, Paul, F. G. Adams and J. J. Seneca. 1966. "The Social Value of Water Recreational Facilities Resulting in Improvement in Water Quality: The Delaware Estuary," in *Water Research,* edited by J. V. Kneese and S. C. Smith (Baltimore: Johns Hopkins University).

Guilkey, David K., C. A. Knox Lovell, and Robin C. Sickles. 1983. "A Comparison of the Performance of Three Flexible Functional Forms," *International Economic Review* 24(October):591–616.

Hotelling, Harold. Dated 1947. Letter to National Park Service in *An Economic Study of the Monetary Evaluation of Recreation in the National Parks* (U.S. Department of the Interior, National Park Service and Recreational Planning Division, 1949).

Kling, Catherine L. 1988a. "Comparing Welfare Estimates of Environmental Quality Changes from Recreation Demand Models," *Journal of Environmental economics and Management* 15(September):331–40.

Kling, Catherine L. 1988b. "The Reliability of Estimates of Environmental Benefits from Recreation Demand Models," *American Journal of Agricultural Economics* 70(November):892–901.

Kopp, Raymond J. and V. Kerry Smith. 1989. "Benefit Estimation Goes to Court: The Case of Natural Resource Damage Assessments," *Journal of Policy Analysis and Management,* 8:(Fall): 593–612.

Loomis, John and Cindy Sorg. 1982. "A Critical Summary of Empirical Estimates of the Values of Wildlife, Wilderness and General Recreation Related to National Forest Regions," unpublished paper, U.S. Forest Service, Denver Colorado.

McFadden, Daniel. 1974. "Conditional Logit Analysis of Qualitative Choice Behavior," in *Frontiers in Econometrics,* edited by P. Zarembka (New York: Academic Press).

Morey, Edward R. 1981. "The Demand for Site-Specific Recreational Activities: A Characteristic Approach," Journal of Environmental Economics and Management 8(December):345–71.

Smith, V. Kerry and Yoshiaki Kaoru. 1990. "Signals or Noise? Explaining the Variation in Recreation Benefit Estimates," *American Journal of Agricultural Economics* (May), in press.

Smith, V. Kerry, William H. Desvousges, and Ann Fisher. 1986. "A Comparison of Direct and Indirect Methods for Estimating Environmental Benefits," *American Journal of Agricultural Economics* 68(May):280–89.

Wales, T. J. and A. D. Woodland. 1983. "Estimation of Consumer Demand Systems with Binding Non-Negativity Constraints," *Journal of Econometrics* 21(No. 3, April):263–86.

EVALUATING ESTIMATES OF ENVIRONMENTAL BENEFITS BASED ON MULTIPLE SITE RECREATION DEMAND MODELS:

A SIMULATION APPROACH

Catherine L. Kling and Marca Weinberg

Recreation demand models have become an important tool for economists interested in valuing environmental amenities. Since the path-breaking work of Clawson (1959), Clawson and Knetsch (1966), and Cesario (1969, 1973), these models have progressed considerably in complexity and generality. Now often referred to as travel cost models due to their use of travel costs in calculating the price of a recreation day, these models are being applied with increasing frequency to an increasing variety of environmental goods. Originally used primarily to predict visitation rates, recreation demand models have been em-

Advances in Applied Micro-Economics, Volume 5, pages 139–165.

ISBN: 0-89232-797-9

ployed more recently to estimate the welfare effects of price and quality changes.

A number of technical issues associated with estimating the benefits of recreational demand models have been addressed. One issue that has received careful attention is the correct measure of the opportunity cost of a recreationist's time to be used in calculating the total cost of accessing a recreation site (McConnell and Strand, 1981; Bockstael et al., 1987b). A second difficult issue that researchers have tackled is the incorporation of variations in the length of time spent at the recreation site into recreation models (Kealy and Bishop, 1986; Wilman, 1987). Another issue that has received attention is how best to include environmental quality variables (Brown and Mendelsohn, 1984; Morey, 1981). These are just a few examples of the complexities that researchers have made great strides in incorporating into recreational models.

Despite considerable progress on these fronts, the applied researcher has little guidance in selecting a model from the array that economists have suggested. For example, a researcher interested in valuing an improvement in environmental quality associated with multiple recreation sites may choose from among a varying parameter model (Vaughan and Russell, 1982; Smith and Desvousges, 1985; Smith et al., 1986), a system of demand equations (Burt and Brewer, 1971; Cicchetti et al., 1976), a multinomial logit model (Binkley and Hanemann, 1978; Feenberg and Mills, 1980; Caulkins et al., 1986; Bockstael et al., 1987a), single equation pooled models (Reiling et al., 1973; Binkley and Hanemann, 1978; Wegge et al., 1985; Caulkins et al., 1986), and the hedonic travel cost model (Brown and Mendelsohn, 1984; Mendelsohn, 1984; Wilman, 1985). Each of these varied approaches is capable of generating welfare estimates associated with environmental quality improvements at a set of recreation sites. However, little is known about the relative accuracy of the welfare estimates resulting from the applications of these models, and the choice of recreation model is likely to have a major influence on the resulting welfare estimates. If these welfare estimates are used for policy-making, the choice of model may be critical.

Several authors have compared the welfare estimates resulting from two or more recreation models by estimating several of the models using the same data set (Caulkins et al., 1986; Smith et al., 1986; Bockstael et al., 1987a). Additionally, several studies compare the results of a recreation demand model with the results of a contingent valuation experiment (Bishop and Heberlein, 1981; Thayer, 1981;

Brookshire et al., 1982; Sellar et al., 1985; Smith et al., 1986). Unfortunately, comparisons of this sort cannot determine which model provides the best estimates of welfare (that is, closest to the truth) since the truth is unknown. These comparisons are able to determine only whether the recreation demand models generate widely disparate estimates of welfare when applied to a single set of data, or whether the recreation demand models generate welfare estimates that differ greatly from those generated by a contingent valuation experiment; they are not able to determine which models generate welfare estimates that are closest to the welfare changes recreationists truly experience.

One potential approach is to choose among the models based on a goodness-of-fit test; however, these methods have not been applied in the recreation demand literature. For linear, nonnested models a Cox (1961) test could be performed. For those models that are nonnested and nonlinear, a modification of the Cox test developed by Pesaran and Deaton (1978) could be employed. Finally, nonnested, discrete choice model tests discussed by Horowitz (1983) may be applicable. One difficulty with such an approach is that the recreation demand literature contains models from all three categories, but these tests are able to distinguish only among models within each category. A larger problem with using goodness-of-fit tests to distinguish among recreation demand models is that these tests compare the predictive ability of the models, while the relevant comparison is between welfare estimates that are functions of the estimated parameters.[1] Goodness-of-fit tests can answer questions concerning functional form, the appropriate variables to be included, and perhaps the correct specification of the error term; however, they are limited in their ability to determine how well various models estimate welfare associated with environmental quality changes.

A second approach to choosing among models is through the use of a simulation experiment. A simulation experiment allows direct comparisons of welfare estimates from recreation demand models to actual welfare changes calculated from a simulated recreation population. The general procedure entails constructing a population of simulated recreation users by choosing a utility function and combining it with data on prices, income, and site characteristics to solve for the number of visits the simulated recreation users will take to each available recreation site. The optimal solutions and the information on prices, income, and site quality make up a simulated data set. Since the utility functions are known, measures of compensating or equivalent variation associated with a quality change can be calculated. Recreation demand models are estimated on the simulated data set and the resulting estimates of welfare are then compared directly with the true (that is, simulated) welfare measures. Monte Carlo repetitions are performed to examine the robustness of the results.

This simulation approach is employed in Kling (1989) to examine the reliability of two recreation demand models applied to a simulated data set based on a linear expenditure system utility function (LES). In Kling (1987), the simulation procedure is employed and the sensitivity of welfare estimates to changes in the utility function used to create the simulated data is explored. This sensitivity analysis is accomplished by generating simulated data sets with three different utility functions, a translog, a Cobb–Douglas, and an LES.

The purpose of this paper is to describe the steps involved in a simulation experiment of the sort described above, and to present the results of a simulation experiment that examines the sensitivity of the simulation results to the choice of parameter values used to generate the simulated data. The sensitivity of the simulation results to the error distribution and parameters of the utility function used to create the simulated date is examined by repeating the simulation experiment employing the same utility function, but using different parameter values and error distributions. The model of recreation behavior used to construct the simulated data sets is presented in Section I. The construction of the simulation experiments is described in Section II and the recreation demand models used in the simulation experiment are described in Section III. The estimation results and welfare estimates from the recreation demand models are contained in Sections IV and V. Although simulation experiments of this sort generate results that are specific to the particular construction of the experiment, some results that may be generally applicable are discussed in Section VI.

I. THE RECREATION DEMAND MODEL

In constructing a simulation experiment, it is necessary to start with a model of recreational behavior. Hanemann (1986) presents a model of consumer choice among quality differentiated goods that can be used to describe recreational choices. The individual is assumed to choose $x_1, \ldots, x_N$ and z to

$$\text{Max } U(x_1, \ldots, x_n, q_1, \ldots, q_N, z) \quad \text{s.t. } 1. \sum_i p_i x_i + z = y \quad (1)$$

$$2.\ x_i \geq 0$$
$$z \geq 0,$$

where x_i is the number of trips the individual takes to site i, p_i is the cost of accessing the site, z is a numeraire good, y is personal income, and q_i is a measure of the environmental quality associated with site i.

If the solution to the maximization problem (1) yields an interior solution for each of the x_i and z, then the solution to this problem is characterized by a set of demand functions

$$x_i = x_i(p_1, \ldots, p_N, q_1, \ldots, q_N, y), \; i = 1, \ldots, N. \quad (2)$$

This describes the optimal number of visits to each recreation site based on prices, site qualities, and income.

If some of the (N + 1) inequality constraints in the maximization problem (1) are binding, the solution is characterized by a set of Kuhn–Tucker conditions. In this case, an individual chooses to visit one of the sites or some, but not all, of the sites. Hanemann terms the former an extreme corner solution and the latter a generalized corner solution.

To examine the properties of corner solutions in more detail, it is convenient to think of the solution to the maximization problem (1) as the optimum from a series of conditional maximization problems. A conditional maximization problem can be constructed for each possible combination of nonzero x_i's. For example, for x_1 and x_2 nonzero and $x_3, \ldots, x_N = 0$ the conditional maximization problem is

$$\text{Max } U(x_1, x_2, q_1, \ldots, q_N, z) \qquad \text{s.t. } 1. \sum_{i=1}^{2} p_i x_i + z = y \quad (3)$$

$$2. \; z \geq 0, \; x_i \geq 0, \; i = 1,2.$$

From the solution to (3), a conditional indirect utility function can be written as

$$V^j = V^j(p_1, p_2, q_1, \ldots, q_N, y), \quad (4)$$

where the superscript indexes which choice of x_i's the indirect utility function is conditioned on. For N sites there are 2^N conditional maximization problems. The individual chooses the combination of sites to visit that maximizes his utility. The resulting indirect utility function

$$V = \text{Max}\{V^1, \ldots, V^{2^N}\}. \quad (5)$$

This expression determines the optimal choice of sites. The application of Roy's identity to (5) yields demand functions that determine how often the chosen sites are visited.

In the maximization problem (1), the individual simultaneously chooses which recreation sites to visit and how often to visit them. In this way, the model incorporates both the discrete and continuous choices involved in determining an optimal pattern of commodity use.

This model describes, in rich detail, an individual's choice of recreation sites. Unfortunately, for purposes of estimation, the model must be simplified. There have been two basic routes to simplification: (1) models focusing on estimation of the continuous choices such as the varying parameter model, a system of demand equations approach, pooled models, or (2) models focusing on the estimation of the discrete choice such as the logit model. These two classes of models will be referred to as continuous and discrete choice models, respectively.

The continuous models postulate a single demand equation or a system of equations that is then estimated. As such, these models presume that the solution to the maximization problem is characterized by (2) and proceed from there. Although not explicitly requiring an interior solution, the continuous models are based on the estimation of demand functions, which are derived from interior solutions.

There has been some attempt to recognize the discrete component of the decision in estimating the continuous models. This aspect has been introduced by the use of the Tobit estimator. With the employment of the Tobit, the individual is assumed to choose whether to visit a site and, if so, how often. At first glance, this appears to describe the complete model of (1)–(5). However, there is an important distinction. The use of the Tobit estimator implies that individuals make independent decisions about whether to visit each site. That is, first the individual decides whether or not to visit site 1 and how often, then he decides whether or not to visit site 2, etc. This differs sharply from the complete model, which implies that individuals choose simultaneously the combination of sites to visit and how often to visit each of them. The Tobit estimator introduces the flavor of the discrete nature of the problem, but it captures only a piece of it.

In contrast to the continuous models, the discrete choice model assumes that the individual is attempting to choose which recreation site to visit. Typically, an indirect utility function is postulated that describes the utility attained from visiting each site. The individual is assumed to visit the site that yields the highest utility. This is similar to the decision modeled in (5) in the complete model, except that in (5) the conditional indirect utility functions correspond to a combination of sites, whereas in the discrete choice models, only extreme corner solutions are considered. That is, each indirect utility function describes the utility from visiting only one site.

To capture an element of the continuous choice, some applications of the logit discrete choice model include the estimation of a participation equation. This equation is used to predict how the total number of visits to all sites varies with environmental quality and other variables. Although this approach recognizes that the total number of visits to all sites varies with quality, it does not indicate how the number of visits to each site individually varies with quality, as the complete model does.

Researchers employing both types of recreation demand models have recognized the need to incorporate both the continuous and discrete nature of the problem and have modified the models in attempts to do so. However, despite these advances, the fundamental distinctions between the continuous and discrete choice models remain. Since neither approach fully captures the discrete/continuous nature of the problem, neither can be chosen on theoretical grounds. One purpose of the following simulation experiment is to compare the two classes of recreation demand models on empirical grounds.

II. CONSTRUCTING THE SIMULATED DATA

The conclusions of a simulation experiment such as the one presented here depend critically on the model and data used to generate the simulated recreation data. The model in Section I provides a utility theoretic foundation for the construction of simulated data sets. The model is general enough to encompass both the discrete and continuous choice elements of the recreation decision; as a result, simulated data sets based on this model should provide a good representation of actual data sets where generalized corner solutions are often predominant.

It is also important that the data used for the exogenous variables such as income, travel costs, and site qualities in the simulation imitate the characteristics of actual recreationists. For this reason, actual recreation data have been employed whenever possible. These data come from two sources. The data on each individual's travel costs and income were gathered in a Chesapeake Bay beach survey conducted by Research Triangle Institute for the University of Maryland (Bockstael et al., 1986). The respondents were residents of the Washington D.C.

or Baltimore SMSA's, so that the information collected pertains primarily to 1-day trips to the Bay. Individuals provided information about round-trip travel costs and distances to the beaches they visited, but not to the beaches they did not. To complete the data set, round-trip distances were calculated from each individual's origin to each beach using road maps. Regression analysis was used to estimate the relationship between round-trip distances and round-trip travel costs and then used to predict travel costs to sites not visited.

The environmental data come from actual measures of water quality associated with five beaches along the Chesapeake Bay. Measures of fecal coliform counts (F) and secchi depth (S) were obtained for each of the beaches. These measures are objective measures of water quality, but since secchi depth is a measure of turbidity and fecal coliform levels are indicators of odor, they are likely to reflect characteristics perceivable by recreationists. The two water quality measures are defined so that increases in the measure corresponds to an improvement in quality. The two measures exhibit a moderate degree of correlation; the simple correlation coefficient between secchi depth and fecal coliform count is −0.51.

To operationalize the model described in Section I, a modified translog utility function is employed. The utility function is

$$U = \sum_{i} a_i \log(x_i + 1) + 1/2 \sum_{i}\sum_{j} \beta_{ij} \log(x_i + 1) \log(x_j + 1) + a_z \log(z + 1) + 1/2\beta_z[\log(z + 1)]^2, \quad i, j = 1, \ldots, 5, \tag{6}$$

where $a_i = \beta_0 + \beta_1 S_i + \beta_2 F_i + \epsilon_i$. The β_i's are parameters of the utility function and ϵ_i is a normally distributed random error.

Utility function (6) has several properties that make it appealing for use in the simulation experiment. First, the inclusion of (x + 1) inside the logarithm instead of x alone implies that the x's are not necessary goods. As a result, depending on the parameter values chosen for (6), generalized corner solutions can result from the maximization of (6) subject to a budget constraint.

A second desirable property of the utility function is that it exhibits the property of weak complementarity (Maler, 1974). This also arises from the addition of 1 to the x's. Weak complementarity occurs between visits to a site and site quality, if, when an individual does not visit a site ($x_i = 0$), the marginal utility of quality of that site is also zero. One implication of this property is that there is no existence or nonuse value associated with a recreation site. Since only use values can possibly be revealed through recreation demand models, it seems desirable to employ a utility function that does not exhibit nonuse values in the construction of the simulation experiment.

A final property of utility function (6) worth noting is the way in which site quality enters. To introduce quality into the translog utility function, the a_i's are assumed to depend linearly on, in this case two, site characteristics. Further, an additive normal error is introduced at this point. The introduction of the error into the quality index suggests that the error arises from the omission of other quality variables or from measurement error of the quality index. In either case, it is assumed that the quality index is known with certainty to the individual recreationist and is unknown only to the researcher.[2]

To solve the optimization problem described in Section I using the translog utility function, a nonlinear optimization routine in the software package GAMS is employed. This routine is used to solve for the optimal solutions for x_1–x_5 for 100 simulated individuals given the income, price, and site quality data described above, and a set of normal errors generated by the random number generator in GAMS. This completes one simulated data set. To create repetitions for the Monte Carlo experiment, the 100 optimization problems are solved 19 more times using different draws of the error, effectively creating 20 simulated data sets.

Once the optimization problems are solved, a measure of compensating variation associated with a 10% improvement in site quality at all of the recreation sites is calculated for each simulated individual in each data set. Compensating variation (cv) is defined as

$$V(p, q^0, y) = V(p, q^1, y - cv) \tag{7}$$

The calculation of cv for each individual in each data set completes the construction of the simulated data.

The preceding discussion describes the construction of a single simulation experiment. To examine the sensitivity of the simulation results to the parameter values used to generate the data, two different simulation experiments are undertaken. The two experiments differ only in their choice of parameter values and error distribution in (6). In the first experiment, the parameter values and errors are chosen so that relatively few corner solutions occur in the data set. In contrast, the second experiment is based on parameter values and errors that generate more than twice as many corner solutions. By comparing the results of these two simulations, in addition to examining the sensitivity of the results to the parameter values, it should be possible to make some inferences about the effect of corner solutions on the reliability of welfare estimates.

In the first simulation, the parameter values chosen for the utility function are $\beta_0 = 0.65$, $\beta_1 = 0.55$, $\beta_2 = 0.00085$, $a_z = 2100$, $\beta_z = -0.001$, and, for simplicity, each of the $\beta_{ij} = \beta_{ji} = 0$, $i \neq j$, and $\beta_{ii} = -0.5$, for all i. The errors are drawn from a normal distribution with a mean of zero and a standard deviation of 0.1. The average number of visits to each site in the simulated data is about 2. The income levels range from $7500 to $120,000 and the travel costs range from $1.00 to $54.50. In this data set, most of the recreation sites are visited by most of the simulated recreationists. Only about 17% of the x's are zeros.

For the second simulation, the parameter values are $\beta_0 = 0.2$, $\beta_1 = 0.58$, $\beta_2 = 0.00088$, $a_z = 2700$, $\beta_z = -0.001$, and, again, each of the $\beta_{ij} = \beta_{ji} = 0$, $i \neq j$, and $\beta_{ii} = -0.5$, for all i. The errors are again drawn from a normal distribution with a mean of zero, but this time the standard deviation is 0.4. The income levels and prices are the same as those used in the first simulation.

Table 1 shows the means and ranges of the x's associated with the first data set of each simulation as well as the income and price data common to both simulations. The most notable difference between the

Table 1. Summary of the First Data Sets for Both Simulation Experiments

	Variable	*Minimum*	*Maximum*	*Mean*	*SD*
	p_1	1.00	30.00	11.29	5.47
	p_2	2.00	24.99	11.50	6.19
	p_3	2.00	28.00	11.20	5.83
	p_4	4.50	54.50	15.71	7.90
	p_5	2.50	25.10	15.11	6.22
	y	7,500	120,000	42,975	23,521.15
Simulation 1	x_1	0	9.00	2.16	1.85
	x_2	0	8.00	1.85	1.61
	x_3	0	8.00	1.75	1.60
	x_4	0	7.00	1.35	1.37
	x_5	0	7.00	1.55	1.61
	cv	1.08	81.08	16.85	14.30
Simulation 2	x_1	0	8.00	1.30	1.35
	x_2	0	5.00	1.09	1.08
	x_3	0	6.00	1.03	1.19
	x_4	0	4.00	0.74	1.01
	x_5	0	8.00	0.97	1.37
	cv	0.67	54.71	10.84	9.54

data generated by the two simulations is that the average x's are larger in the first simulation and there are more zeros in the second. In fact, there are more than twice as many zeros in the second simulation (about 40%).

III. THE RECREATION DEMAND MODELS

This section describes the recreation demand models that are estimated using the two sets of simulated data described above. Since one of the purposes of this experiment is to examine the effect of corner solutions on welfare estimates, two commonly used models of recreation demand are chosen based on the dissimilar way in which they model recreation behavior and incorporate corner solutions: a pooled demand function model and a logit model.

In the pooled model, the numbers of visits each individual takes to each site are treated as distinct observations and are pooled together to estimate a single equation (Binkley and Hanemann, 1978; Freeman, 1979; Smith et al., 1986). In the estimated demand function, the dependent variable is the number of visits individual i takes to site j (x_{ij}), and the independent variables are income (y_i), the corresponding travel costs (p_{ij}), and the two quality characteristics (S_j) and (F_j); that is

$$x_{ij} = f(p_{ij}, F_j, S_j, y_i, \epsilon_{ij}), \qquad \begin{array}{l} i = 1, \ldots, M, \\ j = 1, \ldots, N, \end{array} \tag{8}$$

where M is the number of individuals in the data set, j is the number of recreation sites, and ϵ_{ij} is an error term.

The pooled demand equation can be thought of as a simple version of the varying parameter model of Vaughan and Russell (1982) and Smith and Desvousges (1985), where only the intercept in the system of equations is assumed to vary with quality. Additionally, Eq. (8) can be considered a simplification of the systems of equations approach suggested by Burt and Brewer (1971) and Cicchetti et al. (1976) where the coefficients across the equations are constrained to be equal.

One significant drawback of the estimation of a demand equation like (8) is that substitute site prices and qualities cannot be readily introduced into the model. The pooling of the data across recreation sites creates this problem since it seems clear that own price and own qualities should be grouped together in the estimation of (8), but it is not clear how substitutes should be grouped together.

Two functional forms for (8) are estimated due to their relatively common usage in recreation demand models; they are the linear (Burt and Brewer, 1971; Cicchetti et al., 1976; Kealy and Bishop, 1986) and the semilog (Binkley and Hanemann, 1978; Vaughan and Russell, 1981; Smith et al., 1986). In addition, each functional form is estimated twice; first, employing a correction for heteroskedasticity and second, employing a Tobit estimator to correct for the censoring of the data set caused by corner solutions.

For the linear version of the pooled model, a Marshallian consumer surplus (cs) measure of welfare change is constructed. For the semilog version, both Marshallian and Hicksian measures of welfare change are calculated. A compensating variation measure is constructed

$$cv = e(p_{ij}, S_j^0, F_j^0, u^0) - e(p_{ij}, S_j^1, F_j^1, u^0), \tag{9}$$

where $e(\cdot)$ is the expenditure function, u^0 is the utility level associated with the original levels of S and F, and S_j^0, F_j^0 and S_j^1, F_j^1 are the site qualities before and after the quality change, respectively. The formula for the expenditure function can be found in Bockstael et al. (1986) and Smith et al. (1986).

In addition, since the semilog demand function is asymptotic to the price axis, some researchers have calculated welfare measures using the highest observed price rather than considering the entire area under the demand curve. Here, the welfare measures are calculated both ways to examine the importance of this truncation.

The second model estimated is a logit model (Binkley and Hanemann, 1978; Feenberg and Mills, 1980; Caulkins et al., 1986; Bockstael et al., 1986; Rowe et al., 1985). The logit model assumes that the recreationist decides on each choice occasion whether to visit a recreation site, and, if so, which site to visit. This decision is presumed to depend on the site's qualities and travel costs. Unlike the pooled model, which predicts *how often* an individual will visit the chosen site, the logit models predicts *which* site he will choose to visit.

In the logit model, the individual's indirect utility function associated with the choice of alternative j is usually written as linear in variables

$$\begin{aligned} V_{ij} &= V(p_{ij}, S_j, F_j) + \mu_{ij} \\ &= \beta_0 + \beta_1 p_{ij} + \beta_2 S_j + \beta_3 F_j + \mu_{ij}, \end{aligned} \tag{10}$$

where the β's are parameters and the μ_{ij}'s are error terms. The recreationist will choose to visit site j if the utility from visiting site j is greater than the utility from visiting each of the other sites. This implies that the probability of visiting site j is equivalent to the probability that j yields the greatest utility, that is,

$$\pi_{ij} = \text{Prob}[\mu_{ij} - \mu_{ik} \geq V(p_{ik}, S_k, F_k) - V(p_{ij}, S_j, F_j), \quad \text{all } k \neq j], \tag{11}$$

where π_{ij} is the probability that recreationist i chooses to visit site j. If the μ_{ij} are i.i.d. with a type 1 extreme value distribution, the logit model results and this probability can be written

$$\pi_{ij} = \exp[V(p_{ij}, S_j, F_j)] / \sum_K \exp[V(p_{ik}, S_k, F_k)]. \tag{12}$$

The likelihood function for a sample of individuals is the product of the individual probability statements over all recreationists. Maximum likelihood techniques are used to estimate the parameters of the indirect utility function.

Estimates of welfare change for a single recreation visit can be calculated based on the parameter estimates. Hanemann (1982) shows that the compensating and equivalent variation from the logit model can be approximated by

$$cv = ev = (1/\beta_1)[\log(\sum_j \exp V_j^0) - \log(\sum_j \exp V_j^1)] \tag{13}$$

where V_j^0 and V_j^1 are the indirect utility before and after the quality improvement, respectively. The cv and ev are identical since the form of the indirect utility function implies that there are no income effects in the choice between recreation sites. Total willingness to pay for a change in environmental quality over an entire season can be estimated by multiplying the estimate from (13) by the total number of trips taken in a season. However, with an increase in quality, recreationists may choose to take more visits each season.

To reflect the expected increase in visits due to an increase in quality, a participation function relating total visits to site quality is estimated. Bockstael et al. (1986) employ a Tobit estimator to predict how the total number of visits recreationists take in a season varies with income and an inclusive value. The inclusive value is a variable representing the utility of visiting each of the recreation sites weighted by their probabilities of being chosen. It is a measure of the recreational opportunities available to the recreationist. Based on the participation equation, the predicted number of trips taken due to a quality improvement can to used to obtain a seasonal welfare estimate for each individual.

One disadvantage of the logit model is that it presumes that individuals compare the utility of visiting a site to the utility of visiting all other sites on each recreation day, so each choice is modeled independently of every other choice. Whereas individuals may, in fact, choose a combination of sites to visit at the beginning of a season; decisions may not be independent of every other. This feature of the logit model may make it inappropriate for the estimation of data that contain few corner solutions.

IV. ESTIMATION RESULTS

The models described in Section III are estimated using each of the 20 data sets generated in the two simulation experiments. The two experiments will be denoted experiment 1 and experiment 2 to distinguish them. Rather than present all of the coefficient estimates and relevant statistics associated with estimating the five versions of the models on two sets of 20 simulated data sets, a summary of the results is presented here. It is interesting that, in all models estimated in each experiment, the coefficients on price and income are significant at the 5% level. It is only for the quality variables that coefficients are sometimes statistically insignificant.

In experiment 1, the WLS estimator of the pooled linear model provides a relatively good fit of the data with the R^2 statistics ranging from 0.66 to 0.74. Unfortunately, although the price and income coefficients are all significant at the 5% level, the quality coefficients are not; only 5 of 40 exhibit significance. The use of the Tobit estimator yields quality coefficients that are significant in all cases.

The estimation of the pooled model as a semilog function also yields more significant coefficient estimates than the linear model; in this case, only 6 of 40 coefficients are not significant. The R^2s are again high, ranging from 0.79 to 0.81. For the Tobit estimator of the semilog model all of the coefficients are significant.

The logit model also generates fairly good fits of the data in experiment 1. All of the price coefficients and most of the quality coefficients are significant (2 coefficients on S and 7 on F are not). The χ^2 statistics range from 191 to 212 and indicate that the model is significant at the 1% level in all repetitions.

In general, the model fits in experiment 1 are superior to those in experiment 2. This may be due to the increased variance of the error term used to generate the simulated data in experiment 2. Also, the coefficient estimates across the repetitions of a given model exhibit more variation in this experiment than in the first.

For the linear form of the pooled model there are 5 occurrences of coefficients on S that are not significant and 11 cases where the coefficient on F is not significant, one of which is negative. The R^2s range from 0.49 to 0.57. Again, the use of the Tobit estimator results in a larger number of significant coefficients. There are only 2 coefficients on S that are not significant and 5 on F.

The semilog form of the pooled model generates similar results. There are 13 cases of insignificant quality coefficient estimates and a negative sign on one of them. The R^2s range from 0.57 to 0.64. This time, the use of the Tobit estimator does not do much better; there are still 11 coefficients on the two quality variables that are not significant.

The logit model fits the data fairly well, but there are 18 coefficients on quality that are not significant, 8 on S and 10 on F. The χ^2 statistics range from 156 to 200, again indicating that the model is significant in all repetitions.

V. WELFARE ESTIMATES

Unlike most Monte Carlo studies in which the truth does not vary across repetitions, in this experiment the true welfare varies from observation to observation and from repetition to repetition. The comparisons of the predicted and true welfare measures are made on a case by case basis to incorporate this variability. To facilitate cross-model comparisons, the individual estimates are averaged and this average is reported for each repetition of experiment 1 in Table 2. Summary statistics, likewise averaged, for these estimates are contained in Table 3.

The linear version of the pooled model generates a consumer surplus estimate averaged over the 20 repetitions of \$10.67. In contrast, the simulated data generate a "true" average cv of \$16.90. The mean error (ME) associated with the linear pooled model is −\$6.23. The mean error is defined as

$$ME = (1/N)\sum_{i}(C_i^p - C_i^a), \qquad i = 1, \ldots, N, \tag{14}$$

where C_i^p is the predicted welfare change for recreationist i, C_i^a is the simulated welfare change, and N is the total number of recreationists. The ME is a measure of the average deviation of the simulated welfare change from the predicted welfare measure. Since, in many cases, economists and policy makers are interested in estimating total recreation benefits, the error associated with predicting the total welfare change is of primary importance. The mean error statistic addresses this concern by providing an indication of how far off, on average, the predicted welfare measures are from the simulated welfare changes.[3]

The ratio of error to the simulated cv is also calculated

$$MEC = ME/CA \tag{15}$$

where CA is the average simulated compensating variation. The MEC is useful for the purposes of the simulation experiment since it presents the mean error as a fraction of the simulated welfare measure, generating a statistic that is independent of scale. The MECs can then be compared across simulations where the simulated welfare measures differ. The MEC associated with the linear pooled model is −0.37, indicating that the mean error as a percentage of the simulated compensating variation is −37%.

The final statistic calculated and presented in Table 3 is the root mean square error (RMSE), which is defined as

$$RMSE = \sqrt{(1/N)\sum_{i}(C_i^p - C_i^a)^2}. \tag{16}$$

In addition to capturing the bias associated with the welfare estimate, the RMSE measures the variability. The statistic is presented for completeness; however, primary attention is paid to the ME and MEC statistics in assessing the reliability of the models.

The pooled model is also estimated using a semilog functional form. Four welfare estimates are presented for the semilog form. The first two correspond to Marshallian consumer surplus estimates and the second two are Hicksian compensating variation measures. Marshallian consumer surplus is defined as the area between the semilog demand function at the original quality levels and at the 10%

Table 2. Average Welfare Estimates for the Recreation Demand Models in Experiment 1

Repetition	Simulated compensating variation	Pooled model					Pooled Tobit					
			Semilog					Semilog				
		Linear	cs	cst	cv	cvt	Linear	cs	cst	cv	cvt	Logit
1	16.85	11.18	21.32	19.05	21.34	19.07	20.11	4.42	4.30	4.43	4.31	21.17
2	16.89	10.68	21.70	19.35	21.71	19.37	21.86	3.78	3.67	3.78	3.67	22.27
3	17.51	7.95	28.05	24.92	28.07	24.94	21.56	6.23	6.05	6.25	6.07	24.09
4	17.10	10.25	19.13	17.08	19.14	17.10	21.33	3.48	3.37	3.48	3.38	21.11
5	16.68	12.09	20.84	18.58	20.85	18.60	20.38	4.13	4.01	4.14	4.02	20.25
6	16.86	9.89	21.76	19.40	21.78	19.42	19.50	3.76	3.65	3.77	3.66	19.58
7	16.79	11.70	23.41	20.93	23.43	20.95	21.80	6.04	5.37	6.07	5.89	21.64
8	16.84	13.82	23.49	20.91	23.50	20.93	24.16	5.18	5.02	5.29	5.03	24.14
9	16.95	10.42	21.57	19.23	21.59	19.25	22.88	4.93	4.78	4.94	4.79	21.35
10	16.93	8.97	16.77	14.94	16.78	14.96	18.01	3.31	3.21	3.31	3.21	17.80
11	16.77	7.26	14.76	13.13	14.77	13.14	17.38	3.46	3.35	3.46	3.36	17.82
12	16.73	13.67	23.72	21.04	23.74	21.07	23.49	4.17	4.03	4.17	4.04	24.73
13	17.25	15.54	26.63	24.18	26.65	24.21	22.14	5.08	4.93	5.09	4.94	21.71
14	16.74	10.88	17.67	15.69	17.69	15.71	20.29	3.54	3.43	3.54	3.43	21.51
15	17.14	6.28	12.40	11.08	12.41	11.09	16.96	2.63	2.56	2.63	2.56	17.33
16	16.71	12.93	22.52	20.09	22.54	20.11	21.31	4.20	4.08	4.21	4.09	22.10
17	16.83	12.63	25.30	22.70	25.32	22.73	22.21	5.95	5.80	5.97	5.82	22.01
18	16.39	11.57	21.47	19.10	21.49	19.12	21.49	3.58	3.47	3.59	3.48	21.21
19	17.19	6.28	12.40	11.08	12.41	11.09	16.96	2.63	2.56	2.63	2.56	17.33
20	16.92	9.43	20.88	18.70	20.89	18.72	18.89	4.82	4.69	4.83	4.70	17.75
Mean	16.90	10.67	20.79	18.55	20.81	18.58	20.64	4.27	4.14	4.27	4.15	20.84

Table 3. Summary Statistics for Experiment 1 Averaged over the 20 Repetitions

Model	*Mean simulated cv*	*Mean welfare estimate*	*ME*	*MEC*	*RMSE*
Pooled					
Linear	16.90	10.67	−6.23	−0.37	10.93
Semilog					
cs	16.90	20.79	3.89	0.23	8.28
cst	16.90	18.55	1.65	0.10	7.87
cv	16.90	20.81	3.91	0.23	8.28
cvt	16.90	18.58	1.68	0.10	7.87
Pooled Tobit					
Linear	16.90	20.64	3.74	0.22	7.31
Semilog					
cs	16.90	4.27	−12.63	−0.75	18.81
cst	16.90	4.14	−12.76	−0.76	18.80
cv	16.90	4.27	−12.63	−0.75	17.94
cvt	16.90	4.15	−12.75	−0.75	18.82
Logit	16.90	20.84	3.94	0.23	8.80

improved quality levels. For the first Marshallian measure, the entire area under the demand curve is used (cs); for the second, only the area under the demand curve below the highest observed price is used (cst). This second estimate is intuitively appealing. If no recreationists are observed to visit the recreation site faced with a price greater than p* then the use of the demand curve above p* may lead to erroneous welfare measures since the demand curve is not estimated using these prices.

Hicksian compensating variation is calculated as the difference between the expenditure function implied by the semilog demand function evaluated at the original quality level and the higher quality level. This measure is calculated using both the highest observed price (cvt) and infinity as the price that drives trips to zero (cv).

The average welfare estimates for the semilog functions are contained in Table 2, columns 4–7, and the summary statistics in Table 3, rows 2–5. The mean welfare estimate for cs is $20.79 and the mean cv is $20.81. In this case, the cs and cv estimates are quite close. Truncating the welfare estimate generates slightly lower estimates of welfare with a cst of $18.55 and a cvt of $18.58. Since all of these measures overestimate the simulated welfare, recall that the "true" average cv is $16.90, the truncated measures are more accurate in this case resulting in a mean error of $1.65. This translates into an MEC of only 0.10.

The welfare estimates resulting from the linear and semilog versions of the pooled model estimated with the Tobit are presented in columns 8–12 of Table 2 and are summarized in column 2 of Table 3. In the linear model, the use of the Tobit estimator almost doubles the size of the welfare estimate from $10.67 to $20.64 resulting in a mean error of $3.74. All four of the average welfare measures associated with the semilog model are quite small ranging from a mean of $4.14 for cst and $4.27 for cs. These estimates correspond to quite large mean errors. The MECs are all approximately −0.75, that is, the average mean errors are about 75% of the simulated cv's.

The logit model generates an average welfare estimate of $20.84, corresponding to a mean error of $3.94 averaged across the repetitions.

Cross-model comparisons can be made with reference to the MECs. In experiment 1, the semilog pooled model generates the best estimates of welfare using either of the truncated measures, resulting in an MEC of 0.10. The next best estimates of welfare are from the linear pooled Tobit model with an MEC of 0.22 and the logit model with an MEC of 0.23. The semilog version of the Tobit model generates fairly large errors with MECs of about −0.75.

The extent to which these results depend on the parameter values and error distribution used to generate the simulated data is examined in experiment 2. In this experiment, the variance of the error is slightly larger than in the first simulation and some of the parameter values differ. These differences result in data sets containing more zeros, as noted above.

Tables 4 and 5 contain the average welfare estimates for the recreation demand models estimated using the second set of simulated data. The linear pooled model generates an average welfare estimate of $13.01, as compared with a "true" average cv of $11.07, which results in a mean error of $1.95. For repetition 10, welfare estimates are not calculated since the coefficient on F is negative.

In experiment 2, the estimation of a semilog demand function generates average welfare estimates of about $20.93 for cs and cv and about $20.18 for the truncated measures. These estimates are quite erroneous leading to MEC's of 1.07 and 0.82, respectively.

The use of the Tobit estimator improves the welfare estimates in all cases in this experiment. The linear Tobit model results in a mean welfare estimate of $12.03, closely approximating the true value of $11.07, resulting in an MEC of only 0.09. The semilog measures range from $18.99 to $19.56. In this experiment, the MECs are almost the same magnitude (approximately 0.75 in absolute value), although of opposite sign, as they are in the first experiment.

Table 4. Average Welfare Estimates for the Recreation Demand Models in Experiment 2

Repetition	Simulated compensating variation	Pooled model					Pooled Tobit					Logit
			Semilog					Semilog				
		Linear	*cs*	*cst*	*cv*	*cvt*	*Linear*	*cs*	*cst*	*cv*	*cvt*	
1	10.84	16.19	30.81	26.82	30.82	26.83	17.54	30.05	29.18	30.06	29.20	17.89
2	11.03	25.15	38.11	33.96	38.13	33.98	20.02	29.84	28.89	29.85	28.91	18.91
3	11.14	5.28	11.41	10.05	11.41	10.05	8.24	11.00	10.76	11.01	10.77	8.33
4	11.02	13.03	18.75	16.03	18.76	16.04	11.61	14.97	14.58	14.98	14.59	11.65
5	11.31	8.83	16.84	14.82	16.85	14.83	7.82	16.77	16.31	16.77	16.32	7.28
6	10.79	2.33	4.17	3.61	4.17	3.61	3.04	4.71	4.60	4.71	4.61	1.61
7	11.15	21.38	36.10	32.27	36.12	32.29	17.57	33.14	32.16	33.15	32.18	16.55
8	11.46	23.23	42.23	37.69	42.25	37.71	20.94	38.03	37.00	38.05	37.02	24.06
9	10.86	8.35	13.09	11.52	13.10	11.53	9.14	9.42	9.20	9.43	9.21	8.14
10	11.14	*a*	*a*	*a*	*a*	*a*	1.81	2.16	2.11	2.16	2.11	2.69
11	11.37	17.23	28.83	25.68	28.83	25.70	16.55	26.66	25.81	26.68	25.83	18.50
12	10.91	13.38	29.37	25.54	29.38	25.56	15.52	26.72	26.09	26.73	26.10	17.50
13	10.98	15.32	25.91	22.54	25.92	22.55	15.50	23.51	22.72	23.52	22.74	14.38
14	11.50	10.47	20.39	17.64	20.40	17.65	11.11	17.19	16.56	17.19	16.57	13.46
15	10.73	11.42	21.50	19.00	21.50	19.01	14.57	21.91	21.36	21.92	21.37	12.14
16	10.75	16.44	27.89	24.14	27.89	24.16	13.22	23.91	23.06	23.92	23.07	13.83
17	11.13	11.09	17.36	15.48	17.37	15.48	8.03	13.77	13.44	13.78	13.45	6.48
18	10.67	5.49	15.57	13.69	15.57	13.69	7.33	17.13	16.74	17.14	16.75	7.13
19	11.07	11.39	19.18	16.60	19.18	16.61	9.68	14.91	14.43	14.91	14.44	10.22
20	11.47	11.23	19.03	16.45	19.03	16.46	11.38	11.47	14.73	15.31	14.73	13.00
Mean	11.07	13.01	22.93	20.18	22.94	20.19	12.03	19.36	18.99	19.56	19.00	12.19

[a]Welfare estimates are not calculated in these cases because the coefficients on F are incorrectly signed.

Table 5. Summary Statistics for Experiment 2 Averaged over the 20 Repetitions

Model	*Mean simulated cv*	*Mean welfare estimate*	*ME*	*MEC*	*RMSE*
Pooled					
Linear	11.07	13.01	1.95	0.18	7.08
Semilog					
cs	11.07	22.93	11.86	1.07	14.00
cst	11.07	20.18	9.11	0.82	11.94
cv	11.07	22.94	14.00	1.07	14.00
cvt	11.07	20.19	9.12	0.82	11.95
Pooled Tobit					
Linear	11.07	12.03	0.96	0.09	7.38
Semilog					
cs	11.07	19.36	8.29	0.75	12.48
cst	11.07	18.99	7.92	0.72	12.02
cv	11.07	19.56	8.49	0.77	12.19
cvt	11.07	19.00	7.93	0.72	12.03
Logit	11.07	12.19	1.13	0.10	7.46

Another good performer in this experiment is the logit model. The average welfare estimate across the repetitions is $12.19. This results in an MEC of 0.10. The logit model generates closer estimates of welfare in this experiment than in the first, in which the MEC was 0.23.

VI. CONCLUSIONS OF THE SIMULATION EXPERIMENTS

The two simulation experiments described above differ only in the choice of parameters used to generate the simulated data and the size of the variance of the error. Despite these relatively minor differences, the recreation demand models perform quite differently in their ability to accurately estimate the welfare effects associated with a 10% improvement in site quality. Since the MECs are independent of units, they are used to compare the performance of the recreation models between the two experiments.

Table 6 contains the MECs for both simulation experiments for each of the recreation models. A quick perusal of Table 6 makes it clear that the choice of parameter values and error variance does make a difference in the results of the simulation experiments. This result is fairly disheartening, since it suggests that the results of the simulation experiment depend on the particular values chosen for these parameters.

Table 6. The Average MECs for the Recreation Demand Models for Both Simulations

Model	*Experiment 1*	*Experiment 2*
Pooled		
Linear	−0.37	0.18
Semilog		
cs	0.23	1.07
cst	0.10	0.82
cv	0.23	1.07
cvt	0.10	0.82
Pooled Tobit		
Linear	0.22	0.09
Semilog		
cs	−0.75	0.75
cst	−0.76	0.72
cv	−0.75	0.77
cvt	−0.75	0.72
Logit	0.23	0.10

In addition, it suggests that welfare estimates based on real data may be highly sensitive to slight variations in the underlying data. However, the MECs contained in Table 6 exhibit a predictable pattern, which makes the results more appealing.

In the first simulation experiment, there are relatively few zeros in the data; as a result, the pooled model (particularly, the semilog) without the use of the Tobit estimator provides fairly accurate estimates of welfare. The MEC's range from −0.37 for the linear model to 0.10 to 0.23 for the semilog model. In contrast, the welfare estimates associated with the Tobit estimator result in fairly large MECs, ranging from 0.22 to −0.76 in the linear and semilog cases, respectively. Finally, the logit model generates an MEC of 0.23. In this experiment, corner solutions are the exception and the models such as the logit and Tobit that attempt to incorporate corner solutions do not perform particularly well.

This result is in stark contrast to the results for experiment 2 where the simulated data sets exhibit more than twice as many zeros. In this experiment, the models that incorporate corner solutions explicitly into the estimation procedure perform better than those that do not. The linear pooled model without the Tobit correction yields an MEC of 0.18. With the Tobit estimator this drops in half to 0.09. Likewise, the semilog pooled model with the Tobit estimator results in MECs of 0.82 and 1.07. The employment of the Tobit again results in improved estimates with MECs ranging from 0.72 to 0.77. Finally, the logit estimator, which is primarily intended for corner solutions, generates the lowest MEC in this model of 0.10.

The simulation results appear to be sensitive to the parameter values and error distribution chosen in the simulation. However, the different errors in welfare measurement generated by the two simulation experiments and thus the optimal model choice can be explained by the different types of solutions to the recreationists' optimization problems. In particular, the results suggest that even when corner solutions appear relatively infrequently in the data, it is important to use a model that accounts for the zeros. In fact, in many recreation data sets corner solutions are quite abundant, so the use of a model that accounts for corner solutions may be even more important.

Despite the ability to at least partially explain the changes in the MECs between the two experiments based on corner solutions, there is, in both experiments, a significant amount of error associated with the welfare estimates from all of the simulation experiments. The best estimates have MECs of 0.10 (the pooled semilog) in experiment 1 and 0.09 (the linear Tobit) in experiment 2. The best estimate in both cases still contains average errors that are about 10% of the simulated cv.

Although simulation experiments cannot conclusively discriminate among the various recreation demand models, they can be used by researchers to examine the reliability of models under an array of circumstances. One such circumstance is examined in the experiments presented here. In these two experiments, two different recreation demand models, a logit and a pooled model, are estimated using two sets of simulated data. Although the results of the simulations are sensitive to the parameters and error distributions used in the construction of the simulation experiment, they depend on those parameters in a predictable way. When the parameters generate, in this case, about 40% corner solutions, the Tobit and logit models provide superior estimates of welfare. This result suggests that it is important to employ a model that accounts for the abundance of zeros in recreation data, even when less than half of the observations on site visits are zeros.

Although the results presented here are suggestive, they do not definitively discriminate among recreation demand models. Given the potential importance of welfare estimates in policy decisions affecting the use of natural resources, it would be desirable to continue lines of inquiry along this path. In particular, the sensitivity of the simulation results to the way the error is introduced into the utility function, different error distributions, the importance of the correct specification of functional form for the utility and demand functions and the importance of calculating Hicksian vs Marshallian measures of welfare are all issues that warrant further consideration. One potential avenue for such consideration takes the form of simulation experiments such as the one presented here.

ACKNOWLEDGMENTS

The authors would like to thank V. Kerry Smith, Nancy Bockstael, Maureen Cropper, Wallace Oates, Peter Berck, and an anonymous reviewer for stimulating comments and suggestions on this and related work. This is Giannini Foundation Research Paper #859.

NOTES

1. One means of resolving this problem as suggested by Kerry Smith is to specify an objective function for choosing the parameters of a model based on minimizing the error associated with incorrect estimates of welfare. For example, a traditional least-squares application of the travel cost model minimizes the squared error loss associated with incorrect estimation of the coefficients. In contrast, it would be possible to specify the loss function to describe the risk associated with incorrect estimation of welfare and choose parameter values based on minimizing this loss. Rather than consider variants of current models as this paper does, this procedure suggests that new estimators be derived and employed when the purpose of estimation is welfare measurement.

2. This method for incorporating the error is only one of many possible ways the error could be assumed to enter the utility function. Another possible method for incorporating this error is to assume that individuals misperceive prices as well as site qualities. A third possibility is to assume that consumers have random preferences concerning quantities. Each method has different implications for the resulting distribution of site visits. Additionally, it should be noted that, though the errors themselves are normally distributed, it cannot be assumed that the site visits follow a normal distribution since they are nonlinear functions of the errors. This has important implications for the simulation experiment since in the statistical models, a particular distribution for the errors is assumed for each of the estimation methods (normal or logistic). It may be desirable to repeat the simulation experiment in such a way that the resulting site visits can be assumed to be normally distributed.

3. There are several sources of error that this and the following statistics are capturing. First, there is error in the consumer surplus estimates due to the random error introduced into the maximization process. Second, there is error in the surplus estimates due to the mismatching functional form and model specification used to estimate the statistical models. Third, there are differences in the form of the error in the simulated data (see note 2) and the form assumed in the statistical models. Finally, there is a difference in some cases between the type of welfare measures used (Hicksian vs. Marshallian).

REFERENCES

Binkley, Clark S. and W. Michael Hanemann, *The Recreation Benefits of Water Quality Improvements: An Analysis of Day Trips in an Urban Setting,* Washington DC, EPA 60075-78-010, 1978.

Bishop, Richard and T. A. Herberlein, "Simulated Markets, Hypothetical Markets and Travel Cost Analysis: Alternative Methods of Estimating Outdoor Recreation Demand." University of Wisconsin, Department of Agricultural Economics Working Paper No. 187, 1981.

Bockstael, Nancy, Michael Hanemann and Ivar Strand, *Measuring the Benefits of Water Quality Improvements Using Recreation Demand Models.* Report Presented to the EPA under Cooperative Agreement CR-81143-01-1, Vol. II, 1986.

Bockstael, Nancy E., W. Michael Hanemann and Catherine L. Kling, "An Evaluation of Multiple Site Model Development." *Water Resources Research* 3(1987a):951–960.

Bockstael, Nancy, Michael Hanemann and Ivar Strand, "Time and the Recreational Demand Model." *American Journal of Agricultural Economics* 69(1987b):273–302.

Brookshire, David, L. Eubanks and Alan Randall, "Estimating Option Prices and Existing Values for Wildlife Resources." *Land Economics* 58(1982):1–15.

Brown, Gardner and Robert Mendelsohn, "The Hedonic Travel Cost Method." *Review of Economics and Statistics* 66(1984):427–433.

Burt, Oscar and Durward Brewer, "Estimation of Net Social Benefits from Outdoor Recreation." *Econometrica* 39(1971):813.

Caulkins, Peter, Richard Bishop and Nicolaas Bouwes, "The Travel Cost Model for Lake Recreation: A Comparison of Two Methods for Incorporating Site Quality and Substitution Effects." *AJAE* 66(1986):291–298.

Cesario, Frank, "Operation Research in Outdoor Recreation." *Journal of Leisure Research* 1(1969):33–52.

Cesario, Frank, "A Generalized Trip Distribution Model." *Journal of Regional Science* 13(1973):233–248.

Cicchetti, Charles, Anthony Fisher and V. Kerry Smith, "An Econometric Evaluation of a Generalized Consumer Surplus Measure: The Mineral King Controversy." *Econometrica* 44(1976):1259–1276.

Clawson, Marion, *Methods for Measuring the Demand for and Value of Outdoor Recreation.* Resources for the Future, Inc., Reprint No. 10, 1959.

Clawson, Marion and Jack Knetsch, *Economics of Outdoor Recreation.* Resources for the Future, Washington, DC, 1966.

Cox, D. R., "Tests of Separate Families of Hypotheses." *Proceedings of the Fourth Berkeley Symposium on Mathematical Statistics and Probability,* Vol. 1, University of California, 1961.

Domencich, Thomas and Daniel McFadden, *Urban Travel Demand: A Behavioral Analysis.* Amsterdam: North-Holland, 1975.

Feenberg, Daniel and Edwin Mills, *Measuring the Benefits of Water Pollution Abatement.* New York: Academic Press, 1980.

Freeman, Myrick A., *The Benefits of Environmental Improvement: Theory and Practice.* Baltimore, MD: Johns Hopkins Press for Resources for the Future, 1979.

Hanemann, W. Michael, "Applied Welfare Analysis with Qualitative Response Models." California Agricultural Experiment Station working paper No. 241, 1982.

Hanemann, W. Michael, "The Properties of the Multiple Site Recreation Decision." *Measuring the Benefits of Water Quality Improvements Using Recreation Demand Models,* Chapter 8. Report presented to E.P.A. Under Cooperative Agreement CR-80043-01-0, Vol. II, 1986.

Horowitz, Joel, "Statistical Comparison of Non-nested Probabilistic Discrete Choice Models." *Transportation Science* 17(1983):319–350.

Kealy, Mary Jo and Richard Bishop, "Theoretical and Empirical Specification Issues in Travel Cost Demand Studies." *American Journal Of Agricultural Economics* 68(1986):660–667.

Kling, Catherine L., "The Reliability of Estimates of Environmental Benefits from Recreation Demand Models." University of California, Draft manuscript, 1987.

Kling, Catherine L., "Comparing Welfare Estimates of Environmental Quality Changes from Recreation Demand Models." *Journal of Environmental Economics and Management,* 15(1988): 331–340.

Madalla, F. S., *Limited Dependent and Qualitative Variables in Econometrics.* New York: Cambridge University Press, 1983.

Maler, Karl-Goran, *Environmental Economics: A Theoretical Inquiry.* Baltimore, MD: John Hopkins University Press for Resources for the Future, 1974.

McConnell, Kenneth E. and Ivar E. Strand, "Measuring the Cost of Time in Recreation Demand Analysis: An Application to Sportfishing." *American Journal of Agricultural Economics* 63(1981):153–156.

Mendelsohn, Robert, "Estimating the Structural Evaluations of Implicit Markets and Household Production Functions." *Review of Economics and Statistics* 66(1984):673–677.

Morey, Edward, "The Demand for Site-Specific Recreational Activities: A Characteristics Approach." *Journal of Environmental Economics and Management* 8(1981):345–371.

Pesaran, M. H. and A. S. Deaton, "Testing Non-nested Non-linear Regression Models." *Econometrica* 46(1978):677–695.

Reiling, S. D., K. C. Gibbs and H. H. Stoevner, *Economic Benefits from an Improvement in Water Quality.* Washington, DC: US EPA, 1973.

Sellar, Christine, John Stoll and Jean-Paul Chavas, "Variation of Empirical Measures of Welfare Change: A Comparison of Nonmarket Techniques." *Land Economics* 61(1985):156–175.

Smith, V. Kerry and William H. Desvousges, "The Generalized Travel Cost Model and Water Quality Benefits: A Reconsideration." *Southern Economic Journal* (1985):371–381.

Smith, V. Kerry, William H. Desvousges and Ann Fisher, "A Comparison of Direct and Indirect Methods for Estimating Environmental Benefits." *American Journal of Agricultural Economics* (1986):280–290.

Thayer, Mark, "Contingent Valuation Techniques for Assessing Environmental Impacts: Further Evidence." *Journal of Environmental Economics and Management* 8(1981):27–44.

Tobin, James, "Estimation of Relationships for Limited Dependent Variables." *Econometrica* 26(1958):24–36.

Vaughan, W. J. and C. S. Russell, "Valuing a Fishing Day: An Application of a Systematic Varying Parameter Model." *Land Economics* 58(1982):450–462.

Wegge, Thomas, W. Michael Hanemann and Ivar Strand, "An Economic Assessment of Marine Recreational Fishing in Southern California." Report submitted to National Fisheries Service Southwest Regional Office, 1985.

Wilman, Elizabeth, "Valuing Quality Changes in Recreation Resources." Papers presented at the AERE Workshop on Recreation Demand Modeling, Boulder, Colorado, 1985.

Wilman, Elizabeth, "A Simple Repackaging Model of Recreational Choices." *American Journal of Agricultural Economics* 69(1987):603–612.

NONMARKET VALUES FROM TWO DECADES OF RESEARCH ON RECREATION DEMAND

Richard G. Walsh, Donn M. Johnson, and John R. McKean

I. INTRODUCTION

In the last two decades, interest in nonmarket valuation of natural resource use for outdoor recreation has substantially increased. This is true in the federal government where, for example, the Forest Service, Environmental Protection Agency, and Fish and Wildlife Service now have extensive responsibilities in an area that was once the province of the National Park Service and the Corps of Engineers. Also, nonmarket valuation work has been stimulated by increased interest from state government, particularly water development, environmental quality, forestry, wildlife, and recreation resource management divisions. Perhaps the most important reason for this expanded interest has

Advances in Applied Micro-Economics, Volume 5, pages 167–193.

ISBN: 0-89232-797-9

been growing pressure from both inside and outside government for improvement in the criteria on which public expenditure decisions are made. This general reforming trend has stimulated interest in nonmarket valuation since many governmental projects and programs affect recreational opportunities.

In the past, most studies focused on questions of management at a specific location. Although there is a growing body of findings from such studies, the increased demand for research results has far outpaced supply, which has been severely constrained by reduced budgets of domestic funding agencies (President's Commission on Americans Outdoors, 1987). Concurrently, reduced budgets increase the urgency of valuation estimates to make the difficult decisions with respect to the effectiveness of alternative programs. The policy application must be done quickly and with resources that are usually not sufficient to permit generation of new value estimates based on application of advanced nonmarket valuation methods (for example, Walsh and Loomis, 1986). There will rarely be time or budget to permit a new empirical study.

As a result, there is reason to believe that past nonmarket value studies will play an increasingly important role in future resource policy decisions. This means that evaluation of the adequacy of available research becomes an important question. In a keynote address celebrating the thirty-fifth anniversary of Resources for the Future, Smith (1988) emphasized the problem of *information transfer*. He concluded that as experience is accumulated in valuing nonmarket resources, we must learn how to learn from that research and integrate the findings into improved use of what is on the "research shelf." Such learning would result in a better match between off-the-shelf estimates when they are applied to new valuation problems as well as better understanding of the research needed to make what is on the shelf more useful.

This paper addresses some of the issues in past application of nonmarket value analyses and their relative importance from the perspective of future policy decisions. It is a retrospective glance at 20 years of empirical research using the contingent valuation (CVM), travel cost (TCM), and related methods. What is at issue is defining standards that allow these values to be compared. This paper evaluates the effectiveness of a recent attempt to review the reported values and adjust them not only for inflation but for some of the important variations in method. There are sufficient studies so that they can be pooled and statistical methods applied to improve our understanding of the variables explaining some of the observed variation in the benefit estimates. This should enable the debate over best practices to be more clearly defined.

II. THE INFORMATION TRANSFER PROBLEM

The promulgation of standards for estimation of nonmarket values has a relatively short history. Interest was stimulated by the authorization of Senate Document 97 (U.S. Water Resources Council, 1962), which established benefit–cost methods to be used in planning water and related resource development by federal agencies. Supplement No. 1 to Senate Document 97 was signed by President Kennedy and published by the Water Resources Council (1964) authorizing use of the unit day value method. He also set up the Water Resources Council as an interagency committee to administer the guidelines. Subsequently, the Council revised the guidelines in 1973 under President Nixon to authorize use of the TCM. They were revised again in 1979, when use of the CVM was approved by President Carter. Authorization of the three methods was reaffirmed in a 1983 edition of the guidelines signed by President Reagan and authorized by the Department of Interior in 1986. The bipartisan political support in the past indicates their broad acceptability within and outside of government. It seems likely that future revisions in the guidelines will occur as improved methods are developed.

This study focuses on the problem of estimating a range of unit-day values for major recreation activities in Forest Service Regions as part of long-run (50-year) resource planning. Initially, the unit-day value approach relied on expert judgment to develop an approximation of the average willingness to pay for recreation activities. An estimate adjusted for characteristics of the study site was selected from a range of values approved by the federal guidelines. Based on estimates from a survey of entrance fees at private recreation areas in 1962, the unit-day values recommended by the guidelines have been adjusted for changes in the consumer price index since then. Of particular interest here, the Forest Service has based unit-day values on periodic review (1975, 1980, and 1985) of empirical studies using the CVM, TCM, and related methods.[1] The values have been adjusted by the administration to reflect the concept of reasonable and proper levels for the purposes intended. The literature review on which this paper is based was designed to contribute to the Forest Service 1990 resource planning values for recreation.

There have been hundreds of empirical estimates by studies designed to determine the benefit of an outdoor recreation activity. But there remain many National Forest service areas in which no studies have been made. If the existing studies produced the same set of findings, then the agency could with confidence predict the net benefit of each forest recreation activity in each of the Forest Regions. However, if the studies produced widely varying results for unexplainable reasons, the agency could not easily predict the value of forest recreation based on the available literature (Smith, 1986). Adjustments would have to be made to facilitate the transfer of findings from the locations where studies were performed to areas where they were not. Even where studies were conducted, improved data transfer procedures could increase the precision of net benefit estimates. In a nutshell, these issues comprise the information transfer problem.

Detailed descriptions and evaluations of the design aspects of the studies completed from 1968 to 1982 were prepared by Sorg and Loomis (1984) on behalf of the Forest Service 1985 resource planning program. As might be expected, many of the early studies were of dubious quality from the standpoint of being able to make valid benefit inferences from them. Only midway in the review period did the federal government (Water Resources Council, 1973, 1979, 1983) issue guidelines on statistical sampling, vehicle travel cost, travel time cost, substitutes, and other aspects of experimental design to be used by new studies. These guidelines clearly were minimal when judged by the standards of some of the best studies. Even so, several of the studies did not meet them in important respects, and therefore were of almost no value in establishing comparable measures of the net benefits of recreation activities. The consensus judgment of a panel of evaluators was that substantial adjustment should be made in the reported values before presentation of the summary statistics.[2]

As a result, Sorg and Loomis (1984) increased the reported TCM values by 30% for the omission of travel time; both TCM and CVM values were increased by 15% for omission of out-of-state users; and TCM values were decreased 15% for application of the individual observation approach. Omission of travel time from the TCM demand function leads to a downward bias in estimated benefits. The cost of time spent traveling represents the difference between sightseeing benefits enroute and the opportunity cost of the time in an alternative activity. Although there is unanimity in the need to include travel time, the exact size of the correction of benefit estimates when travel time is not included is difficult to determine. Similarly, omission of out-of-state users tends to understate the number of visits to most resource-based sites at relatively higher travel costs. If they travel further than instate users, the upper limit of travel cost in the demand curve will be understated and benefits will be biased downward. The individual observation approach uses annual trips per participant as the dependent variable. Although this is statistically more efficient than the zonal approach, it omits the effect of travel costs on the probability of participating. The resulting demand curve is often less elastic (steeper), which results in overstating recreation benefits of some activities when the probability of participation decreases significantly at higher travel costs. Information is needed on the effect of travel cost on the probability of visiting a particular site across different recreation activities. Unfortunately such information is not readily available.

Table 1 illustrates the resulting summary statistics for the recreation use categories of the National Forest Service. The net economic values per day reported by outdoor recreation demand studies from 1968 to 1988 are updated to the third quarter 1987 dollars and adjusted for method as in Sorg and Loomis (1984). Mean value of the 287 estimates is $34 per day with a 95% confidence interval of $31 to $37 and a range of $4 to $220.[3] The median is $27. These values are shown for each activity along with output of the agency. Average benefit of activities range from $12 to $72 per day with the highest values reported for hunting, fishing, nonmotorized boating, hiking, and winter sports. Ideally, the distribution of values would approximate normality with outliers at both the high and low ends. Given sufficient number of studies, the solid core of values in the middle would be the most reasonable estimate. This approach assumes that socioeconomic variables and characteristics of the study sites are sufficiently similar that a common pattern of consumption applies to each.

A number of problems should be considered before analysts could reasonably apply this information to policy decisions. First, for most recreation activities, an insufficient number of studies have been completed to obtain reasonable estimates of value by this method. Even where there are a large number of studies, the frequency distribution is often skewed with the majority of estimates clustered near the bottom of the range in values and a relatively few extremely high estimates. This substantially increases the sample mean and thus it is questionable whether the mean truly reflects the sample as a whole. The median would be a more appropriate measure to use if the purpose of the analysis is to determine a representative estimate rather than calculate the net economic value of the estimates.

Table 1. Net Economic Values per Day Reported by TCM and CVM Demand Studies from 1968 to 1988 Applied to National Forest Recreation Use Categories, United States (Third Quarter, 1987 Dollars)

Activity	*Visitor, days 1000*[a]	*Number of estimates*	*Mean*	*Median*	*Standard error of the mean*	*95% confidence interval*	*Range*
Total	226,533 (100.0%)	287 (100.0%)	$33.95	$27.02	1.67	30.68–37.22	3.91–219.65
Camping, picnicking, and swimming	66,811 (29.5)	36 (12.5)	20.14	17.80	1.80	16.61–23.67	7.05–46.69
Camping	53,666 (23.7)	18 (6.3)	19.50	18.92	2.03	15.52–23.48	8.26–34.89
Picnicking	7,838 (3.5)	7 (2.4)	17.33	12.82	5.08	7.37–27.29	7.05–46.69
Swimming	5,405 (2.3)	11 (3.8)	22.97	18.60	3.79	15.54–30.40	7.05–42.94
Mechanical travel and viewing	68,423 (30.2)	11 (3.8)	25.42	21.44	5.14	15.35–35.49	8.27–68.65
Sightseeing and offroad driving	62,451 (27.6)	6 (2.1)	20.29	19.72	3.73	12.98–27.60	10.33–31.84
Boating, motorized	4,301 (1.5)	5 (1.7)	31.56	25.67	10.36	11.25–51.87	8.27–68.65
Hiking, horseback riding, and water travel	19,900 (8.8)	17 (5.9)	41.74	24.72	10.53	21.10–62.38	10.26–183.36
Hiking	12,740 (5.6)	6 (2.1)	29.08	23.62	5.82	17.67–40.49	15.71–55.81
Boating, nonmotorized	3,419 (1.5)	11 (3.8)	48.68	25.36	15.85	17.61–79.75	10.26–183.36
Winter sports	14,730 (6.5)	12 (4.2)	28.50	24.39	4.48	19.72–37.28	11.27–66.69

Resorts, cabins, and organized camps[b]	15,117	2	12.48	—	—	—	3.91–19.93
	(6.7)	(0.7)					
Hunting	15,276	83	41.69	34.88	2.72	36.36–47.02	16.58–142.40
	(6.7)	(28.9)					
Big game hunting	10,729	56	45.47	37.87	3.47	38.67–52.27	19.81–142.40
	(4.7)	(19.5)					
Small game hunting	4,015	10	30.82	27.48	3.51	23.94–37.70	18.72–52.04
	(1.8)	(3.5)					
Migratory waterfowl hunting	532	17	35.64	25.27	5.87	24.13–47.15	16.58–102.88
	(0.2)	(5.9)					
Fishing	15,208	88	39.25	29.59	3.80	31.80–46.70	8.13–219.65
	(6.7)	(30.7)					
Cold water fishing	10,687	39	30.62	28.49	3.24	24.27–36.97	10.07–118.12
	(4.7)	(13.59)					
Anadromous fishing[c]	—	9	54.01	46.24	11.01	32.43–75.59	16.85–127.26
	—	(3.1)					
Warm water fishing	4,072	23	23.55	22.50	2.46	18.73–28.37	8.13–59.42
	(1.8)	(8.0)					
Salt water fishing	226	17	72.49	53.35	14.05	44.95–100.03	18.69–219.65
	(0.1)	(5.9)					
Nonconsumptive fish and wildlife	1,532	14	22.20	20.49	2.30	17.69–26.71	5.27–38.06
	(0.7)	(4.9)					
Other recreation activities	9,537	9	18.82	16.06	3.65	11.67–25.97	6.81–43.39
	(4.2)	(3.1)					
Wilderness	12,014[d]	15	24.58	19.26	6.10	12.62–36.54	8.72–106.26
	(4.5)	(5.2)					

[a]Thousands of 12-hour recreation visitor days reported by the Forest Service, USDA, for the year ending September 30, 1986 (U.S. Dept. of Commerce, 1988, p. 212).

[b]Resorts were 1.83% valued at $19.93 per day; seasonal and year around cabins were 3.06% valued at $3.91 per day; and organized camps were 1.79% valued the same as camping.

[c]Anadromous fishing estimates included in cold water fishing. Estimated as roughly 5.0%.

[d]Included above.

Second, the approach does not reveal what is causing the extreme range in values, whether variation in characteristics of users, quality of sites, or research methods. A potentially useful approach to the data transfer problem would be to pool the data from existing studies and apply multiple regression analysis. If the basic model specification was complete, that is, if it included all the relevant explanatory variables in the correct functional form, then it could explain the variation in benefits embodied in differences among the explanatory variables. The net benefit estimated for a site lacking data would then be predicted by inserting appropriate values of explanatory variables into the model fitted to data from the other study sites.

In the future, it seems likely that an ever larger number of studies will be accumulated that carefully apply microeconomic theory to the demand for outdoor recreation. In this case, the growing science of reviewing research, so-called meta-analysis, should be considered (Cooper, 1984; Light and Pillemer, 1984). The approach introduces precision into the analysis with respect to specific purpose of the literature review, the selection of the studies for review, the similarity of the units of analysis and subject matter across studies, the distribution of study values, and the relationship of study values to research design, characteristics of participants, quality of the sites, and management programs.

The primary purpose of meta-analysis is to provide guidelines for future research. A single review can examine many possible variables that might be important, and provide a basis for eliminating some of them as serious candidates for new research. Using prior reviews to reduce the number of experimental variables should improve the statistical analysis and allocation of resources in new studies. Thus, each succeeding literature review should build upon previous ones. No single review can possibly consider everything since the available regression techniques limit the number of possible significant variables in each new effort.

In the early stages of this evolving process, the critical problem will be to correctly specify the variables that are expected to influence the benefit estimates. For if important determinants are omitted, the statistical equation will not predict the effects accurately, as illustrated by Allen et al. (1981). Thus, the early review efforts should be treated with caution since by leaving important variables out of the regression analysis, they may attribute more or less of the variation to those that are included than would be the case with a more complete specification, as illustrated by Smith and Kaoru (1988).

Ideally, the empirical model used to explain the variation in benefit estimates would be based primarily on applied microeconomic theory (McKean and Walsh, 1986). In an ordinary demand function for a recreation site, the dependent variable to be explained is the quantity demanded. The list of independent variables that influence demand includes a proxy for direct cost or price and factors such as travel distance or the value of time, the price and availability of substitutes, consumer income, other socioeconomic variables such as age, quality, or attractiveness of the site, population of the consuming group, individual taste or preference, expectations and experience with respect to crowding or congestion.[4] Other variables related to research method may include recreation activity, sample size and coverage, CVM, TCM or other method, statistical model, econometric estimators, type of CVM question, and site administration.

The possible affect of the specification of each of these variables should be carefully evaluated. For example, measurement of quantity demanded in different units may affect the benefit estimate, whether trips, hours, visitor days per person, or per capita. Specification of own price as distance with variable travel costs per mile from the U.S. Department of Transportation or reported by respondents may also affect benefit estimates (Duffield, 1988). The effect of travel time cost on benefit estimates has been shown to vary with the percentage of wage rate used (McCollum et al., 1988). Smith and Kaoru (1988) make an important contribution to understanding the effects of alternative methods of estimating travel time cost, presence of a substitute price term, use of a regional model, type of site studied, statistical models (linear, log-linear, or semilog), and estimators (ordinary least squares, generalized least squares, or maximum likelihood-tobit) used in TCM studies.[5] They conclude that these methodological variations significantly affect benefit estimates. The question remains whether method would have as much effect in a regression model holding constant the effects of other important variables including recreation activity, time on site, quality of the site, location of the site, variable cost per mile, travel time cost per hour, income and other socioeconomic variables, or sample size and coverage.

III. RESEARCH PROCEDURE

A systematic search of the available literature was conducted in an effort to review all available empirical studies from 1968 to 1988. The selection process was designed to fairly represent all of the research on the topic in the United States. Included were studies in journals, chapters in books, unpublished research reports, masters and doctoral theses, research reports from private organizations and government agencies, and conference papers. In a number of cases, the authors were contacted by phone to clarify a methodological question or to obtain the results of unpublished studies. The overall effect of the selection process was to provide sufficient studies to identify interesting trends and get a broad flavor of the findings from both published and unpublished studies.

The values reported here represent consumer surplus calculated by the authors of each study from the demand functions they reported. The net economic values are equivalent to the dollar amount participants would be willing to pay over and above their current expenditures to ensure continued availability of the opportunity to use recreation resources. The review is limited to studies measuring the onsite recreation use benefits provided by a natural resource of given quality. Many of the studies also estimate the change in benefits with changes in the quality of the resource and interested readers are referred to the detailed descriptions of the original studies for estimates (Walsh et al., 1988). The values reported here do not include the public benefits from preservation of resource quality such as option values of future use and existence values to the general population of users and nonusers.[6]

The standard unit of measurement is an activity day, defined as one person onsite for any part of a calendar day. When values are reported on any basis other than per activity day, they are adjusted to this common unit. For TCM demand functions, the appropriate unit of analysis often is number of trips, but most authors also report the results in terms of value per activity day. Or we divide values per trip by the reported number of days per trip. Similarly, annual values are divided by the reported days of participation. Household group values are divided by the number of persons and days of participation per person. Where the value of recreation activities are reported for hypothetical quality changes, the base value for current site quality is used. There is a problem of defining recreation activity days at some sites, notably reservoirs with camping, swimming, boating, and fishing on the same trip. In this case, the concept of recreation use is based on the standard procedure of the U.S. Census in which an activity is defined as primary use when it represents over 50% of total individual activity while at the site.

Table 2 defines the explanatory variables included in the equations. Most are standard measures and require no further explanation. They

Table 2. Description of Variables in the Analysis

Name	*Definition of variable*
Dependent variable	Consumer surplus estimated by each study, standardized to average values per activity day, adjusted to third quarter 1987 dollars
Site quality	Qualitative variable = 1 if site was rated by each study as uniquely high quality, 0 if medium or low
Forest Service administered	Qualitative variable = 1 if the study sites were Forest Service administered, 0 if otherwise
Mixed public and private sites	Qualitative variable = 1 if household survey of participants in an activity at public and private sites, 0 if otherwise (the omitted categories were other wholly public and wholly private)
Specialized activity	Continuous variable = percent. Proportion of total recreation use of U.S. Forest Service resources in the activity category. Proxy of taste and preference for specialized vs generalized activities
Inflationary adjustment	Qualitative variable = 1 if data were collected for each study prior to 1980, 0 if 1980–1988
Sample coverage	Qualitative variable = 1 if only instate residents were included in the sample of users, 0 if out-of-state residents were also included
Method	Qualitative variable = 1 if CVM, 0 if TCM or other method
Substitution	Qualitative variable = 1 if a substitute price term was included in the TCM demand specification, 0 if otherwise
Travel time	Qualitative variable = 1 if travel time cost was omitted in the TCM demand specification, 0 if time was included
Individual observation	Qualitative variable = 1 if TCM sample units were individual observations, 0 if otherwise
Household production and hedonic price	Qualitative variable = 1 if household production or hedonic price TCM procedure, 0 if otherwise (the omitted category was the zonal group approach)
Open-ended question	Qualitative variable = 1 if noniterative open-ended question was asked in a CVM, 0 if otherwise
Dichotomous choice question	Qualitative variable = 1 if dichotomous choice CVM question was used, 0 if otherwise (the omitted category was the iterative question)
Socioeconomic characteristics	Proxy for socioeconomic characteristics of participants in the service area of the study site. The nine Forest Regions are qualitative variables. Alaska is the omitted region
Recreation activity	The 19 national recreation use categories are potential qualitative variables for activities. Omitted categories include activities with limited representation in the studies, i.e., resorts, cabins, and organized camps

represent the usual determinants of demand in applied microeconomics and research methods described elsewhere. Most of the variables are qualitative, indicating that a particular treatment is either present or absent. Of primary interest are the three adjustments by Sorg and Loomis (1984) for omission of travel time, the use of individual observations, and instate sample coverage discussed earlier in this paper. Other important determinants of demand are included to hold constant their effects and to estimate the single effect of each of these variables and other possible candidates for adjustment in benefit estimates. Other variables are recreation activity, whether specialized or general, site administration, quality, location, inflationary adjustment, method, open-ended, iterative, or dichotomous choice question, and zonal, household production, or hedonic price approach. Some potentially important variables are omitted: direct travel cost per mile, travel time cost per hour, income and other socioeconomic variables, sample size, statistical model, and estimator used.

A quality variable is included to control for specific quality characteristics of sites that vary among recreation activities and expectations of individual participants. Sufficient information is available in the studies to apply a rough index of site quality in three categories—uniquely low, ordinary, and uniquely high—based on a review of the physical and biological information provided. A site administration variable is included to test the hypothesis that Forest Service administered site benefits are not significantly different from other public and private sites. A mixed public–private site variable tests the hypothesis that household surveys are more effective than site-specific studies, whether public or private. A specialized activity variable tests the hypothesis that benefits are lower for general activities than for specialized activities. This may be interpreted as a proxy for taste and preference. The federal guidelines (Water Resources Council, 1983) differentiate between general recreation activities engaged in by a large number of persons and specialized recreation limited to fewer participants with unique preference patterns. The guidelines associate specialized recreation with higher unit-day values and general recreation lower.

An inflationary adjustment variable is intended to begin examining the question whether recreation values increase at the same rate as changes in the purchasing power of the dollar. For comparison purposes, the reported values must be adjusted for inflation. However, this is equivalent to assuming constant real prices, which would not be consistent with increased crowding and relative scarcity of natural resources available for resource-based recreation activities (President's Commission on Americans Outdoors, 1987). Moreover, the procedure assumes an equal proportional change in the reported values for any given year, which tends to dampen (enlarge) the absolute dollar adjustment for studies reporting low (high) values. This is evident for surveys from 1968 to 1979 when the inflation rate was 6.9%, compared to 4.8% from 1980 to 1987. Finally, willingness to pay is, in part, a function of ability to pay, which suggests that secular adjustments for per capita real income would be useful.

A method variable is included to test the hypothesis that intended willingness to pay CVM estimates are lower than behavior-based TCM. This is based on the observation that TCM values the entire trip including the primary activity and secondary activities while the CVM usually values the primary activity alone. For example, TCM always values the entire time onsite per calendar day of a weekend or vacation trip while CVM usually values only that part of the day that pertains to the primary activity, e.g., the 4 hours devoted to fishing each day.

A variable indicating location of the study sites in Forest Regions is included as a proxy for socioeconomic characteristics of the user population. Since the regression model controls for site quality, the other important effect of location is the distribution of income and other socioeconomic characteristics of the population in the relevant market for use of the study site. While extensive data on household demographics and equipment ownership are available for outdoor recreation activities from national and state samples, similar information is available only for a small fraction of the studies reviewed here. Thus, this important feature of variation in benefits would have to be ignored without an effective proxy variable.

IV. TOWARD UNDERSTANDING VARIATION IN THE ESTIMATES

With the increased output of empirical studies in recent years, there are enough data to begin understanding the variables that explain the observed variation in benefit estimates. Table 3 includes three functions showing the statistical relationship of recreation benefits to some important explanatory variables. These are for the total sample of 287 benefit estimates, 156 TCM and related estimates, and 129 CVM. The number of observations is sufficient for statistically significant analysis. The R^2, adjusted for degrees of freedom, indicates that 36–44% of the total variation in the values is explained by the variables included in the functions. The overall equations are significant at the 0.01 level. The T statistics shown in parentheses beneath the coefficients indicate that about two-thirds of the variables (27 of 42) are significant at the 0.10 level or above. Omission of a variable indicates that it is not related to benefits.

The panel nature of the data render the usual statistical tests of the

Table 3. OLS Regressions of Recreational Values on Several Important Explanatory Variables, United States, 1987

Independent variable	Description of variable	Total		Travel cost method		Contingent valuation method	
		Mean	Coefficient [a]	Mean	Coefficient [a]	Mean	Coefficient [a]
Site quality	1 = High	0.129	33.568*	0.154	39.171*	0.101	25.082*
	0 = Other		(7.51)		(6.06)		(4.42)
Specialized activity	Percent of Forest Service output	4.917	−0.574*	5.235	−0.679*	4.571	−0.147
			(−2.23)		(−1.83)		(−0.519)
Forest Service administered	1 = Forest Service	0.230	4.931	0.218	6.204	0.248	2.594
	0 = Other		(0.98)		(0.84)		(0.42)
Mixed public and private sites	1 = Mixed	0.596	9.891*	0.571	6.933*	0.636	13.539*
	0 = Other		(2.29)		(1.12)		(2.46)
Inflationary adjustment	1 = 1980–88	0.564	−7.971*	0.436	−10.579*	0.721	−16.582*
	0 = 1965–79		(−2.35)		(−2.03)		(−3.31)
Sample coverage	1 = Instate sample	0.115	−6.892	0.186	−11.759*	0.031	−7.464
	0 = Other		(−1.33)		(−1.77)		(−0.86)
Method	1 = CVM	0.449	−8.098*		—		—
	0 = TCM		(−2.34)				
Sorg–Loomis adjustments	1 = Not adjusted	0.578	−4.290		—		—
	0 = Adjusted		(−1.09)				
Travel time cost	1 = Omitted		—	0.192	−13.333*		—
	0 = Included				(−1.90)		
Substitution variable	1 = Included			0.647	−10.831*		—
	0 = Omitted				(−2.05)		
Individual observation	1 = Indiv. obs.		—	0.333	17.950*		—
	0 = Other				(3.44)		

Household production	1 = HP		—	0.083	9.499		—
and hedonic price	0 = Other				(1.03)		
Open-ended question	1 = Open-ended		—		—	0.333	−3.659*
	0 = Other						(−0.76)
Dichotomous choice	1 = Dichotomous		—		—	0.101	3.503
question	0 = Other						(0.62)
Southern region	1 = Southern	0.094	−13.089*	0.122	−12.333*	0.062	−10.998*
	0 = Other		(−2.48)		(−1.66)		(−1.67)
Northwest region	1 = Northwest	0.052	−10.676		—	0.039	−12.186*
	0 = Other		(−1.47)				(−1.53)
Pacific SW region	1 = Pacific SW	0.059	−10.683*		—		—
	0 = Other		(−1.66)				
Intermountain region	1 = Intermountain	0.171	−9.252*		—	0.155	−13.517*
	0 = Other		(−2.18)				(−2.98)
Salt water and ana-	1 = S-A fishing	0.091	34.566*	0.096	42.939*	0.085	24.454*
dromous fishing	0 = Other		(6.20)		(5.10)		(4.02)
Big game hunting	1 = Big game	0.199	21.817*	0.186	23.037*	0.209	16.664*
	0 = Other		(5.33)		(3.58)		(4.04)
Waterfowl hunting	1 = Waterfowl	0.063	11.325*		—	0.093	7.042*
	0 = Other		(1.80)				(1.28)
Constant			33.579*		33.769*		28.543*
			(6.89)		(4.24)		(3.98)
Sample size			287		156		129
Adjusted R^2			0.36		0.39		0.44

[a]T ratios are shown in parentheses; an asterisk indicates that the coefficient is significant at the 90% level or greater.

models approximations rather than precise estimates. Although the residuals are close to normally distributed, in any study with parameters drawn from different data sets, heteroscedasticity is likely to be present. Even though review of the correlation matrixes indicates mostly low levels with few near a maximum of 0.70, autocorrelation is likely to result from inclusion of more than one benefit estimate from the same study.[7] The *t*-statistics somewhat over- or underestimate variable significance based on a Smith and Kaoru (1988) comparison of OLS estimates with the Newey and West (1987) variation of the White (1980) consistent covariance estimates of standard errors used in calculating *t*-statistics.

Of primary interest here are the variables estimating the effect of the three adjustments in benefits by Sorg and Loomis (1984), namely, for omission of travel time cost, use of the individual observation approach, and instate samples at sites with out-of-state users. The increase in reported values by 30% for omission of travel time cost seems to be about right. The statistically significant coefficient indicates that TCM benefits are about 34% less for the 30 studies omitting travel time cost, other variables in the equation held constant. On the other hand, the decrease in reported benefits by 15% for use of the individual observation approach seems quite conservative. The significant coefficient indicates that benefits are 46% greater for the 52 TCM studies using individual observations. The increase of both TCM and CVM values by 15% for omission of out-of-state users appears to be about right for the total sample where the coefficient shows a 20% increase, although not statistically significant. The 15% adjustment seems conservative for TCM studies where the significant coefficient indicates the correct adjustment would be an increase of about 30%. Thus, while the three adjustments appear about right or to err on the low side, the overall effect is reasonably correct. There is no significant difference between the mean values of adjusted and unadjusted studies because of offsetting effects.

Another critical issue, of course, in the evaluation of the Sorg and Loomis (1984) adjustments is whether they are supported by applied microeconomic theory, accepted econometric procedures, and guidelines of best practice. Obviously, some adjustment for the omission of travel time is required, however, the precise level is not known and would vary for each study site. The statistical effect of the travel time cost variable could be improved if specified as a continuous variable in dollars per hour rather than as a qualitative variable indicating presence or absence of the adjustment. With respect to the adjustment for use of individual observations in TCM studies, some observers argue that values from zonal studies should be increased rather than those from individual observation studies decreased because of the dampening effect of aggregation in the zonal approach (McConnell and Bockstael, 1984). Finally, limitation of the sample to instate residents originates in the institutional constraints of researchers and has no other basis. The precise level of adjustment for sample truncation would vary with the actual origin of the user population of each site.

The regression results indicate other prime candidates for adjustment not considered by the earlier work. Benefit estimates from TCM studies omitting an effective cross-price term for substitution should be decreased by 30%. If the behavior-based TCM results are accepted as the standard for benefit estimation, then the CVM estimates of intended willingness to pay should be increased by an average of 20–25%. Although the coefficient is not significant, the results suggest that benefit estimates from CVM studies using dichotomous choice questions are closer to TCM benefit estimates and require about half as much adjustment. However, benefit estimates from CVM studies asking open-ended willingness to pay questions should be increased by 10–15% more based on the preliminary regression results considered here. These are but a few of the possible adjustments that should be considered in applying the Sorg and Loomis (1984) approach of making adjustments before presenting statistical summaries of the data.

An important question raised by the Forest Service in applying the data to policy decisions is whether the benefit estimates from other public and private recreation sites are applicable to Forest Service resources. The insignificant coefficient for study sites administered by the agency suggests that there is no appreciable difference. Apparently, the benefit estimates from the literature review apply to valuation of the agency's recreation program. In theory, benefit estimates for a forest lacking data can be predicted by inserting appropriate values of explanatory variables into the regressions. Unfortunately, an insufficient number of studies have been completed to obtain more than a few estimates of value by this method. The agency requires benefit estimates for 19 national recreation use categories in 9 Forest Regions, or a total of 171. However, only 3 of the 19 national recreation use categories and 4 of the 9 Forest Regions are significant in the models fitted to data from the study sites. The specialized activity variable could provide a rough indication of the benefit for some activities with few studies. For example, the benefit of sightseeing and offroad driving, the largest single recreation activity with 27.6% of total output, would be $20 per day [= 39−(27.6 × .679)] based on the TCM equation. This compares favorably to the mean of $20 for six studies of this activity in Table 1. It seems likely that the agency will need to rely on a combination of several approaches until a much larger number of studies of most recreation activities has been completed.

V. ISSUES IN NONMARKET VALUATION

There are several other questions that should be addressed in the application of nonmarket valuation research to public policy decisions of resource-based recreation agencies such as the Forest Service (Stoll et al., 1983). Perhaps most important are questions having to do with tailoring research methods to the nature of the resource and behavior of the users. The recreation sites studied in most of the literature reviewed here are resource-based while some are intermediate areas. This follows the Clawson and Knetsch (1966) classification of outdoor recreation resources as resource-based, intermediate, and user-oriented. The dominant characteristics of resource-based areas are their physical resources. Resource-based sites include national forests, mountains, deserts, national parks, wildlife refuges, historic sites, swamps, seashores, and major lakes that provide sightseeing, camping, hiking, mountain climbing, fishing, hunting, boating, etc. primarily on vacation trips. The major areas of this type are usually located a considerable distance from concentrations of population. Of course, a few people live nearby and can use them as user-oriented or intermediate sites for day outings and weekend trips. For most people, however, visiting resource-based areas involves considerable travel, and thus both time and money in moderately large amounts. Intermediate sites include federal reservoirs and state parks that provide hiking, camping, fishing, boating, and hunting on day outings and weekend trips within 2 or 3 hour drives from home. User-oriented sites include city and county parks, golf courses, tennis courts, swimming pools, zoos, playgrounds, and the like within 1 hour travel from home.

The TCM has been the preferred approach for estimating the benefits from recreation activities at existing, new, and expanded sites, and it can be an acceptable approach for estimating the recreation benefits from changes in the quality of resources (Ward and Loomis, 1986; Rosenthal et al., 1984). The method has been successfully applied to intermediate areas located within 100–150 miles from the homes of most users, primarily state parks and reservoirs. However, the federal guidelines (U.S. Water Resources Council, 1983), recommend that TCM not be used to estimate the benefits of resource-based recreation sites. Because several sites are usually visited on a single vacation trip, the distance-traveled proxy for price cannot be assigned to a single destination.

The limited applicability of the TCM is a continuing problem in nonmarket valuation research. However, recent innovations in the study of resource-based sites indicate that it may be possible to learn how to adjust the method so that future revision of the guidelines will recommend it as providing acceptable measures. Haspel and Johnson (1982) illustrate how the proxy for price could be adjusted to apply to resource-based sites. The authors assign an equal proportion of the total distance traveled on a single trip to each of several resource-based recreation destinations in the Southwest. They conclude that the procedure provides a reasonably accurate demand curve. Others obtain satisfactory results by allocating travel costs on the basis of the number of days at each site. In future studies, consumers could be asked to provide the perceived allocation of trip costs among destinations.

Most of our research methods have been designed to study intermediate sites. Procedures have been developed to adjust regional demand studies to apply to proposed new intermediate sites. The Corps of Engineers, for example, adjusts values for the size of the proposed reservoir and population in the market area. Some studies adjust for differences in socioeconomic variables such as income in the new market area. An adjustment for quality of the proposed site also is included in some studies of new or proposed changes in existing recreation sites. Many of these procedures developed for the study of intermediate sites will be directly transferable to resource-based sites.[8] Others will not.

In the past, most studies of resource-based sites treated demand for them as if they were intermediate sites. Samples often have been restricted to day-use, single-purpose trips, or instate residents. Nearly all studies have truncated the demand curve, ignoring as much as 50% of annual use. This means that studies have nearly always neglected tourists on vacation trips to multisites, driving or flying considerable distance, staying in commercial lodging, eating in restaurants, and paying various user fees. Tourists were excluded despite the fact that most states have found that they make a significant contribution to economic development. Tourism is especially important in western states with resource-based recreation sites on public land.

Typically, researchers decide on the appropriate travel cost per mile for a party or household group in a single vehicle. Most intermediate-site studies reviewed here define travel cost as the average variable costs of operating an auto, based on national estimates for gas, oil, maintenance, and parts per vehicle-mile for the year of the study (13.4 cents per mile in 1986). For longer trips to resource-based sites, there are often other travel costs such as added food, lodging, equipment rental, and recreation supplies that are necessary to obtain the recreation experience. Such costs have been included in some studies (Burt and Brewer, 1981) and can result in travel costs per mile that are up to four times those limited to vehicle operating costs. Recreation economists have known for some time that vehicle operating costs average only about one-fourth of the cost of recreation travel (Clawson and Knetsch, 1966). Limiting specification of the TCM price variable can have a significant effect on estimation of recreation values of resource-based sites (Duffield, 1984). The reason is that a proportional change in travel cost tends to result in a similar proportional change in consumer surplus.[9]

It would be useful to explore the possibility that there may be other adjustments that would improve the application of TCM to resource-based sites. Since vacation users tend to travel further it would be interesting to test for the possibility of increasing out-of-pocket and time cost with added distance. The hypotheses of increasing disutility of travel time would be consistent with the observation that people get more and more tired of riding on longer trips. Out-of-pocket costs are expected to be an increasing function of distance for the following reasons. For local users who live within 100 miles, the variable auto cost assumption may be satisfactory since they probably arrive at the few available free campsites earlier and, in that case, 13.4 cents per mile could be increased by some amount to account for the higher costs of transportation in resource-based areas. For more distant users, camping fees, commercial overnight lodging, and added restaurant meals are often necessary expenditures for access to resource-based sites.

Studies show that time onsite becomes more variable for trips to resource-based sites and tends to increase with distance traveled. The effect on demand for trips can be controlled by including onsite time as an independent variable in TCM demand equations. The concept of substitutes may have less meaning for vacation users of resource-based sites. Although they have considerable choice among possible alternative sites, by definition, they seem to have less interest in or knowledge of their availability and tend to arrive at popular resource-based sites during the peak holiday season. For these users, there may be external benefits of expanded access to new sites that relieve peak congestion at existing sites.

The CVM is the preferred approach for estimating the effect of changes in the quality of resources at recreation sites. It is also an acceptable approach for estimating the recreation demand for existing sites and the effects of changes in the availability of recreation opportunities, such as from the development of new and expanded access to resource-based sites. Although the CVM approach is gaining broad acceptance, it is generally recognized that it requires careful wording of questions and well-defined market structures including substitutes with which respondents are familiar. Several procedures have been used and none has emerged as superior in all cases.

The federal guidelines suggest that methods of payment such as taxes, utility bills, and hunting or fishing license fees usually should be avoided because they may result in an emotional reaction against the method of payment. Apparently, the subjective value of a dollar depends on what it is spent for. From the individual's perspective, a dollar spent on utility bills, user fees, or taxes may be valued differently than a dollar spent for direct trip costs or for the purchase of goods and services in general. For example, Davis (1963), who originated the CVM, initially tried a user fee but abandoned it after a pretest showed that willingness to pay direct trip expenses proved more realistic and acceptable to households engaged in fishing, hunting, and camping in the Maine woods. There is a need for further research to test the effectiveness of alternative willingness to pay questions.

In the past decade, an extensive body of literature has developed assessing the accuracy of CVM estimates of individual willingness to pay for the recreational use of resources. Initial results were challenged on the grounds that what people say they are willing to pay contingent on the availability of a resource represents behavioral intentions rather than a directly observable action or historical fact. The relationship between intentions and actual behavior has been submitted to systematic empirical investigation. Despite some continuing controversies and unsettled points, CVM studies of the user benefits of familiar recreation resources have performed reasonably well when compared to the available empirical evidence from travel behavior, actual cash transactions, and controlled laboratory experiments (Cummings et al., 1986). Levels of accuracy have been consistent with levels obtained in other areas of economics and in other disciplines.

Finally, the task remains to discover how far these results can be generalized. The importance of continued research is illustrated by the conceptual and empirical difficulties associated with their estimation and the potential importance of recreation benefits in the economic assessment of programs such as long-run forest recreation.

VI. SUMMARY AND CONCLUSION

Although issues in estimating nonmarket values continue to cause concern, America's resource economists now have more reason to be optimistic than ever before. More progress toward improved measurement has been made in the past 5 years than in the previous quarter century since development of the TCM and CVM. The output of studies measuring the onsite recreation benefits of resource-based areas has quadrupled from an average of three studies per year during the 15-year period from 1968 to 1982, to more than a dozen studies per year from 1983 to 1988.

This paper addressed the problem of information transfer, that is, the possibility of adjusting past studies to estimate benefits for long-run policy analysis. The process involves developing an understanding of the important variables that explain the observed differences in benefit estimates. As a first step, we updated and evaluated a previous literature review that adjusted reported benefits for omission of the opportunity cost of travel time, sample truncation to instate residents, and use of the individual observation approach. The travel time adjustment was supported by the regression results and the other adjustments were somewhat lower than suggested by these results. Overall, they did not significantly change average benefit estimates because of offsetting effects. It is encouraging that, since 1982, fewer studies have required adjustments for these reasons.

Newer methods of controlling for the effects of these and related variations in estimation give reason to believe that it may be possible to resolve many of the issues. These include adjusting for variations in the treatment of monetary and time cost of travel, substitution, site quality, and the functional form used in TCM applications. CVM problems include adjusting for variations in the method of payment, functional form used to analyze dichotomous choice questions, and information on resource quality, uncertainty, and substitution possibilities. In both the TCM and CVM approaches, the tie between consumer theory and statistical estimation is being improved via use of discrete choice models, qualitative response models, and maximum likelihood statistical techniques.

The challenge is to learn how to adjust the TCM to treat the unique characteristics of demand for resource-based sites, and how to adjust previous studies to approximate the demand for new or proposed resource-based sites. We illustrated how the current results thus far could be adjusted to develop tentative estimates of the recreation use value of Forest Service resources. A number of additional variables should be considered before the agency could reasonably apply this information to policy decisions. For some activities, insufficient studies have been completed to understand the variables explaining the observed differences in benefit estimates. This knowledge would be essential to adjust existing benefit estimates to fit the requirements imposed by new situations addressed in policy analysis.

In the future, more research projects should provide for the translation of findings to answer policy questions. Most of the studies reviewed here were designed to answer a specific question at a particular recreation site. As a result, certain types of research on some recreation activities have claimed substantial amounts of public support although they offer little prospect of affecting a basic change in recreation opportunities for the future. In those instances, there may be new lines of emphasis that promise larger returns. The new problem becomes to design dual purpose studies, with a direct use in policy application at the study sites and an indirect use to answer policy questions at other times and places.

ACKNOWLEDGMENTS

An earlier version of this paper was presented at the Western Agricultural Economic Association Annual Meeting, University of Hawaii, Honolulu, July 1988, summarized in Walsh et al. (1989). The study was funded, in part, by Purchase Order No. 43-82FT-7-1253, Rocky Mountain Forest and Range Experiment Station, Forest Service, U.S. Department of Agriculture, Fort Collins, and by the Colorado Agricultural Experiment Station, Western Regional Project W-133, Benefits and Costs in Resource Planning. We are grateful for the assistance of Kun H. John and helpful comments by V. K. Smith, J. B. Loomis, O. Bergland, J. E. Keith, G. H. Elsner, and G. L. Peterson. Errors and omissions are, of course, the sole responsibility of the authors.

NOTES

1. For example, Dwyer et al. (1977) reviewed the TCM and CVM literature as a contribution to estimation of unit-day values for the Forest Service 1980 resource plans (RPA), as did Sorg and Loomis (1984) for the 1985 RPA.

2. The adjustments were based on a review of the literature by a panel of economists working in nonmarket benefit estimation, including Professor William Brown, Oregon State University; David King, University of Arizona; Elizabeth Wilman, University of Calgary, formerly Resources for the Future; Richard Walsh, Colorado State University; and Dennis Schweitzer, Gary Elsner, and Don Rosenthal, Forest Service, USDA.

3. By Comparison, Smith and Kaoru (1988) review 77 TCM studies from 1967 to 1986 with 734 benefit estimates averaging $73.40 per day or trip with a range of $0.30 to $1,023 (1987 dollars). The fact that the data sets are aggregated in a slightly different way causes some difficulty in interpreting the results, since there are a different number of days in each trip. Using trips and days as the unit of measure has the added problem that onsite sampling procedures tend to draw a disproportionate number of persons with longer length of stay (Shaw, 1988).

4. For review of problems in measurement of the variables, see Walsh (1977, 1986).

5. McConnell (1985) discusses these and related TCM models.

6. The omission of these offsite benefits is a significant limitation since they may be equal to or greater than onsite recreation benefits, particularly for sites with unique natural resources (Walsh, 1986; Peterson and Sorg, 1987).

7. The problem is expected to be less severe since we used fewer data points from each study. For example, the data set contains 287 estimates from 120 studies, often selecting an average best estimate, or minimum and maximum of the reported values. The Smith and Kaoru (1988) TCM data set includes 722 estimates from 77 studies.

8. The most notable example of improvement in method is a series of bulletins (Sorg et al., 1985) published by the Rocky Mountain Forest and Range Experiment Station in cooperation with the Idaho Department of Fish and Game, University of Idaho, and the U.S. Fish and Wildlife Service. These regional TCM demand studies for fishing and hunting in Idaho include nonresident participation, substitution, site quality, travel time cost, user reported travel costs, and income.

9. The relationship between travel cost per mile and consumer surplus estimates is illustrated in a series of wildlife recreation studies in Montana. For example, Duffield et al. (1987) show that TCM benefit estimates for elk hunting in the state increase from $28 per day with standard travel cost of 5.8 cents per mile to $68 with hunter-reported travel cost averaging 34.6 cents per mile. Duffield (1988) reported that TCM benefit estimated for river fishing in the state increase from $49 per day with standard travel cost of 5.6 cents per mile to $103 with angler reported travel cost averaging 22.4 cents per mile. Also, there appears to be a direct relationship between the value of travel time and consumer surplus estimates. Bishop and Heberlein (1979) show that TCM benefit estimates for goose hunting increase from $11 per day without travel time to $28 with time valued at 25% of the wage rate and $45 at 50%. McCollum et al. (1988) show that deer hunting benefit estimates increase from $29 per day without travel time to $46 with travel time at 50% of the wage rate and $69 at 100%. Generally, the effect

depends on the proportion of travel time cost to total trip cost. The higher the proportion, the greater the charge in consumer surplus resulting from a change in the value of travel time.

REFERENCES

Allen, P. G., T. H. Stevens and S. A. Barrett, "The Effects of Variable Omission in the Travel Cost Technique." *Land Economics* 57(1981):173–180.

Bishop, R. C. and T. A. Heberlein, "Measuring Values of Extra-Market Goods: Are Indirect Measures Biased?" *American Journal of Agricultural Economics* 61(1979):926–930.

Burt, O. R. and D. Brewer, "Estimation of Net Social Benefits from Outdoor Recreation." *Econometrica* 39(1981):813–827.

Clawson, M. and J. L. Knetsch, *Economics of Outdoor Recreation.* Baltimore: Johns Hopkins University Press, 1966.

Cooper, M. H., *The Integrative Research Review: A Systematic Approach.* Beverly Hills, CA: Sage Publications, 1984.

Cummings, R. G., D. S. Brookshire and W. D. Schulze (eds.), *Valuing Environmental Goods: An Assessment of the Contingent Valuation Method.* Totowa, NJ: Rowman and Allanheld, 1986.

Davis, R. K., "Recreation Planning as an Economic Problem." *Natural Resources Journal* 3(1963):239–249.

Duffield, J., "Travel Cost and Contingent Valuation: A Comparative Analysis." In V. K. Smith and A. D. Witte (eds.), *Advances in Applied Micro-Economics,* Vol. 3. Greenwich, CN: JAI Press, 1984.

Duffield, J., "The Net Economic Value of Elk Hunting in Montana." Report by the Montana Department of Fish, Wildlife and Parks, Helena, 1988.

Duffield, J., J. Loomis, R. Brooks, J. Holliman and J. Cooper, "The Net Economic Value of Fishing in Montana." Draft Report. University of Montana, Helena, 1987.

Dwyer, J., J. Kelly and M. Bowes, "Improved Procedures for Valuation of the Contribution of Recreation to National Economic Development." Water Resources Center Report Number 128. University of Illinois, Champaign, 1977.

Haspel, A. E. and F. R. Johnson, "Multiple Destination Trip Bias in Recreation Benefit Estimation." *Land Economics* 58(1982):364–372.

Light, J. R. and D. B. Pillemer, *Summing Up: The Science of Reviewing Research.* Cambridge, MA: Harvard University Press, 1984.

McCollum, W. D., R. C. Bishop and M. P. Welsh, "A Probabilistic Travel Cost Model." Draft, Dept. of Agricultural Economics, University of Wisconsin, Madison, 1988.

McConnell, K. E., "The Economics of Outdoor Recreation." In A. V. Kneese and J. L. Sweeney (eds.), *Handbook of Natural Resource and Energy Economics,* Vol. II. New York: Elsevier, 1985.

McConnell, K. E. and N. E. Bockstael, "Aggregation in Recreation Economics: Issues of Estimation and Benefit Measurement." *Northeastern Journal of Agricultural and Resource Economics* 13(1984):181–186.

McKean, J. R. and R. G. Walsh, "Neoclassical Foundations for Nonmarket Benefits Estimation." *Natural Resource Modeling* 1(1986):153–170.

Newey, W. K. and K. D. West, "A Simple, Positive Semi-Definite, Heteroscedasticity and Autocorrelation Consistent Covariance Matrix." *Econometrica* 55(1987): 703–708.

Peterson, G. L. and C. F. Sorg, "Toward the Measurement of Total Economic Value." General Technical Rpt. RM-148, Rocky Mountain Forest and Range Experiment Station, Forest Service, U.S. Dept. of Agriculture, Fort Collins, Colorado, 1987.

President's Commission on Americans Outdoors, *Americans Outdoors: the Legacy, the Challenge*. Washington, DC: Island Press, 1987.

Rosenthal, D. H., J. B. Loomis and G. L. Peterson, "The Travel Cost Model: Concepts and Applications." General Technical Rpt. RM-109, Rocky Mountain Forest and Range Experiment Station, U.S. Dept. of Agriculture, Fort Collins, Colorado, 1984.

Shaw, D., "On-Site Samples' Regression: Problems of Non-Negative Integers, Truncation, and Endogenous Stratification." *Journal of Econometrics* 37(1988):211–224.

Smith, V. K., "Benefit Estimation and Recreation Policy." *Policy Studies Review* 7(1986):432–442.

Smith, V. K., "Resource Evaluation at the Crossroads." *Resources* (1988):2–6.

Smith, V. K. and Y. Kaoru, "Signals or Noise? Explaining the Variation in Environmental Benefit Estimates." Unpublished draft, Dept. of Economics, North Carolina State University, Raleigh, 1988.

Sorg, C. F. and J. B. Loomis, "Empirical Estimates of Amenity Forest Values: A Comparative Review." General Technical Rpt. RM-107, Rocky Mountain Forest and Range Experiment Station, Forest Service, U.S. Dept. of Agriculture, Fort Collins, Colorado, 1984.

Sorg, C. F., J. B. Loomis, D. M. Donnelly, G. L. Peterson and L. J. Nelson, "Net Economic Value of Cold and Warm Water Fishing in Idaho." Resource Bulletin No. RM-11, Rocky Mountain Forest and Range Experiment Station, U.S. Dept. of Agriculture, Fort Collins, Colorado, 1985.

Stoll, J. R., R. N. Shulstad and W. M. Smathers Jr. (eds.), "Nonmarket Valuation: Current Status and Future Directions." Southern Natural Resource Economics Committee Publication No. 18, College Station, Texas, 1983.

U.S. Dept. of Commerce, "Statistical Abstract of the United States, 1988." Bureau of the Census, Washington, DC, 1988.

U.S. Dept. of Interior, "Natural Resource Damage Assessments: Final Rule." *Federal Register* 44:242(Dec. 14, 1986):950–1965.

U.S. Water Resources Council, "Policies, Standards, and Procedures in the Formulation, Evaluation, and Review of Plans for Use and Development of Water and Related Land Resources." 87th Congress, Second Session, Senate Document 97. Washington, DC, May 1962.

U.S. Water Resources Council, "Evaluation Standards for Primary Outdoor Recreation Benefits." Supplement No. 1 to Senate Document 97. Washington, DC, June 1964.

U.S. Water Resources Council, "Principles, Standards, and Procedures for Water and Related Land Resource Planning." *Federal Register* 38(Sept. 10, 1973):174, Part III.

U.S. Water Resources Council, "Procedures for Evaluation of National Economic

Development (NED) Benefits and Costs in Water Resources Planning." *Federal Register* 44:242(Dec. 14, 1979):72, 950–965.

U.S. Water Resources Council, "Economic and Environmental Principles and Guidelines for Water and Related Land Resources Implementation Studies." U.S. Government Printing Office, Washington, DC, 1983.

Walsh R. G. "Effect of Improved Research Method on the Value of Recreational Benefits." In Jay Hughes and R. Duane Lloyd (eds.), *Outdoor Recreation: Advances in Application of Economics,* pp. 145–153. General Technical Report WO-2. Washington, DC: Forest Service, USDA, 1977.

Walsh, R. G., *Recreation Economic Decisions: Comparing Benefits and Costs.* State College, PA: Venture Publishing, 1986.

Walsh, R. G., D. M. Johnson and J. R. McKean, "Review of Outdoor Recreation Demand Studies with Nonmarket Benefit Estimates, 1968–1988." Technical Rpt. No. 54, Colorado Water Resources Research Institute, Colorado State University, Fort Collins, Colorado, 1988.

Walsh, R. G., D. M. Johnson and J. R. McKean, "Issues in Nonmarket Valuation and Policy Application: A Retrospective Glance." *Western Journal of Agricultural Economics* 14(1989):178–188.

Walsh, R. G. and J. B. Loomis, "Contribution of Outdoor Recreation to National Economic Development." *A Literature Review,* pp. 35–46. The President's Commission on Americans Outdoors, Washington, DC, 1986.

Ward, F. A. and J. B. Loomis, "The Travel Cost Demand Model as an Environmental Policy Assessment Tool: A Review of Literature." *Western Journal of Agricultural Economics* 11(1986):164–178.

White, H., "A Heteroscedasticity-Consistent Covariance Matrix Estimator and a Direct Test for Heteroscedasticity." *Econometrica* 48(1980):817–838.

AN ECONOMIC MODEL TO ASSESS THE IMPACT OF ACID RAIN:

A CHARACTERISTICS APPROACH TO ESTIMATING THE DEMAND FOR AND BENEFITS FROM RECREATIONAL FISHING

Edward R. Morey and W. Douglass Shaw

I. INTRODUCTION

This paper specifies and estimates a characteristics-based utility-theoretic model of site-specific recreational fishing demand. The estimated parameters are used to calculate the conditional compensating variations (CCVs) that different individuals would associate with the changes in the availability of fish that might result from changes in the level of acid deposition. The almost universally ignored, but policy relevant, standard deviations of these consumer's surplus measures are also reported. These results indicate that the benefits recreational fish-

Advances in Applied Micro-Economics, Volume 5, pages 195–216.

ISBN: 0-89232-797-9

ermen would receive from reduced acid deposition are significantly positive but possibly quite small.

The lakes and ponds considered are all in the Adirondacks State Park, an area where the general adverse impacts of acid rain are well documented.[1] The specifics of the linkage between acid deposition and stock sizes are not well known, but Brook and Lake Trout are the species most affected and acid rain has already caused their extinction in many of the area's high-altitude lakes.

Policymakers have been grappling with ways to estimate the consumer's surplus fishermen associated with the availability of these species. One method, supposedly suggested by a former U.S. Director of the Budget, is to value them at their retail price at the grocery store. The intent of this paper is to provide and implement a superior method of valuation. The CCVs for changes in the availability of trout at a site (or sites) are found to vary extensively across fishermen as a function of their species preference, ability level, location of residence, value of time, and fishing budget. For example, the individual CCVs for a simultaneous 25% increase in the catch rates for trout at all the sites considered average \$3.56, but vary from zero to \$159.46 as a function of the above factors. This illustrates the danger of just reporting average or aggregate benefit measures, though attempts to do so are common in the literature (see Vaughan and Russell (1982) and Mullen and Menz (1985) for examples).

A utility function for fishing activities is derived by assuming that fishing activities are weakly separable from all other activities in the individual's preference ordering. Weak separability is assumed because data do not exist to estimate the marginal rate of substitution (MRS) between fishing and nonfishing activities, i.e., the sample of individuals does not contain data on the prices or quantities consumed of the nonfishing activities.

The characteristics of the fishing sites, and the individual's fishing ability and species preference, are explicit arguments in the utility function for fishing. The three characteristics considered are acreage, and two average catch rates that vary across individuals for a given site as a function of their ability level and species preferences. The individual maximizes fishing utility subject to his fishing budget and the parametric costs of fishing at each of the sites (including travel costs, on-site costs, and the opportunity cost of his time) to obtain a system of "partial" share equations for the fishing sites. Each share (a site's share being the proportion of fishing days that the individual will spend at the site) is a function of the costs and characteristics of all the sites. The share equations are "partial" in that they are conditional on the total budget allocation to fishing so do not measure the marginal rate of substitution between fishing and nonfishing activities. This system of partial share equations is estimated and used to obtain an estimate of the expenditure function for fishing. This fishing expenditure function is then used to estimate the CCVs that different individuals would associate with different changes in catch rates at the different sites. Each CCV is a lower bound estimate of the CV an individual would associate with an improvement in one or more of the sites.

The correct management of acid rain and many other environmental issues that impact on recreators requires that policymakers have a way of estimating the consumer's surplus that different individuals would associate with changes in the number, locations, and characteristics of the sites where they recreate. Unfortunately, the data needed to estimate the exact CVs are usually not available; most recreational data sets contain no information on the costs or the amounts of the non-recreational activities that individuals consume.[2] However, the available data are often sufficient to estimate a utility-theoretic lower bound on each CV. This paper provides one policy-relevant example.

The model is linked to acid deposition through the catch rates for the different species at the different sites. Acid rain impacts on the stocks of the different species at the different sites, which in turn affects the catch rates. Once these biological links are modeled, our model can be used to estimate lower bounds on the CVs that each fisherman would associate with different amounts of reduction in the level of acid deposition. For a given level of improvement, a lower bound estimate of total fishing benefits can then be obtained by summing the CCVs of the individual fishermen.

II. THE MODEL

Suppose there are M potential activities, the quantity of the mth activity consumed by the ith consumer being denoted by v^i_m. Let $V^i \equiv [v^i_m]$ denote individual i's consumption vector. Assume that activities are nonjointly produced subject to constant returns to scale. Associated with each activity is a vector of L effective physical characteristics, $z^i_{.m} \equiv (z^i_{1m}, \ldots, z^i_{\ell m}, \ldots, z^i_{Lm})^T$ where L is assumed to include all the characteristics of all the activities.[3] These characteristics vary across activities for a given individual because different activities are produced from goods with different physical characteristics and they vary across individuals for a given activity as a function of the characteristics of the individuals. The complete matrix of characteristics for individual i is $Z^i \equiv [z^i_{\ell m}]$. The individual ranks bundles of activities on the basis of the quantities of the different activities in each bundle and their characteristics, not on the basis of the activities names. Assume individual i's ranking can be represented with some direct utility function, $U^i = U(V^i, Z^i)$. Since all the characteristics of the activities are explicitly included as exogenous variables, the mathematical form of $U(V^i, Z^i)$ is invariant to which activity is associated with each of the m subscripts.[4] This preference ordering can also be represented with its indirect utility function, $\chi(Y^i, P^i, Z^i)$, or its expenditure function, $E(U^i, P^i, Z^i)$, where Y^i is individual i's total income and $P^i \equiv [p^i_m]$ such that p^i_m is the parametric cost to individual i of producing one unit of activity m.

This expenditure function, $E(U^i, P^i, Z^i)$, can be used to determine the dollar amount that must be given to, or taken from, individual i to make him indifferent between two alternative cost-characteristic configurations. Assume that individual i initially faces the constraints $Y^{i\prime}$, $P^{i\prime}$, and $Z^{i\prime}$. These constraints allow the consumer to achieve some maximum utility level $U^{i\prime}$. Costs and characteristics then exogenously change to $P^{i\prime\prime}$ and $Z^{i\prime\prime}$. The compensating variation, CV^i, that individual i associates with the change is

$$CV^i = E(U^{i\prime}, P^{i\prime}, Z^{i\prime}) - E(U^{i\prime}, P^{i\prime\prime}, Z^{i\prime\prime}). \tag{1}$$

The CV^i is the amount of money that would make individual i indifferent between facing the set of exogenous parameters $(P^{i\prime}, Z^{i\prime}, Y^{i\prime})$ and the set $(P^{i\prime\prime}, Z^{i\prime\prime}, Y^i - CV^i)$. The CV^i is positive for improvements and negative for deteriorations.

Order the M activities so that the first J activities are site-specific fishing activities, i.e., partition V^i such that

$$V^i \equiv [X^i, W^i] \tag{2}$$

where $X^i \equiv (x^i_1, x^i_2, \ldots, x^i_J)^T$, where x^i_j is the quantity of fishing activity j consumed by individual i. Fishing activity j is produced and consumed at site j and

$W^i \equiv (w^i_1, w^i_2, \ldots, w^i_{M-J})^T$, where w^i_m is the quantity of nonfishing activity m consumed by individual i.

The price vector, P^i, can therefore be partitioned

$$P^i \equiv [C^i, D^i] \tag{3}$$

where $C^i \equiv (c^i_1, c^i_2, \ldots, c^i_J)^T$, where c^i_j is the parametric cost to individual i of producing one unit of fishing activity j, and

$D^i \equiv (d^i_1, d^i_2, \ldots, d^i_{M-J})^T$, where d^i_m is the parametric cost to individual i of producing one unit of nonfishing activity m.

Order the L characteristics so that the first K characteristics are the characteristics of the fishing activities and the last L − K characteristics are the characteristics of the nonfishing activities; i.e., partition Z^i such that

$$Z^i \equiv \begin{bmatrix} A^i & 0 \\ 0 & B^i \end{bmatrix} \tag{4}$$

where $A^i \equiv [a^i_{kj}]$, where a^i_{kj} is the amount of characteristic k that individual i associates with fishing activity j, $k = 1, 2, \ldots, K$ and $j = 1, 2, \ldots, J$, and

$B^i \equiv [b^i_{\ell m}]$, where $b^i_{\ell m}$ is the amount of characteristic ℓ that individual i associates with nonfishing activity m, $\ell = 1, 2, \ldots, L - K$ and $m = 1, 2, \ldots, M - J$.

The CV^i that individual i would associate with a change in the costs and characteristics of the fishing activities from $(C^{i\prime}, A^{i\prime})$ to $(C^{i\prime\prime}, A^{i\prime\prime})$ is therefore

$$\begin{aligned} CV^i = {} & E(U^{i\prime}, C^{i\prime}, D^{i\prime}, A^{i\prime}, B^{i\prime}) \\ & - E(U^{i\prime}, C^{i\prime\prime}, D^{i\prime\prime}, A^{i\prime\prime}, B^{i\prime}). \end{aligned} \tag{5}$$

Estimation of the CV^i for a general change in the cost-characteristic configuration of the fishing activities is not possible because samples of fishermen do not contain data on the costs, D^i, and quantities, W^i, of the nonfishing activities consumed by each fisherman sampled, but this information is needed to estimate the expenditure function, $E(U, P^i, Z^i)$.[5]

One, however, can proceed by assuming that fishing activities are weakly separable from all other activities, i.e.,

$$U^i = U[U_f(X^i, A^i), W^i, B^i] \tag{6}$$

where the function $U_f^i = U_f(X^i, A^i)$, is the direct utility function for fishing activities. Individual i's system of partial demand functions for the J fishing activities can be obtained as the solution to the constrained optimization problem

$$\max_{\text{wrt } X^i} U_f(X^i, A^i) \qquad \text{s.t. } Y_f^i = C^{i^T} X^i \tag{7}$$

where Y_f^i is individuals i's total expenditures on fishing activities.

The demand equations are partial in that they are conditional on the budget allocation to fishing. Substituting this system of partial demand functions into the direct utility function for fishing, one obtains the indirect utility function for fishing activities, $\chi_f(Y_f^i, C^i, A^i)$, which may be inverted to obtain the expenditure function for fishing activities, $E_f^i = E_f(U_f^i, C^i, A^i)$.

The conditional CV^i, CCV^i, that individual i would associate with a change in the costs and characteristics of the fishing activities from $(C^{i\prime}, A^{i\prime})$ to $(C^{i\prime\prime}, A^{i\prime\prime})$ is therefore

$$CCV^i = E_f(U_f^{i\prime}, C^{i\prime}, A^{i\prime}) - E_f(U_f^{i\prime}, C^{i\prime\prime}, A^{i\prime\prime}) \tag{8}$$

where $U_f^{i\prime}$ is the maximum fishing utility that individual i can achieve from the fishing activities given $(C^{i\prime}, A^{i\prime}, Y_f^{i\prime})$, where $Y_f^{i\prime}$ is the utility maximizing budget allocation to fishing given $(C^{i\prime}, D^{i\prime}, A^{i\prime}, B^{i\prime}, Y^i)$. The CCV^i is the amount of money that would make individual i indifferent between facing the set of exogenous parameters $(C^{i\prime}, A^{i\prime}, Y_f^{i\prime})$ and the set $(C^{i\prime\prime}, A^{i\prime\prime}, Y_f^{i\prime} - CCV^i)$.

Hanemann and Morey (1989) have proven that $CCV^i \leq CV^i$, so if $(C^{i\prime\prime}, A^{i\prime\prime})$ is preferred to $(C^{i\prime}, A^{i\prime})$, CCV^i provides a lower bound estimate of the CV^i associated with the improvement. Morey (1981, 1985) failed to recognize this relationship in previous work. The CV^i and CCV^i are equal if the costs and characteristics of only some of the fishing activities change and if the partial demand functions for that subset of fishing activities have zero income effects. This is unlikely. Intuitively, the CCV^i provides, in absolute terms, a lower bound estimate because improvements or deteriorations in the fishing activities will most likely cause the individual to change his fishing budget. The CV^i, but not the CCV^i, incorporates this adjustment that the individual makes to the change. An individual will pay less to bring about an improvement, $(C^{i'}, A^{i'})$ to $(C^{i''}, A^{i''})$, if they are constrained in their ability to take advantage of that improvement. Holding the fishing budget at $Y_f^{i'}$ is one such constraint.

III. EMPIRICAL IMPLEMENTATION

A. Characteristics

It is assumed that each of the J site-specific fishing activities can be completely described in terms of the magnitudes of three effective physical characteristics, a_{1j}^i, a_{2j}^i, and a_{3j}. Characteristic a_{1j}^i is the average catch rate at site j for individual i's most preferred species for everyone of individual i's fishing ability (novice, intermediate, or advanced). The characteristic a_{1j}^i is a function of site j's stock size for each species, and individual i's most preferred species and ability level. It varies across sites for a given individual because stock sizes vary across the sites, and it vary across individuals for a given site because species preference and ability vary across individuals. Characteristics a_{2j}^i is the average catch rate at site j for individual i's second most preferred species for everyone of individual i's ability level. Characteristic a_{3j} is the total amount of fishable acreage at site j. Total acreage, a_{3j}, captures some elements of the fishing experience that the catch rates may not, such as scenery and open space. Anglers may enjoy aspects of the fishing experience other than the act of catching a fish. Previous literature shows that the demand for fishing sites can be explained fairly well with these few principal characteristics (see Mullen and Menz (1985) or Vaughan and Russell (1982)).

B. The Utility Function for the J Site-Specific Fishing Activities

The CES functional form is used to approximate the direct utility function for the fishing activities, $U_f(X^i, A^i)$. This choice is motivated by the fact that it is well-known, relatively simple, and easily allows for the incorporation of characteristics.[6]

$$U_f(X^i, A^i) = \sum_{j=1}^{J} (x_j^i)^{\beta}\, h(a_{1j}^i, a_{2j}^i, a_{3j}) \tag{9}$$

where

$$h(a^i_{1j}, a^i_{2j}, a_{3j}) = [\alpha_0 + \alpha_1 a^i_{1j} + \alpha_2(a^i_{1j})^{1/2} + \alpha_3(a^i_{1j}a^i_{2j})^{1/2} + \alpha_4 a^i_{2j} + \alpha_5(a^i_{2j})^{1/2} + \alpha_6(a^i_{2j}a_{3j})^{1/2} + \alpha_7 a_{3j} + \alpha_8(a_{3j})^{1/2} + \alpha_9(a^i_{1j}a_{3j})^{1/2}]^2. \quad (10)$$

The CES form constrains all the Hicks–Allen elasticities of substitution to equal $1/(1 - \beta)$. The function $h(a^i_{1j}, a^i_{2j}, a_{3j})$ can be viewed as a second-order approximation to any nonnegative function of the three characteristics. The CES function is a well-behaved direct utility function if $1 > \beta \neq 0$.

Assuming a CES utility function for fishing activities, the solutions to maximization problem (7) can best be derived in share form

$$s^{i*}_j = \frac{x^{i*}_j}{x^*} = [h(\tfrac{i}{j})/c^i_j]^\sigma / \sum_{m=1}^{J} [h(\tfrac{i}{m})/c^i_m]^\sigma \quad j = 1, 2, \cdots, J \quad (11)$$

where

$$x^* = \sum_j x^{i*}_j, \sigma = 1/(1 - \beta), \text{and } h(\tfrac{i}{j}) = h(a^i_{1j}, a^i_{2j}, a_{3j}).$$

Site j's share, s^{i*}_j, is the proportion of fishing days that we expect individual i desires to spend at site j. Note that all the share equations are identical. The only thing that varies from one site's shares equation to another is the value of the exogenous variables $(c^i_j, a^i_{1j}, a^i_{2j}, a_{3j})$. Demand equations are ordinarily allowed to differ between goods, in this case between site-specific fishing activities. However, when all the characteristics that explain variations in demand are included in the analysis, there is no reason to have different demand equations for different goods.[7]

The characteristics approach that we propose is attractive for a number of reasons. First, there is only one equation to estimate, yet the model is compatible with a system-wide approach and with an underlying preference ordering for fishing activities. The number of parameters that must be estimated depends only on the number of characteristics. Hence, our approach is particularly useful if the number of activities exceeds the number of characteristics as it does in the Adirondacks where there are hundreds of lakes from which to choose.

A second advantage is that it is possible to estimate how the demand for the different sites will change as the costs and characteristics of the fishing activities change. For example, the estimated model can be used to predict how the conditional demand (conditional on the initial budget allocation to fishing) for the different sites will change if a decrease in acid deposition increases the catch rates for trout at some of the high-altitude lakes.

Third, it should be emphasized that when estimating Eq. (11), it is not necessary to include data on every one of the J site-specific fishing activities. Estimation of all the unknown parameters can be done with data from a subset of the J sites.[8] This follows from the assumption of weak separability in the fishing utility function, i.e., the MRS between site 1 and site 2 does not depend upon attributes of any J + 1th site. This is very important when there are hundreds of sites. The parameter estimates can nevertheless be used to estimate an individual's share for a site, including those omitted from the sample, as a function of its cost and characteristics.

Finally, the approach allows us to estimate the CCV^i for any change in the costs or characteristics of the fishing sites. The incorporation of characteristics that depend on the stock sizes of the different species at the different lakes provides the link to acid rain and makes the model capable of estimating, through its effect on the catch rates, the CCV^is that different individuals would associate with a change in the level of acid deposition. An expenditure function for fishing that is dual to our CES direct utility function for fishing is

$$E_f(U_f^i, C^i, A^i) = -e(C^i, A^i)/U_f^i \tag{12}$$

where

$$e(C^i, A^i) = [\sum_{j=1}^{J} h(\frac{i}{j})^{-1/(\beta-1)} c_j^{i\,\beta/(\beta-1)}]^{(\beta-1)/\beta}. \tag{13}$$

The CCV^i that individual i would associate with a change in the costs and characteristics of the fishing activities from $(C^{i\prime}, A^{i\prime})$ to $(C^{i\prime\prime}, A^{i\prime\prime})$ is, by substitution of Eq. (12) into Eq. (8),

$$CCV^i = [e(C^{i\prime\prime}, A^{i\prime\prime}) - e(C^{i\prime}, A^{i\prime})]/U_f^{i\prime}. \tag{14}$$

The estimated CCV^is are easily calculated using the data and the estimated parameters of the share equation.[9]

C. Stochastic Specification

We assume that utility is deterministic from the individual's perspective but random from our perspective because we do not observe everything that the individual observes. We further assume that $U_f(x^i, A^i)$ represents the expected value of individual i's utility. Therefore, from our perspective, the observed share for individual i at site j is a random variable with the expected value s_j^{i*}. Rather than explicitly introduce the distributional properties of the random component at the level of the utility function, it is easier to append a random term to the expected shares. This is due to the fact that many of the distributional properties of the observed shares are well known. For each observation, the J stochastic shares must sum to one and each must be in the zero–one range. One would also expect the distribution of the shares to be skewed, especially for shares with expected values near zero or one.

It is therefore assumed that individual i's density function for the observed shares; s_j^i, j = 1, 2, . . . , J, is

$$f(s_1^i, s_2^i, \ldots, s_J^i; x^i; \theta) = \left(x^i! \Big/ \prod_{j=1}^{J} x_j^i! \right) \left(\prod_{j=1}^{J} (s_j^{i*})^{(x_j^i)} \right) \qquad (15)$$

where $\theta \equiv (\beta, \alpha_1, \alpha_2, \ldots, \alpha_9)$ is the parameter vector and x^i is the total number of fishing trips that individual i took during the year. This density function has the mathematical form of the multinomial distribution; however, it is not assumed that s_j^{i*} is the probability that individual i will choose site j on a given trip, and it is not assumed that the site choice for each trip is independent. This qualified multinomial was chosen as the appropriate density function because it is simple and because it maintains the inherent properties of the shares. The standard normality assumption is inappropriate because many of the observed shares in the sample are zero.[10]

If it is assumed that the choice of sites by one individual is independent of any other individual's choice of sites, the likelihood function for a sample of N individuals is

$$L = \prod_{i=1}^{N} f(s_1^i, s_2^i, \ldots, s_J^i; x^i; \theta). \qquad (16)$$

The maximum likelihood parameter estimates for a particular sample is the $\hat{\theta}$ which globally maximizes the likelihood function (16).

D. Data

Estimation of the share equation, (11), requires a cross-sectional survey of fishermen which details where each individual fished during an entire season and the costs they incurred to visit each of the sites. Data on the surface acres and catch rates (by species and ability level) at each site are also required.

Data on New York anglers have been collected by the New York State Department of Environmental Conservation (1977). For most of the individuals sampled, there is a complete record of where they fished during the 1976/77 season, the number of fish of each species they caught on each trip, their species preferences, their site expenditures, their years of fishing experience, their income, and the location of their residence.

These individuals visited many sites in the Adirondacks State Park but to ease the problem of estimation we restricted the analysis to seven fishing sites. Remember that the parameters can be estimated using data on only a subset of the J sites. The sites chosen were popular with many of the fishermen and exhibit a lot of cross-sectional variation in the costs and characteristics. The sites vary in terms of location, size and species caught. The seven sites are listed in Table 1. Lake Placid and Lake Saratoga are single lakes but each of the other sites is an aggregate of a number of adjacent lakes. Lakes were aggregated into a single site if the lakes were located in a small cluster such that they could all be easily fished in a single day and if they were all at approximately the same altitude. Lakes were aggregated so as to increase the number of visits to each site.

Fishermen with incomplete records and fishermen whose distance to the farthest site was greater than 200 miles were eliminated from the sample.[11] This left 607 fishermen. Our results therefore apply only to fishermen who are capable of making day trips to any of the sites. Sixty-three of the 607 anglers are classified as beginners (those with 0–10 years of fishing experience), 152 are classified as intermediates (11–20 years of experience), and the remaining 392 are classified as advanced anglers.

The acreage data are reported in Table 1 and are from the Gazetteer

Table 1. Average Daily Catch Rate (Number of Fish Caught per Day)

Site	*Panfish*	*Walleye*	*Pike*	*Smelt*	*Trout 1*[a]	*Bass*	*Trout 2*	*Salmon*	*Total acreage*
A. Beginner[b] catch rates for the eight species									
Saranac[c]	1.482	.0	.029	.0	.224	.093	.10	.405	9,856
Raquette	.864	.0	.0	.0	.004	.175	.053	.0	11,214
Lake George and Brandt Lake	1.353	.0	.028	.555	.040	.205	.016	.0	29,517
Lake Placid	.027	.500	.0	1.111	.427	.0	.026	.0	2,803
Piseco	.363	.0	.0	.0	.093	.128	.0	.0	4,909
Great Sacandaga	2.972	.087	.137	.0	.0	.534	.0	.0	4,096
Lake Saratoga	.52	.261	.050	.002	.0	.258	.192	.0	26,656
B. Intermediate catch rates									
Saranac	1.134	.0	.160	.0	.060	.097	.42	.529	
Raquette	.950	.0	.009	3.93	.310	.35	.35	.0	
Lake George and Brandt Lake	1.367	.0	.186	.174	.031	.565	.052	.011	
Lake Placid	.086	8.960	.088	.0	.835	.817	.087	.0	
Piseco	1.380	.094	.481	.0	.037	.502	.386	.0	
Great Sacandaga	2.306	.145	.399	.0	.051	.619	.0	.0	
Lake Saratoga	.498	.234	.324	.0	.015	.292	.0	.0	
C. Advanced catch rates									
Saranac	2.141	.0	.315	.017	.304	.19	.394	.153	
Raquette	1.012	.0	.014	2.323	.154	.49	.742	.001	
Lake George and Brandt Lake	4.200	.001	.764	.704	.074	.524	.183	.012	
Lake Placid	.006	.0	.0	.0	1.534	.439	.624	.0	
Piseco	.920	.136	.344	.0	.309	.226	.413	.0	
Great Sacandaga	3.166	.157	.282	.0	.0	.696	.0	.0	
Lake Saratoga	.813	.596	.144	.0	.058	.447	.011	.0	

[a] Trout 1 consists of Rainbow and Brown Trout. Trout 2 consists of Lake, Brook Trout, Splake, and Whitefish. Trout 2 is the species most impacted by acid rain.

[b] A beginner has 0–10 years of fishing experience. An intermediate has 11–20 years experience. An advanced has over 20 years experience.

[c] Saranac consists of Colby Lake, St. Regis Lake, and all of the Saranac Lakes. Raquette consists of Blue Mt. Lake, Raquette Lake, Indian Lake, and the Eighth Lake in the Fulton Chain. Piseco consists of Sacadandage Lake, Piseco Lake, and Lake Pleasant. Great Sacandaga consists of Great Sacandaga Lake, Ballston Lake, and Round Lake.

of Lakes, Ponds and Reservoirs prepared by the New York State Department of Environmental Conservation and the U.S. Department of the Interior (1970). The average catch rates for eight species groups and the three ability levels were calculated for each site using the catch data of the over 2000 individuals in the overall sample that visited at least one of the seven sites. These average catch rates are reported in Table 1 and can be interpreted as the expected catch rates for someone of that ability level. Ability level causes catch rates to vary because of ability per sec but also because more experienced fishermen often target harder to catch species and because they often "handicap" themselves with difficult to use equipments such as fly rods.

We assume that individual i's expected cost of producing one unit of site-specific fishing activity j is

$$c_j^i = \delta_{ij}\begin{pmatrix}\text{per mile}\\ \text{transportation}\\ \text{costs}\end{pmatrix} + \begin{pmatrix}\text{opportunity}\\ \text{value of}\\ \text{time}\end{pmatrix}\begin{bmatrix}\text{travel} \\ \text{time}\end{bmatrix. + \left.\begin{matrix}\text{on-site}\\ \text{time}\end{matrix}\right] + \begin{bmatrix}\text{on-site}\\ \text{expenditures}\end{bmatrix} \quad (17)$$

where δ_{ij} is twice the distance from individual i's residence to site j. Transportation costs in 1977 were $.15 per mile (Department of Transportation, 1977). Travel time is calculated assuming an average speed of 40 mph. On-site expenditures were assumed to be $7.29; the per trip average over all 607 fishermen. The average expenditure is used because prices must be exogenous and we estimate demand for the "representative" fisherman. On-site time is assumed to be 4 hours because no data are available. The opportunity value of each fisherman's time is assumed to be their yearly income divided by the number of hours an average individual is expected to work. Hourly wage data were not available.

IV. ESTIMATION

Given the sample of 607 fishermen, maximum likelihood estimates of the parameter vector, $\hat{\theta}$, were obtained by finding those values of θ which maximize

$$\ell^* = \sum_{i=1}^{607} \sum_{j=1}^{7} x_j^i \log(s_j^{i*}) \quad (18)$$

where x_j^i is the actual number of trips that individual took to site j and s_j^{i*} is individual i's predicted share for site j. The shares equations are homogeneous of degree zero with respect to the α parameters so α_0 was set equal to one without loss of generality. The log of the likelihood function was maximized using a quasi-Newton search algorithm developed by Schnabel and Dennis (1985).

The parameter estimates for three models are reported in Table 2. The regularity condition, $1 > \beta \neq 0$ is satisfied in each case. Model 1 assumes that the individual randomly allocates his time among the seven sites. It involves no estimation and assumes that $\sigma = \alpha_1 = \alpha_2 = \ldots = \alpha_9 = 0$. Model 2 allows the costs, but not the characteristics ($\alpha_1 = \alpha_2 = \ldots = \alpha_9 = 0$), to explain the allocation of fishing days. Model 3 is the full model and allows both costs and characteristics to explain each individual's allocation of fishing days. The asymptotic t values for model 3 are shown in parentheses. Likelihood ratio tests show that Model 2 explains the allocation significantly better than Model 1 and that Model 3 explains the allocation significantly better than Model 2. We can therefore reject the null hypothesis that costs and characteristics are not important determinants of where the individual will fish. The psuedo R^2 proposed by Baxter and Cragg (1970) is 0.728 for Model 3 indicating that the Model 3 is explaining a significant proportion of each fisherman's behavior. This is also indicated by examining the actual and the predicted aggregate shares (not reported here) for the seven sites.[12] The parameter estimates from Model 3 are used to estimate the elasticity and consumer surplus measures reported in the rest of the paper.

The expected conditional share elasticities with respect to both costs and characteristics, along with their standard deviations, were calculated for each individual in the sample. These elasticities are conditional in that they do not consider substitution in and out of fishing.[13] These own share elasticities with respect to cost are all significantly negative, varying from -1.75 to -4.47.[14] These cost elasticities vary across individuals for a given site as a function of species preference, ability level, and cost, and vary across sites for a given individual as a function of relative travel costs and the availability of each species at each site. The vast majority of the expected share elasticities with respect to characteristics one and two, a_{1j}^i; and a_{2j}^i, are significantly positive, indicating that, for most fishermen at most sites, a site's share increases as the site's catch rates for the individual's preferred species increase. Most, but not all, of the negative elasticities with respect to the catch rates are significantly negative. This indicates that, at least

Table 2. Maximum Likelihood Estimates for Three Models

Model	ℓ^*	σ	α_1	α_2	α_3	α_4	α_5	α_6	α_7	α_8	α_9
1	−17,009.2										
2	−13,322.8	3.59	—								
3	−11,550.0	4.24	−.200	.386	.0231	−.0652	.2149	.0003	.5E−05	−.3E−09	.0006
		(74.9)[a]	(17.6)	(23.1)	(1.91)	(8.64)	(12.2)	(25.8)	(4,341.0)	(6.8)	(3.6)

[a] Values in parentheses are asymptotic t statistics calculated for Model 3.

for some fishermen, increasing their catch rates for their preferred species at particular sites can make them worse off. A characteristic that is normally an attribute at one site can be bad at another site because of the way it interacts with the site's other characteristics. Like the cost elasticities, the catch rate elasticities vary extensively across sites and individuals. The expected share elasticities with respect to acreage, a_{3j}, are all significantly positive, varying from 0.06 to 1.20.

V. EXPECTED CONSUMER'S SURPLUS

Equation (14) and the estimated parameters, along with individual i's fishing expenditures and initial vectors of fishing costs and characteristics ($C^{i\prime}$, $A^{i\prime}$), can be used to estimate the expected CCV that individual i would associate with any change from ($C^{i\prime}$, $A^{i\prime}$) to ($C^{i\prime\prime}$, $A^{i\prime\prime}$).[15] Our intent is to use these CCV^i measures to assess the impact of acid deposition on recreational fishermen. We have no a priori reason to suspect that the CCV are significantly different than zero. The species most harmed by acid deposition in the Adirondacks are the Brook and Lake Trout (Trout 2), which live in the cold, high-altitude lakes.[16]

Acid rain is a major issue and numerous policies are being considered that could decrease the level of acid deposition in many of the Adirondacks high-altitude lakes. While the exact impact of acid deposition on stock sizes and catch rates is outside the domain of this study, it is clear that different policies have the potential to increase the catch rates for Trout 2 by different amounts at many sites in the Adirondacks.

We concentrate on Brook and Lake Trout (Trout 2) at sites near or above 1500 feet. Four of our seven sites (Saranac, Raquette, Lake Placid, and Piseco) are in this category. Examination of Table 1 shows that most of the trout are caught at these sites. Three policy scenarios are considered, policies that increase the catch rates for Trout 2 at these four sites by 5%, 25%, and 50%. Table 3 contains the expected CCV^is that 10 representative fishermen would associate with these three policies. The asymptotic standard deviations are in parentheses. This is the first empirical demand study that we are aware of that calculates the estimated standard deviations on the estimated consumer's surplus measures when the prices (and characteristics) of more than one activity are simultaneously changing.

The average CCV^is, along with their ranges and aggregate values, are also reported for each of the three scenarios. The CCV^is reported

Table 3. Selected Individual Annual Expected CCV^is for an Increase in the Catch Rates for Brook and Lake Trout (Trout 2) by 5%, 25%, and 50% at Saranac, Raquette, Lake Placid, and Piseco[a]

Origin	*Ability*	*Fishing budget*	*Most preferred species*	*Second most preferred species*	*Increase 5% CCV^i*	*Increase 25% CCV^i*	*Increase 50% CCV^i*
Albany	(A)	$212.76	Trout 2	North. Pike	$0.29	$1.29	$2.21
					(0.06)	(0.26)	(0.49)
	(B)	507.70	Trout 2	Yellow Perch	0.25	1.20	2.30
					(0.04)	(0.27)	(0.34)
	(I)	244.44	Trout 2	Trout 2	0.46	2.16	4.06
					(0.07)	(0.35)	(0.66)
Plattsburg	(I)	179.88	Trout 2	Trout 2	0.89	4.04	7.23
					(0.13)	(0.59)	(1.06)
	(A)	117.90	Trout 2	North. Pike	0.45	1.95	3.37
					(0.07)	(0.30)	(0.56)
	(A)	36.69	Trout 2	Panfish	0.17	0.75	1.30
					(0.03)	(0.11)	(0.21)
Utica	(I)	419.50	Trout 2	Trout 2	2.03	9.12	16.16
					(0.34)	(1.53)	(2.75)
	(I)	422.94	N. Pike	Trout 2	1.17	5.51	10.27
					(0.16)	(0.73)	(1.36)
	(A)	38.07	Bass	Trout 2	0.08	0.37	0.68
					(0.01)	(0.05)	(0.09)
Oneonta	(A)	632.90	Trout 2	Bass	1.59	6.90	11.59
					(0.30)	(1.39)	(2.52)
Range across all individuals with positive CCV^is					$0.01–$35.60	$0.02–$159.46	$0.04–$280.93
Mean across all individuals with positive CCV^is					$1.91	$8.68	$15.51
					(0.05)	(0.21)	(0.36)
The aggregate CCV for the 607 individuals					$475.87	$2162.04	$3862.94
					(11.22)	(51.47)	(89.23)

*The asymptotic standard deviations are in parentheses. The CCV^is are zero for all those individuals who did not specify Trout 2 as either their most or second most preferred species. There are 358 (59% of the sample) individuals in this category.

are quite representative, even though they do not represent the entire range of the estimates. For example, the CCV^is for a 5% improvement range from zero to \$35.60 but 77% of the positive CCV^i are less than \$2.00. The CCV^is at the high end are definite outliers.

The first thing to note is that $CCV^i = CV^i = 0$ if Trout 2 is neither individual i's most or second most preferred species. Acid deposition therefore affects only 41% of the fishermen in our sample. The homotheticity of the CES preference ordering implies that the expected CCV^i that a given type of individual (all those with the same ability, species preference, origin zone, and value of time) associates with a specific change is a constant proportion of their fishing budget. For example, for the 25% increase in the Trout 2 catch rates it is 0.006 for all fishermen who have the same characteristics as the first individual reported in Table 3.

The expected CCV^i are all significantly positive (some in theory could be negative) and vary extensively across individuals as a function of their ability, species preference, origin zone, and value of time. The estimates, however, are in general quite small in magnitude. The estimated standard deviations indicate the degree of error that can be attributed to the different CCV^i estimates. For example, for the 25% increase and the first individual in Table 3, Prob ($\$0.78 \leq CCV^i \leq \$1.79$) = 95%. Without the estimated standard deviations, it would be easy to forget that these CCV^is are stochastic variables. On the basis of the expected CCV^is and their estimated standard deviations, one can reject the null hypothesis that $CV^i \leq 0$ for each individual who specified Trout 2 as a preferred species.

Assuming independence and summing across the 607 individuals in the sample, the aggregate expected CCV for the 50% scenario is \$3,862.92 with an estimated standard deviation of \$89.23. One should bear in mind that his aggregate is the sum of many different CCVs. The aggregate CCV can be interpreted as a lower bound estimate of the total amount of money that would have to be paid by the 607 fishermen to make them each indifferent between the payout with the 50% increase in the Trout 2 catch rates and the original situation. If, for example, there were 10,000 fishermen in the population from which our sample was randomly drawn, the aggregate expected CCV for the population would be \$63,639.54 with an estimated standard deviation of \$1,470.02. Adopting conventional benefit–cost analysis, one would, for example, be at least 95% certain that it is worthwhile to clean up the lakes by an amount that would induce a 50% increase in the Trout 2 catch rates if the total cost of that cleanup is less than

$61,213.98. We would be at least 50% certain if the total cleanup cost is less than $63,639.54. While not telling us everything we would like to know, this is valuable information given that our sample did not contain the information that is required to estimate the marginal rate of substitution between fishing and nonfishing activities. Since the CCV is all that may be calculated when analyzing the impact of a wide spread reduction in acid rain, lower bound measures are what must be used for policy decisions. Our results also point out the importance of how aggregate benefits are distributed.

VI. CONCLUSIONS

This paper has presented lower bound estimates of a benefit measure for individuals that fish at a small group of sites in the Adirondacks. Our measure incorporates use values for the sites only. No attempt was made to estimate option or existence values in this paper. The first implication for policies that might affect acid rain levels is that we present identifiable, statistically significant, positive benefit measures for reductions in acid rain. This, in itself, is significant because there was no a priori reason to suspect that the expected CCVs would be significantly different from zero.

The second implication of this paper for policy is that the CCVs vary greatly across individuals with different recreational abilities. Policy managers may want to take this point into consideration by "targeting" specific sites for cleanup according to the expected willingness to pay of those individuals who frequent the site. The technique used in this paper is ideal for identifying willingness to pay as a function of the individual's characteristics.

The magnitude of the aggregate benefit measure presented here is small, and reflects the fact that only those fishermen who target trout have a positive willingness to pay for trout, the species most likely to be affected by acid rain. Should more results from other studies become available, it will be interesting to see how they compare to the results from our model of constrained individual utility maximization.

ACKNOWLEDGMENTS

This paper stems from the second author's Ph.D dissertation. An earlier version of the paper was presented at the First National Symposium on Social

Science in Resource Management, Corvalis, Oregon. We would like to thank Peter Caulkins, Phil Graves, Chuck Howe, Gary Johnson, Kerry Smith, and Don Waldman for their helpful suggestions and insights, and would like to thank RCG/Hagler Bailly of Boulder, Colorado for providing the raw data.

NOTES

1. For more details on the impact of acid deposition on fish stocks in the Adirondacks and in general, see Cowling (1982), Dahl (1921), Henriksen (1980), Hultberg and Stenson (1970), and LaBastille (1981).

2. Hausman's (1981) methodology can be modified to show that even with such limited data the exact CV may be calculated if one assumes that the quality level changes at only one site, with quality and prices remaining constant for all other commodities (fishing and nonfishing). However, acid rain does not impact on only one site so the Hausman technique cannot, in general, be applied to our problem. Hausman's method could possibly be used to calculate the CV associated with the chemical treatment of a single site. More is known about the chemical treatment of a single site than the general impact of acid rain (see Dutkowsky and Menz (1985).

3. Note that T denotes transpose.

4. For more details see Morey (1985).

5. To our knowledge, no sample of recreators contains data on their nonrecreational activities.

6. The CES with characteristics, Eq. (9), was first specified and estimated by Morey (1981).

7. The assumption that all the characteristics are included in the model is not tested. Its plausibility obviously depends on the analyst's ability to identify and measure the important characteristics. For an application of this characteristics approach to skiing, see Morey (1981, 1984, 1985). For applications to the estimation of import demand functions, see Kohli and Morey (1988 and 1990).

8. Naturally, statistical efficiency increases with the number of sites included.

9. Morey (1985) estimated the CCV^i for the introduction of a new ski area but did not recognize the important distinction between the CCV^i and the CV^i. Morey (1985, p. 228) incorrectly states that "the magnitude of the (estimated) compensating variation does not depend on the fact that skiing activities were assumed weakly separable from all other activities."

10. For more details on this qualified multinomial specification as compared to a normality specification see Morey (1984). Woodland (1979), Wales and Woodland (1983), and Morey (1984) indicate that the distribution of a system of share equations can be approximated with a joint normal distribution if, for each observation, none of the observed shares is near zero, but if many of the observed shares are zero, the normality assumption will lead to nonsensical results. Kohli and Morey (1988 and 1990) estimated import share equations assuming normality but their two samples contained no observed shares of, or near, zero.

11. Observations were not used when data on income were missing. Using only complete observations introduces the possibility of sample selectivity bias. We do not feel that sample selectivity bias is an important issue in this case because we have no reason to expect a systematic correlation between the nonreporting of income and the

site-selection process. See Smith and Kopp (1980) for a discussion of a distance limit for feasible 1 day trips.

12. For example, the correlation coefficient between the predicted share and actual share for average anglers from the cities of Albany, Utica, Saranac, and Blue Mountain Lake is 0.827.

13. Like the CV, the full elasticities cannot be estimated if the data set does not include the prices, characteristics, and consumption levels of the nonfishing activities.

14. The asymptotic variances of the elasticity estimates and the variances of the CCV^i estimates are obtained by noting that for any function $q = q(\Gamma)$, where $\Gamma \equiv [\delta_i]$ is a vector of random variables, the variance of 9 is

$$[\partial q/\partial\delta_1, \partial q/\delta_2, \ldots, \partial q/\partial\delta_N] \quad \Omega \quad \begin{bmatrix} \partial q/\partial\delta_1 \\ \partial q/\partial\delta_2 \\ \vdots \\ \partial q/\partial\delta_N \end{bmatrix}$$

where Ω is the variance–covariance matrix of Γ. For details see Theil (1971).

15. Bockstael and Strand (1987) point out that the source of the randomness can affect the size of consumer surplus estimates. However, their discussion relates to an expected Marshallian measure, which is a function of endogenous variables. Our (expected CCV) measure depends only on exogenous variables so the issue that Bockstael and Strand raise is not relevant here. [Note that the equation for the expected CCV can be replaced with an equation that substitutes the indirect utility function for U_f, so our expected CCV depends only upon prices, income, and characteristic levels.]

16. For more details see Schofield (1976).

REFERENCES

Baxter, N. D. and J. G. Cragg, "Corporate Choice among Long-Term Financing Instruments." *Review of Economics and Statistics* 52(3)(1970):225–235.

Bockstael, N. E. and I. E. Strand, Jr., "The Effect of Common Sources of Regression Error on Benefit Estimates." *Land Economics* 63(1)(1987):11–20.

Cowling, E. B., "An Historical Perspective on Acid Precipitation." In Raymond E. Johnson (ed.), *Acid Rain/Fisheries Northeastern Division*. Bethesda, MD: American Fisheries Society, 1982.

Dahl, K., "Research on the Die-off of Brown Trout in Mountain Lakes in Southwestern Norway." *Norsk Jaeger-og Forenings. Tidsskrift* 49(1921):249–267.

Department of Transportation, "Costs of Owning and Operating an Automobile," 1977.

Dutkowsky, D. and F. C. Menz, "A Cost Function for Neutralizing Acidic Adirondack Surface Waters." *Journal of Environmental Economics and Management* 12(1985):277–285.

Hanemann, W. M. and E. R. Morey, "Separability, Partial Demand Systems and Exact Consumer's Surplus Measures," Discussion Paper, Department of Economics, University of Colorado, Boulder, Colorado, 1989.

Hausman, J. A., "Exact Consumer's Surplus and Deadweight Loss." *American Economic Review* 71(4)(1981):662–676.

Henriksen, A., "Acidification of Freshwaters—A Large Scale Tritation." In D. Drablos and A. Tollan (eds.), *Proceedings of the International Conference on Ecologi-*

cal Impact of Acid Precipitation, pp. 68–74. Aas, Norway: Acid Rain-Forest Fish Project, 1980.

Hultberg, H. and J. Stenson, "Effects of Acidification on the Fish Fauna of Two Small Lakes in Bohnslau, Southwestern Sweden." *Flora Fauna* 1(1970):11.

Kohli, U. R. and E. R. Morey, "U.S. Imports by Country of Origin: A Characteristics Approach." *Kyklos* 41(1)(1988).

Kohli, U. R. and E. R. Morey, "Oil Characteristics and the U.S. Demand for Foreign Crude by Region of Origin." Forthcoming in the *Atlantic Economic Journal*, 1990.

LaBastille, Anne, "Acid Rain: How Great a Menace." *National Geographic* 160(5)(November 1981):652–681.

Mullen, J. R. and F. C. Menz, "The Effect of Acidification Damages on the Economic Value of the Adirondack Fishery to New York Anglers." *American Journal of Agricultural Economics* 67(1)(1985):112–119.

Morey, E. R., "The Demand for Site-Specific Recreational Activities: A Characteristics Approach." *Journal of Environmental Economics and Management* 8(1981):345–371.

Morey, E. R., "The Choice of Ski Areas: Estimation of a Generalized CES Preference Ordering with Characteristics." *The Review of Economics and Statistics* 66(4)(1984):584–590.

Morey, E. R., "Characteristics, Consumer Surplus, and New Activities: A Proposed Ski Area." *Journal of Public Economics* 26(1985):221–236.

Morey, E. R., W. D. Shaw and R. D. Rowe, "Repeated Discrete Choice, Expected Consumer's Surplus, and Option Price." Colorado Discussion Paper in Economics, University of Colorado, Boulder, 1988.

New York State Department of Environmental Conservation Bureau of Fisheries, "1976–1977 New York Resident and Nonresident Angler Surveys" and 1976 "Adirondack Pond and Lake Survey," Albany, N.Y. 12233.

New York State Department of Environmental Conservation Bureau of Fisheries, Characteristics of New York Lakes. Part 1—Gazetteer of Lakes, Ponds, and Reservoirs. Bulletin 68 (in conjunction with U.S. Department of Interior), 1970.

Pollak, R. A., "Conditional Demand Functions and the Implications of Separable Utility." *Southern Economic Journal* 37(1971):432–433.

Schnabel, R. B. and J. E. Dennis, *Numerical Methods for Unconstrained Optimization*. Englewood Cliffs, NJ: Prentice Hall, 1985.

Schofield, C. L., "Historical Fisheries Changes in the United States Related to Decreases in Surface Water pH." In Raymond E. Johnson (ed.), *Acid Rain/Fisheries N.E. Division*. Bethesda, MD: American Fisheries Society, 1982.

Smith, V. K. and R. J. Kopp, "The Spatial Limits of the Travel Cost Recreation Demand Model." *Land Economics* 56(1980):64–71.

Theil, Henri, *Principles of Econometrics*. New York: Wiley, 1971.

Vaughan, W. J. and C. S. Russell, "Valuing a Fishing Day: An Application of a Systematic Varying Parameter Model." *Land Economics* (1982):450–463.

Wales, T. J. and A. D. Woodland, "Estimation of Consumer Demand Systems with Binding Non-Negativity Constraints." *Journal of Econometrics* 21(1983):263–285.

Woodland, A. D., "Stochastic Specification and the Estimation of Share Equations." *Journal of Econometrics* 10(1979):361–383.

HABIT FORMATION AND THE DEMAND FOR RECREATION

ISSUES AND A CASE STUDY

Kenneth E. McConnell, Ivar E. Strand, and Nancy E. Bockstael

I. INTRODUCTION

In the early years of the economics of outdoor recreation, researchers expressed some interest in the role of habit formation and learning-by-doing in the demand for and benefits of outdoor recreation. Davidson et al. (1966) argued that when natural resource facilities are made available, people will learn to use them and future preferences are influenced as a result. This dynamic relation was part of the unmeasurable effects in the Delaware estuary restoration. Krutilla (1967) used this argument when he emphasized the possibility of excessive development of unique natural resources when habit formation is ignored.

Advances in Applied Micro-Economics, Volume 5, pages 217–235.

ISBN: 0-89232-797-9

Munley and Smith (1976, 1977) were among the first to capture the effect of habits in empirical demand analysis. They included years of experience in a model predicting the willingness to undertake recreation travel. A number of others have used other habit "stock" variables such as durable equipment ownership (e.g. Bockstael et al., 1986).

Empirical studies in the demand for recreation have been informal, ignoring much of the emerging literature on habit formation. We explore some of that literature and use it to examine the demand for recreation in general. As one might expect, certain types of recreational experiences turn out to be modeled more easily than others. We choose an easy case, beach use, and estimate a specific habit formation model for it. Finally, we compare estimates of the access value of a beach with and without a habit formation model.

The analysis demonstrates another important reason for investigating habits in recreational use: improving the explanatory power of recreational demand models. Estimated models of recreational demand typically have low explanatory power because demand functions are rather sparsely specified. Functions are often specified as if the neoclassical utility maximization problem were the only guidance. Typical specifications model the quantity demanded as a function of prices and perhaps income. Researchers are interested in the central relationship: quantity as a function of price. Estimating stripped-down demand functions may be justified, because other omitted explanatory variables are frequently uncorrelated with own price, and hence their omission does not bias the estimated coefficients of the more important included variables. But even if omitted variables are uncorrelated, there is the problem of explaining demand. The ability of the standard model to describe behavior, as measured by standard descriptive techniques, is quite low. Given that we can explain only a small percentage of the variation in observed behavior, can we have confidence in our models of recreational demand?

The problem of explaining recreational behavior in models of the demand for outdoor recreation becomes more important as benefit estimates, particularly for pollution control, move from journals to courtrooms in damage cases, to government agencies for rule making, and into the public arena for policy debate. Economists discoursing among themselves are content to debate over stylized fact. But the standard model of the demand for outdoor recreation may be inadequate for many ultimate uses; it explains too little of observed behavior.

Developing models of habit formation is one means of improving the explanatory power of models. Much behavior is governed by habit, and so past behavior is important simply to help explain current behavior. Further, the role of habits requires the investigator to think more carefully about the dynamic aspcets of recreational demand models. And for those who are skeptical about optimizing in the neoclassical model, habitual behavior provides a natural alternative.

II. HABITS AND RECREATION DEMAND

Habits play an important role in recreation demand because the individual's stock of knowledge is a critical element in recreational decisions. In many instances, recreation activities take specific skills, e.g., sportfishing entails the skills of casting, retrieving artificial lures, and handling hooked fish. Such skills are physical and are learned by trial and error. It is natural to think of the stock of these skills as improving with use. Moreover, people make conscious decisions to endure bad first experiences in order to develop skills that will pay off in the long run. Many "skunked" fishermen and "high handicap" golfers understand that experience is necessary in order to enjoy the recreation activity. These "learning-by-doing" activities require a model that captures the individual's stock of skill and the effect of future returns on current use.

Not all temporal dependence in the demand for recreation is associated with skill development. Past experience is perhaps the most important source of information about costs of access to recreational sites and the amenities of the site. Choice of beaches is one such activity where skills are less critical but information is important. The activity of sunbathing or picnicking at a beach requires little skill, but the choice of which site to go to may depend strongly on past experience. Here, there is no formal market to help spread information, and experience plays a different role. Individual perceptions of the amenities of a site help determine the enjoyment and use of the site. And these perceptions are formed most strongly by experience. These experiences are costly so that people typically do not visit many sites. Hence, in this role, temporal dependence of demand is explained by the need for information about sites. In turn, the stock of experience helps explain the choice among sites.

Temporal dependence would also be observed when information about the costs of access to different sites is uncertain. Costs are typically composed of travel and time costs and depend heavily on the distance to the site and speed of travel. This information can be determined most precisely by traveling to the site. There are other conditions of access that are learned from experience. Parking capacity and the distance from parking to the resource are mundane but important. Whether there are capacity constraints typically can be learned only by visiting a site.

Consumer durables play an additional role in making recreational behavior time dependent. When a consumer buys a durable recreational good such as a boat, the implicit price of using the good is reduced. Since the good can be expected to enhance the utility of specific activities, one would expect the demand for that activity (boating) to expand. Thus, the ownership of durables makes recreational behavior temporally dependent.

Thus, there is ample reason to believe that the demand for recreation is determined in part by past behavior. This behavior plays two roles. It helps individuals develop skills and also helps determine the costs and conditions of access.

III. FORMAL MODELS OF HABIT FORMATION

Formal models of habit formation were developed in the early 1970s by Pollak (1970) and Lluch (1974) and more recently by Becker and Murphy (1988). A simple classification of these models can be made on the basis of how the stock variable is derived and whether the individual is myopic or farsighted in planning. The early models (e.g., Pollak, 1970) consider the stock variable to be proportional to previous consumption and the individual to be myopic in his decision making. The recent models (Becker and Murphy, 1988) have nonlinear stock transition equations and a farsighted decision process.

In empirical work, Houthakker and Taylor (1970) demonstrated the role of habits in single-equation models of the consumption of a wide range of work commodities. Manser (1976) as well as Blanciforti and Green (1983) estimate habit formation effects in the systems of the demand for food. In contrast to the theoretical work, all empirical work has estimated models that assume that the consumer is myopic.

A. Simple Habits and Myopic Planning

Pollak (1970) developed several demand models for habit-forming goods by assuming the stock (S_t) of the habit was linearly dependent on past consumption $S_t = c_0 + cx_{t-1}$. Introducing this into a general linear expenditure function by assuming the subsistence quantity of the good equalled the stock, he implied a utility function of the form

$$u(x) = \sum_{i=1}^{N} b_i \ell n(x_{it} - c_{i0} - c_i x_{it-1}) \tag{1}$$

where b and c are vectors of parameters and x_{it} is consumption of commodity i in period t; there are N goods s_i, i = 1, . . . , N. This formulation gives quite reasonable Marshallian demand functions. Demand increases with increases in the past consumption of the same good and decreases with increases in past consumption of other goods. This model has the characteristic of adjacent complementarity, discussed by Ryder and Heal (1973), which implies that increases in the good this period induce increases next period.

From the standpoint of the preference function, habits enter in a quantity-augmenting sense, but they do so in a perverse way. In (1), an increase in x_{t-1}, consumption in the previous year, *reduces* the utility from a given level of consumption in the current year: $\partial u(x_t)/\partial x_{t-1} < 0$. In a dynamic setting, this implies a constant positive marginal rate of substitution between current and past consumption. These features may be useful in describing addictive behavior, but they are not very appealing for a story of habit formation in recreation. It seems more appropriate for past consumption of services to increase utility from current consumption. In fact, past consumption might work well as an aspect of the quality of current consumption, and it ought to increase both the level of current utility and the marginal utility of the consumption of the own good.

Positive analysis of the role of habits has concentrated on adjacent complementarity as a key characteristic. For the demand function to imply desirable preference function characteristics may be of little consequence if one is interested solely in prediction. But the desirability of having past consumption increase both the marginal utility of the own good and the total utility is evident if the demand functions are to be used for welfare measurement.

Welfare measures derive from the problem

$$m(p, x_{t-1}, u) = \min_{x_t}[x_t p_t | u(x_t; x_{t=1}) = u]$$

For outdoor recreation, for example, the existence of habit formation may be taken to imply that the compensating variation for a particular service flow will increase with increases in past service flows. This requires the cost function $m(p, x_{t-1}, u)$ to be decreasing in x_{t-1}, which in turn implies that current utility is increasing in x_{t-1}.

The relationship between current levels of consumption of one good, x_{it}, and past levels of a related good, x_{jt-1}, is also relevant. This is of special interest in outdoor recreation where models of quality-differentiated goods have become prevalent and where habit formation may be an important determinant in site choice. With specific restrictions on the preference function such as additive utility, some rather explicit results can be derived. In the additive utility case, the effect of past consumption of good i on current consumption of good j is

$$\partial x_{jt}/\partial x_{it=1} = -\frac{m_{ij}}{\lambda}\frac{\partial^2 u}{\partial x_{it-t}\partial x_{it}} \qquad (2)$$

where the m_{ij} is the cross-price effect of the Hicksian demand curve and λ is the marginal utility of income. In the additive case, $m_{ij} > 0$ for $i \neq j$ and < 0 for $i = j$. And when marginal utility of the own good increases, we have the standard result for quality-differentiated goods: Marshallian demand increases for past increases of the own good and decreases for past increases of other goods.

Rarely will such specific structure be imposed in an empirical context. However, it is useful to consider the conditions under which past consumption of any given good enters the utility function and thus other demand functions. The concept of weak complementarity, typically applied to the relationship between the demand for a good and its quality, can be applied in the case of habit formation as well. Weak complementarity in the context of quality means that if the current consumption of a good is zero, its quality does not influence the operative utility function. We might define weak complementarity in the case of habits to mean that if current consumption of a good is zero, its past consumption should not enter the preference function. The question arises because the process of habit formation appears to give preferences a memory. Habit formation implies that the effects of past consumption decisions linger on, influencing current preferences and choices. Thus, habit formation appears to contradict this concept of weak complementarity between past and current consumption.

Closer inspection suggests that the imposition of weak complementarity is not contrary to the habit formation model. As an example, consider two roughly comparable recreation sites. An individual visits a particular recreation site regularly, building up his knowledge of and preferences for that site. This process of habit formation, resulting in stronger preferences for one site, implicitly means weaker preferences for another site. Now suppose that access to the preferred site is removed. The individual has fairly weak preferences for the alternative site not directly in response to habits formed for the preferred site, but because he has a low stock of habits for the alternative site. Thus, the preference function "remembers" past use of the preferred site through absence of use of the alternatives. Consequently, in specifying current demand for the alternative site, when the quantity demanded of the preferred site is zero, only the stock of habits at the alternative site belongs in the demand function, not past consumption of the removed site. Weak complementarity should hold.

Both these issues relate to the problem of estimating recreational models with habit formation. As in the case of quality-differentiated goods, properly specified habit formation models are complex. Ideally, the quantity demanded of each good depends on past habits of all goods whose current consumption is positive. Like the problem of including all substitute prices and qualities, this is typically not possible econometrically.

B. Complex Habits

The above discussion incorporates the concept of a "stock" of habits in a simple model. In the habit formation literature, others (e.g., Houthakker and Taylor, 1970) conceived of the stock changing over time according to a difference equation such as

$$S_{it+1} = h(x_{it}) + (1 - \delta)S_{it} \tag{3}$$

where $h(x_{it})$ represents the net effect of use on the stock of habits and δ represents a depreciation factor. This formation makes good sense in the context of recreation demand. Skills will often increase with activity and depreciate without activity. Additionally, it often takes more than 1 year for the complete attachment to a particular site. For example, habit formation in recreational fishing is quite reasonable because one learns about tides, baits, weather, seasons, and the like. And in learning about the effect of seasons, it typically takes more than 1 year of observations, especially if the variation in these elements is important. Houthakker and Taylor (1970), using time-series data, estimate several versions of the process in (3) by assuming that $h(x_{it}) = x_{it}$ and that individuals are myopic. The essential explanatory variables in their demand function are one-period lagged consumption and the present and one-period lagged exogenous variables.

A slightly different stock model has been proposed recently by Becker and Murphy (1988):

$$\dot{S}(t) = c(t) - \delta_1 S(t) - h[D(t)]$$

where $\dot{S}(t)$ is the instantaneous growth in habits, c is the gross investment in "learning," δ_1 is the instantaneous disappearance of the physical and mental stock of previous consumption, and D is expenditure on endogenous depreciation and appreciation of the stock.

The attraction of the Becker–Murphy paper is that it rationalizes addictive behavior such as drug use. It has some relevance for recreation, though one does not need a complex model to induce time-dependent behavior. For skill activities, c may be sportfishing trips where both information is gained about the site and skills sharpened. The endogenous expenditure on appreciation may be classes in fly casting or purchases of outdoor magazines or equipment.

C. Habits and Welfare Analysis

The dynamic nature of habit formation requires especial care in welfare measurment. Here is where the original insights of Davidson et al. (1966) and of Krutilla (1967) are most relevant. With habit formation, future preferences depend on current choices, which are influenced by current regulatory actions. Should current preferences be used for all time, or should one account for the effect of current policy actions on future preferences? By introducing dynamic considerations into the problem, the usual techniques of benefit–cost analysis become questionable.

Although there are many problems relating to welfare analysis in a dynamic setting, we look briefly at the implications of myopia versus farsightedness. This is a useful focus, because in practice we are forced to estimate models that are myopic. The barriers of estimating a consistent farsighted model are immense. By comparing the welfare implications of myopia versus farsightedness, we get a sense of what is (perhaps) missing.

To examine the distinction between myopia and farsightedness, consider a demand function of the sort

$$x_t = f(p, S_t)$$

where p is price of access and S_t is current stock of habits. This demand function implicitly defined benefits as

$$W(S_t) = \int_{p}^{p^*} f(p, S_t)\, dp.$$

Suppose the process of stock formation is

$$S_{t+1} = (1 - \delta)S_t + h(x_t)$$

where

$$h(0) = 0.$$

If myopia is assumed, then the individual's willingness to pay in each period after access is denied should decline. The declining stock of habits lowers the demand for the site in each subsequent period. The loss in welfare declines because of the discount factor β and because the stock variable depreciates each period by the proportion $1 - \delta$. This is not the case when individuals are farsighted. When access is denied in period $t = 0$, the individual's welfare is diminished by the contemporaneous denial of access *plus* the loss in subsequent periods' welfare, which is incurred because the individual cannot "learn" over the time horizon. Thus, the loss from denial of current access must include terms representing the future effects of the denial (see Table 1). The benefit analysis is much more complex in this setting.

Table 1. Lost Value of Access under Myopia and Farsightedness When Access Is Denied in $t = 0$[a]

Myopia	$W(S_0) + \beta W[(1-\delta)S_0] + \beta^2 W[(1-\delta)^2 S_0] + \cdots + \beta^n W[(1-\delta)^n S_0]$
Farsightedness	$W(S_0) + \beta W[(1-\delta)S_0 + h(x_0)] + \beta^2 W[(1-\delta)^2 S_0 + h(x_0) + h(x_1)]$ $+ \cdots + \beta^n W[(1-\delta)^n S_0 + \sum_{i=0}^{n} h(x_i)]$

[a] $\beta^n = 1/(1 + i)^n$.

IV. AN OPERATIONAL HABIT FORMATION MODEL

To illustrate the effects of habit formation in the context of a typical single site, we estimate a simple version of the Houthakker–Taylor model. The model is myopic, but it introduces temporal dependence of preferences. The model shows the welfare implications of habit formation effectively, but it also shows the econometric difficulties of this kind of model. Begin with a simple model of the demand for trips to a single site

$$x_t = \beta w(t) + \gamma S_t + u_t \tag{4}$$

$$S_t = (1 - \delta)S_{t-1} + f(x_{t-1}, b_{t-1}) \tag{5}$$

where β is a vector and γ is a scalar; x_t and S_t now are trips and stocks of habits at one site, w(t) is the vector of exogenous determinants of demand, and $f(\cdot)$ describes how the stock is incremented. The exogenous component of demand is

$$\beta w(t) = \beta_0 + \beta_1 p_t + \beta_2 r_t + \beta_3 ps_t + \beta_4 rs_t. \tag{6}$$

Variables like these typically appear in a static version of demand functions. The variables in period t are

x_t = trips to site
S_t = stock of habits
p_t = travel cost to the site
r_t = time cost of users at corner solutions in labor market
ps_t = substitute site travel costs
rs_t = substitute site time costs
u_t = disturbance term.

One way in which this model falls short of the ideal model is that it excludes the stocks of habits at other sites.

The second equation (5) models the stock of habits. Stocks depreciate over time at the rate of δ but are incremented by a switching function of the form

$$f(x_{t-1}, b_{t-1}) = b_{t-1} + D_t b_{t-1} \tag{7}$$

$$\text{where } D_t = \begin{matrix} 0 \\ 1 \end{matrix} \begin{cases} \text{if } x_{t-1} = 0 \\ \text{if } x_{t-1} > 0 \end{cases}$$

b_t = the square root of the number of years (prior to t) going to beaches in the area

In this formulation, the stock variable grows as long as the person goes to beaches in the area. But it grows more if the person went the previous year. When there is no use in the previous year ($x_{t-1} = 0 = D_t$), then

$$S_t - S_{t-1} = b_{t-1} - \delta S_{t-1}. \tag{8}$$

This may be positive or negative, depending on the history of past activity, embodied in b_{t-1} and S_{t-1}. The square root is chosen so that there is a declining marginal effect of years on the stock variable.

As usual, the stock variable is unobservable, but Eqs. (4) and (5) can be used to develop an expression for it. Expression (4) implies

$$S_{t-1} = (x_{t-1} - \beta w(t-1) - u_{t-1})/\gamma$$

so that the current stock variable is

$$S_t = (1 - \delta)\{x_{t-1} - \beta w(t-1) - u_{t-1}\}/\gamma + f_{t-1}$$

where $f_{t-1} = f(x_{t-1}, b_{t-1})$. Then the demand function becomes

$$x_t = \beta w(t) - (1 - \delta)\beta w(t-1) + (1 - \delta)x_{t-1} + \gamma f_{t-1} + \theta_t, \tag{9}$$

where θ_t is a disturbance term whose properties will be discussed. For movements over several years, travel costs to recreation facilities change only slightly. Assuming $w(t) = w(t-1)$ yields

$$x_t = \alpha_0 + \alpha_1 p + \alpha_2 r + \alpha_3 ps + \alpha_4 rs + \alpha_5 x_{t-1} + \alpha_6 f_{t-1} + \theta_t. \tag{10}$$

This model, when it is estimated, provides estimates of the structural parameters of (4) and (5):

$$\beta_i = \alpha_i/\delta \qquad i = 0, \ldots, 4$$

$$\delta = 1 - \alpha_5$$

$$\gamma = \alpha_6.$$

There is at least one serious econometric problem embedded in this formulation. It relates to the error term, θ. In developing (10) from (4), we have not eliminated endogenous variables from the right-hand side. The error in (10) is

$$\theta_t = u_t - (1 - \delta)u_{t-1}$$

and from the definition of x,

$$x_{t-1} = \beta w(t - 1) + \gamma S_{t-1} + u_{t-1}.$$

Hence, there are two sources of error: x_t and x_{t-1}. A complete maximum likelihood procedure for estimating the parameters of (10) needs to account for the distribution of both error terms. We address the problem by replacing x_{t-1} with estimates that depend on polynomial functions of instruments. This procedure is motivated by the efficacy of an analogous operation on a least-squares model and the fact that a maximum likelihood model is approximately equivalent to a least-squares model with the inverse Mills ratio as a regressor.

Having estimated Eq. (10) and recovered the structural parameters, how does one then obtain welfare estimates in the context of this habit formation model? Given that the form of the demand function is linear, the current period consumer surplus associated with access to the site would be

$$CS_t = -0.5\hat{x}_t{}^2/\beta_1$$

where $\hat{x}_t$ is the predicted value for trips and β_1 is the estimate of the structural coefficient on price derived from the estimated parameters.

With the permanent elimination of the site, the consumer surplus change is the present discounted value of all future losses (where i is the real disounct rate:)

$$PDV = -0.5 \sum_{t=0}^{T} (\hat{x}_t^2/\beta_1)(1 + i)^{-t}$$

The nature of the habit formation model dictates how $\hat{x}_t$, $t > 0$, should be predicted. In the dynamic context of a habit formation model, the usual assumption that $x_{t+j} = x_t$ for all $j > 0$ is no longer viable. The expressions in (10) define how the systematic portion of x_t changes over time. Given that the demand function will likely be estimated in a censored form (i.e., account must be taken of the nonparticipants in the sample), the predicted value of x_t will be

$$\hat{x}_t = \hat{\beta}w(t) + \hat{\gamma}S_t + \sigma_u\phi/\Phi. \tag{11}$$

The last term is the inverse Mills ratio where ϕ and Φ are the unit normal probability density and cumulative distribution functions. The stock variable changes as

$$S_t = (1 - \delta)S_{t-1} + f_{t-1} \tag{12}$$

$$f_t = b_t(1 + D_t). \tag{13}$$

This model allows the calculation of dynamic and static benefit streams.

V. AN EMPIRICAL EXAMPLE

To illustrate the implications of this model for benefit estimation, we estimate the demand for trips to the largest beach on the western shore of the Chesapeake Bay. The data are extracted from a 1984 intercept survey of Maryland western shore beaches, sponsored by EPA and conducted for us by Research Triangle Institute. From May 26, 1984 to August 19, 1984, Research Triangle Institute (RTI) interviewed individuals on Maryland's public access beaches on the western shore of the Chesapeake Bay. The study population consisted of all residents of the Baltimore and Washington, D.C., SMSA's, age 14 or older, who used these beaches for recreation in 1984.[1]

Four hundred and eight individuals were interviewed to learn of their recreational patterns and perception of water quality at these beaches. The individuals were randomly selected from sample beaches and days. The sampling design can be described as a two-stage stratified sample in which a probability sample of beaches and days was selected, and a random systematic sample of persons was interviewed at each sample site (day-beach combination).

Not all households were interviewed at the end of the season. On-site responses included trips in 1984 taken prior to the interview and intentions regarding trips to be taken during the rest of 1984. Follow-up telephone interviews at the end of the season obtained complete

1984 trip information for 251 of the 408 beach users interviewed. For the remaining households, information was obtained solely on-site.

To ensure consistency in our trip measurement, the end of the season information was compared with in-season response so that a correction factor could be applied to households with only "in-season" information. Using data from Sandy Point, a regression of end of the season trips (x_{ie}) on reported and intended trips during the season (x_{ir}) yielded

$$x_{ie} = \underset{(1.40)}{0.686} + \underset{(35.00)}{0.632x_{ir}} + \epsilon \qquad R^2 = 0.89\ (n = 148) \qquad (14)$$

where the t statistics are in parentheses. Equation (14) was used to convert trips to a site for a household interviewed only during the season to trips for the entire season.

Previous studies have considered travel costs to be dependent on the person's (or household's) location relative to a site and their occupational situation. Distance to a site, transformed into transportation costs, is a feature common to all visitors. However, those individuals who forego income in order to take time to recreate incur monetary expenses in excess of transportation costs. For these individuals, these costs can be measured as the foregone wage rate times the time spent traveling to the activity. For households without employed persons or with employed persons with fixed work schedules, there is no direct loss of income incurred when recreation is undertaken. The opportunity costs of recreation time for these individuals is the foregone alternative activity (presumably recreation), which can be measured in hours spent traveling and recreating.[2] In addition to these access costs, most western shore beaches have an admissions fee. Often the fee will vary depending on the day of the week and the size of party. It must, however, be added to the other costs of accessing the site. The access and time costs were computed for both Sandy Point and for the individual best alternative beach site.

In addition, questions were asked concerning how many trips the individual had taken to Sandy Point in the previous year and how many years the individual had been going to beaches on the western shore of Maryland. We did not consider capital equipment, such as RVs or fishing gear, to be important determinants of beach use at Sandy Point, even though those data were available.

Table 2 gives the parameter estimates of a demand model for trips to Sandy Point Beach, which come from estimating the equation

$$x_t = \begin{cases} \alpha_0 + \alpha_1 p + \alpha_2 r + \alpha_3 ps + \alpha_4 rs \\ \quad + \alpha_5 x_{t-1} + \alpha_6 f_{t-1} + \theta & \text{RHS} > 0 \\ 0 & \text{RHS} \leq 0. \end{cases} \tag{15}$$

The coefficients of this Tobit model are estimated via maximum likelihood by assuming θ to be normal with zero mean and constant variance. The estimates shown in Table 2 are for a model in which x_{t-1} is replaced with a polynomial function of exogenous variables.[3] The important structural parameters implied by these estimated coefficients are given in Table 3.

It is interesting to compare dynamic paths with static paths in two ways:

1. How does the inclusion of the habit formation variable in the demand function influence the estimation of the coefficients, and hence the benefit estimates?
2. What happens under different assumptions about the prediction of x_t, given the coefficients?

The first question can be answered in part by estimating $x_t = \beta_0 + \beta_1 p + \beta_2 r + \beta_3 p_s + \beta_4 r_s + u_t$. We refer to this as a habitless model, although it is the usual recreation demand model. The parameters are given in Table 4.

For purposes of benefit analysis, the price coefficients are most important. From Tables 3 and 4 we see that the two models give similar estimates. Hence it is the dynamic effect of habits that will make a difference in the welfare analysis.

Recreational demand models are used by benefit–cost analysts to calculate the economic consequences of various public actions. In the benefit analysis, the researcher typically takes a demand model in conjunction with a discount rate and a time horizon. What are the

Table 2. Reduced Form Parameter Estimates of Eq. (10)[a]

	Coefficient							
	α_0	α_1	α_2	α_3	α_4	α_5	α_6	α_θ
Estimate	−6.67	−0.275	−3.23	3.71	0.200	0.128	2.27	13.97
Standard error	4.79	0.11	1.75	2.55	0.10	0.73	0.28	0.26

[a] n = 368.

Table 3. Structural Parameters Implied by Reduced Form Parameters

Parameters	*Estimate*
$\delta = 1 - \hat{\alpha}_5$	0.872
$\hat{\gamma} = \hat{\alpha}_6$	2.27
$\beta_1 = \hat{\alpha}_1/\delta$	−0.315

implications of habit formation for such an exercise? To see what is implied, we compare a stream of benefits from the habits model (Tables 2 and 3) with the habitless model (Table 4). We give the analyst 5 and 10% discount rates and a 15-year horizon.

We consider the welfare effects of eliminating the Sandy Point site for a representative household in the sample. This household is characterized by 7.1 trips in the year of the sample (1984) and 5.4 trips the previous year (1983). They have been going to western shore beaches for 6 years, so $b_0 = 6^{1/2}$. Present discounted value is calculated according to the formula

$$\mathrm{PDV} = -0.5\sum_{t=0}^{T}(\hat{x}_t^2/\hat{\beta}_1)(1 + i)^{-t} \tag{16}$$

where $T = 15$ and $i = 0.10$. The relatively short horizon is chosen so as not to tax the dynamics of the model in the distant future. Discount rates of 5 and 10% are used to convert returns into present value.

We provide two illustrations of the loss in access for this representative user. The dynamic loss allows the stock variable to decline over time. Thus, each year's willingness to pay for access is based on the fact that the individual did not have access, and hence did not augment the stock variable in the previous year. Thus, the willingness to pay for access in period 9, for example, is based on the assumption of no access for the first eight periods. It is given by

$$x_t = \hat{\beta}w + \hat{\gamma}\, S_t + \sigma_u\phi/\Phi$$
$$S_t = (1 - \delta)S_{t-1} + b_t.$$

The alternative is simply the static benefit. It assumes that trips would always be 7.1, and uses the coefficient of $\hat{\beta}_1 = -0.338$ from

Table 4. Parameter Estimates without Habit Formation

	Coefficient					
	β_0	β_1	β_2	β_3	β_4	σ_u
Estimate	7.69	−0.338	−4.50	0.216	2.46	14.89
Standard Error	2.94	0.083	1.35	0.078	2.20	0.26

Table 4. Over the 15-year horizon, with the 10% discount rate, we calculate the lost value of access to be as follows:

	At 5%	*At 10%*
Habit formation (Tables 2 and 3)	\$120	\$110
Habitless model (Table 4)	\$871	\$616

The economic loss from eliminating access is clearly due to the dynamics. It is evident from comparing the estimates of the price slope from Tables 3 and 4 that the loss from a given quantity demanded is similar. But in the habit formation model, the stock variable declines and leads to a declining potential demand. When the benefit analyst ignores the ability of the user to learn to use his time in other ways, he will overestimate the social losses from eliminating the sites.

We do not argue from this one case that researchers should drop everything and study habits. But the results uncover some strong dynamic effects. They also demonstrate the possibility of specification error. There is some evidence that when recreational behavior is time dependent, welfare losses from the loss of sites are substantially diminished.

VI. CONCLUSIONS

We began this exploration into the role of habits because we have intuitively felt that habits are an important determinant of recreational choice. Our case study demonstrates that there is some empirical relevance to this intuition. Including habits in a site choice demand function has a big impact on the estimates of parameters and substantially reduces the welfare effects of removing access to sites.

The relevance of this impact is tempered by the econometric problems that habit formation causes. Because the stock variable is not observed, econometric practices involve the use of lagged trips in the demand model. This results in a variable whose endogeneity can be purged only with difficulty. Further, if we follow the logic of the habit formation model as implied by utility maximization, we need the stock variable of all other goods chosen. In effect, it creates a much greater specification problem. As a consequence, we find ourselves in the uncomfortable situation of having additional evidence that habit formation matters and an increased awareness that estimating good models with habit formation is a difficult and complex task. As in many cases in economics, we can in a statistical sense be more confident of the numerical estimates of the parameter from intuitively less appealing models.

ACKNOWLEDGMENTS

We thank Kerry Smith for constructive comments and for helping us eliminate a variety of blemishes from an earlier draft. We naturally accept full responsibility for the remaining blemishes.

NOTES

1. A more complete discussion of the sample design is found in Bockstael et al. (1988).
2. As discussed in Bockstael et al (1986), on-site time is difficult to include as a "cost" because it also represents the unit of account for the recreation activity and likely is not predetermined. We thus chose to use only round-trip time in our computation of the opportunity costs of time.
3. The lagged value of trips was estimated via Tobit. The instruments were distance and distance squared to Sandy Point, years going to the Bay, and whether the household went to Ocean City, and the number of family members participating in water sports.

REFERENCES

Becker, G. S. and K. M. Murphy, "A Theory of Rational Addiction." *Journal of Political Economy* 96(1988):675–700.

Blanciforti, L. and R. Green, "An Almost Ideal System Incorporating Habits: An

Analysis of Expenditures on Food and Aggregate Commodity Groups." *Review of Economics and Statistics* 65(1983):511–515.

Bockstael, N. E., W. M. Hanemann and I. E. Strand, "Measuring the Benefits of Water Quality Improvements Using Recreation Demand Models." Report presented to the Environmental Protection Agency under Cooperative Agreement CR-811043-01-0 with the University of Maryland, College Park, 1986.

Bockstael, N. E., K. E. McConnell and I. E. Strand, "Benefits from Improvements in Chesapeake Bay Water Quality." Report presented to the Environmental Protection Agency under Cooperative Agreement CR-811043-01-0 with the University of Maryland, College Park, 1988.

Davidson, P., F. G. Adams and J. Seneca, "The Social Value of Water Recreational Facilities Resulting from an Improvement in Water Quality: The Delaware Estuary." In A. V. Kneese and S. C. Smith (eds.), *Water Research.* Resources for the Future, Inc. Baltimore: Johns Hopkins Press, 1966.

Houthakker, H. S. and L. Taylor, *Consumer Demand in the United States 1929–1970,* 2nd ed. Cambridge: Harvard University Press, 1970.

Krutilla, J. V., "Conservation Reconsidered." *American Economic Review* 57(1967):777–786.

Lluch, C., "Expenditure, Savings and Habit Formation." *International Economic Review* 15(1974):786–797.

Manser, M. E., "Elasticities of Demand for Food: An Analysis Using Non-additive Utility Functions Allowing for Habit Formation." *Southern Economic Journal* 43(1976):879–891.

Munley, V. G. and V. K. Smith, "Learning-by-Doing and Experience: The Case of Whitewater Recreation." *Land Economics* 52(1976):545–553.

Munley, V. G. and V. K. Smith, "A Note on Learning-by-Doing and Willingness-to-Travel." *Annals of Regional Science* 11(1977):61–70.

Pollak, R. A., "Habit Formation and Dynamic Demand Functions." *Journal of Political Economy* 67(1970):745–763.

Pollak, R. A., "Habit Formation and Long-Run Utility Functions." *Journal of Economic Theory* 13(1976):272–297.

Ryder, H. E. and G. M. Heal, "Optimum Growth with Intertemporally Dependent Preferences." *Review of Economic Studies* 49(1973):1–33.

Data: Problems of Design and Statistical Analysis, *G.S. Maddala, University of Florida.* **Estimating Neoclassical Production Technologies with the Use of Experimental Data,** *John Moroney, Texas A&M University.* **Aggregate Summary Functions - Heterogenelty and the Use of Random Coefficient Models,** *Robert C. Bever, Standard Oil of California, James R. Marsden, University of Kentucky, Vicente Salas-Fumas, University of Zaragonza, and Andrew Whinston, Purdue University.* **Stochastic Costs Frontiers and Perceived Technical Inefficiency,** *Raymond J. Kopp, Resources for the Future, V. Kerry Smith, Vanderbilt University, and William J. Vaughan, Resources for the Future.* **A Method of Analysis for Regulatory Impacts in Banking,** *Thomas F. Cargill, University of Nevada, Reno, and Robert A. Meyer, University of California, Berkeley.* **Econometric Representation of Industry Process Analysis Models: An Application to Forecasting Industrial Electricity Generation,** *Ernest H. Manuel, Jr., Marcus C. Duff, Pat Nanda and Daniel E. Cullen.* **A Pseudo-Data Analysis of Input Factor Substitutability: An Application to the Textile Industry,** *Kay K. Lee, Research Triangle Institute, Dan A. Fuller, Weber State University and Stephen A. Johnston, Research Triangle Institute.* **PART II. Conceptual Issues in Modeling Production Technologies. Multiple Use Forestry and the Economics of the Multi-Product Enterprise,** *Michael D. Bowes and John V. Krutilla, Resources for the Future.* **Duality and the Estimation of a Restrictive Technology,** *Thomas G. Cowing, State University of New York, Binghamton.* **A Method and Application of Estimating Long-Run Marginal Cost for an Electric Utility,** *E. Odgers Olsen, Jr., and Paul H. Raab, Ernst & Whinney.*

Volume 3, 1984, 293 pp. $63.50
ISBN 0-89232-398-1

Edited by **V. Kerry Smith,** *Department of Economics and Business Administration, Vanderbilt University* and **Ann Dryden Witte,** *Department of Economics, University of North Carolina, Chapel Hill*

CONTENTS: Overall Introduction to Volume, *V. Kerry Smith.* **PART I. Issues in Modeling and Valuing Amenity Resources—Introduction to PART I,** *V. Kerry Smith.* **An Analysis of Congested Recreation Facilities,** *Kenneth E. McConnell, University of Maryland, and Jon C. Sutinen, University of Rhode Island.* **Intrinsic Benefits of Improved Water Quality: Conceptual and Empirical Perspectives,** *Ann Fisher and Robert Raucher, U.S. Environment Protection Agency.* **Travel Cost and Contingent Valuation: A Comparative Analysis,** *John Duffield, University of Montana.* **An Application of the**

JAI PRESS

JAI PRESS

Hedonic Travel Cost Framework for Recreation Modeling to the Valuation of Deer, *Robert Mendelsohn, University of Michigan.* **PART II. Economic Impact Analysis and Climate Change — Introduction to PART II,** *V. Kerry Smith, Vanderbilt University.* **Modeling the Prospects of Climate Changes, Current State-of-the-Art and Implications,** *William W. Kellogg, National Center for Atmosphereic Research, Boulder.* **Welfare Analysis of Incomplete Adjustment to Climate Change,** *Daniel McFadden, Massachusetts Institute of Technology.* **The Dedonic Price Technique and the Value of Climate as a Resource,** *A. Myrick Freeman III, Bowdoin College.* **PART III. Issues in Modeling Public Provision of Education and Crime Protection — Introduction to PART III,** *Ann Dryden Witte, University of North Carolina, Chapel Hill.* **Improving the Use of Empirical Research as a Policy Tool: Replication of Educational Production Functions,** *Anita A. Summers, University of Pennsylvania and Barbara L. Wolfe, University of Wisconsin.* **Crime in Sweden: Causality, Control Effects and Economic Efficiency,** *Harold L. Votey Jr., University of California, Santa Barbara.* **A Dynamic Model of the Provision of Public Safety and Justice,** *Llad Philips, University of California, Santa Barbara.*

Volume 4, Risk, Uncertainty and the Valuation of Benefits and Costs
1986, 216 pp. $63.50
ISBN 0-89232-577-1

CONTENTS: List of Contributors. Introduction to the Volume, V. Kerry Smith. PART I. Risk Assessment and Benefit-Cost Analysis. The Old-New Risk Dichotomy and Environment Policy: A Case Study of Electric Power in the Courts, *Peter Huber, Science Concepts, Inc.* **Benefit-Cost Analysis and Risk Assessment,** *V. Kerry Smith, Vanderbilt University.* **The Dangers of Caution: Conservation in Assessment and the Mismanagement of Risk,** *Albert L. Nichols, U.S. Environmental Protection Agency and Richard J. Zeckhauser, Harvard University.* **Cigarette Smoking, Air Pollution, and Respiratory Illness: An Analysis of Relative Risks,** *John Mullahy and Paul R. Portney, Resources for the Future.* **Uncertainty in Risk Analysis: A Retrospective Assessment of the Osha Cotton Dust Standard,** *Paul W. Kolp, Centaur Associates and W. Kip Viscusi, Northwestern University.* **PART II. Valuation Under Uncertainty. Resource Valuation Under Uncertainty: Theoretical Principles for Empirical Reserach,** *Ricahrd C. Bishop, University of Wisconsin.* **Uncertainty and Environmental Policy: The Role of Option and Quasi — Option Values,** *A. Myrick Freeman III, Bowdoin College.* **Option Value and the Extinction of Species,** *Anthony C. Fisher and W. Michael Hanemann, University of California, Berkeley.*

Volume 5, 1990, 247 pp. $63.50
ISBN 0-89232-797-7

Edited by **Albert N. Link,** *University of North Carolina, Greensboro* and **V. Kerry Smith,** *North Carolina State University*

Volume 6, In preparation, Summer 1991
ISBN 1-55938-208-2 Approx. $63.50